WISDOM *and* MONEY

WISDOM *and* MONEY

Applying the
7 Laws of Highest Prosperity
To Make the Most of Your Money

CECIL O. KEMP JR.

W

Franklin, Tennessee
The Wisdom Company

Published by:

THE WISDOM COMPANY
P.O. Box 681351
Franklin, TN 37068-1351
Telephone: 1-800-728-1145
Fax: 1-615-791-5836
E-mail: cecil@hopestore.com

Cecil's books are sold on the Internet at www.hopestore.com and in local bookstores and gift shops. Bookstores or gift shops that don't already carry his books can order them from FaithWorks/National Book Network by calling toll free 1-877-323-4550.

Warning:
If financial advice or assistance is required, the services of a competent professional should be sought. The author and publisher have not written or sold this publication representing or intending it to be financial or investment advice.

Biblical quotations are paraphrases by the author, using modern language.

Library of Congress Cataloging-in-Publication Data Applied For
ISBN 1-893668-21-5

Printed in Canada

Patty and I dedicate this book to our children and grandchildren. You are precious treasure, daily reminders to make our lives count for what really counts!

CONTENTS

ACKNOWLEDGMENTS

Highest thanks and praise go to my heavenly Father.

To the reader, thank you for buying this book. My hopes and prayers are that it inspires and encourages you, empowering you to make wise, honorable, and hopeful decisions with your life and money.

And last but certainly not least, a very special thanks to Diana Donovan, Marilyn Williams, and Kathryn Knight for your effort and contributions. On the pages of this book readers learn what I have been so blessed and privileged to learn through experience. Diana, Marilyn, and Kathryn are exceptional ladies, extraordinarily enlightened, insightful, and passionate souls who see through the eternal scope of spiritually wise hearts that are directly connected to God.

Introduction

Fables are not always for children. The companion to this book, *7 Laws of Highest Prosperity*, is a fable about a creative soul striving to find his way in the world. It gives a feel for what a life of true prosperity is really like. I recount its basics here for the sake of those who have not yet read it, and for those who may have read it sometime ago and need a reminder.

Sam, a young wood gatherer, finds himself unhappy about aspects of his life in the village. He wants to try out his ideas about what life is about, ideas that have come to him in the solitude of the forest. In time, Sam braves criticism from his fellow villagers and moves to the unfamiliar city, where he puts some of these ideas into action . . . and does very well—for a while.

But like most of us the very strengths that helped him find initial success eventually become weaknesses and lead to a fall—and to the beginning of true success. With the support of experienced advisers and with the forgiveness and love of his wife, Suzette, and of his friends and coworkers, Sam learns to embrace a new definition of success—one that includes Life as well as money. He learns to listen to God's guidance through prayer and through the words of others on this same path to making life count. Step by step, he begins to live by the 7 Laws of Highest Prosperity and reap the benefits— peace, financial security, fulfillment, and joy.

"Yes, but *7 Laws* is a fable," you may be tempted to think. "In the real world . . ."

I would respond gently but firmly, "This type of reaction comes from the very fear that keeps so many of us in our 'real world' from applying the 7 Laws of Highest Prosperity to our lives, from extending the principles further into the areas of our lives not in line with them. I urge you to start applying some or all of the 7 Laws to your life today."

And that is where *Wisdom and Money* comes in.

Wisdom and Money is a textbook with hands-on worksheets to help you apply the 7 Laws to your life. It is not a fable, but a plan of action based on over thirty years of living the laws myself and of teaching the laws and seeing others begin to live them too. They work, I assure you.

A few cautions:

Although *Wisdom and Money* outlines how to act in real life on the principles for budgeting, saving, investing, and spending shown in the fictional *7 Laws of Highest Prosperity*, it is not meant to be a substitute for using real-world financial advisers like the fable's Magowin and Suzette and Geoffrey. The solid guidelines in *Wisdom and Money* are meant to be general. I urge you to look for an adviser to help you make specific decisions for your situation at this time of your life. How to choose such an adviser is discussed in chapter 13, "Investment Wisdom."

The story and language of a fable are fairly simple. Examples and language for real-world advice can be complex. I have tried to use general examples—sometimes framed in terms of being a single person or a couple, male or female, young or old—that apply to situations most readers will encounter. Any generality, however, is going to apply (or not apply) to any individual in varying degrees. Any generality holds the possibility of being seen as a judgment on some other specific. It is not my intent to show any one quality, gender, generation, or type of mentor as superior or inferior to another. If you find yourself reading my examples as judgmental or politically incorrect, please put that irritating aspect aside and try to focus on the part of the example that applies to you. My goal is to help you see Truth, which is reality at its highest level. Nothing more or less.

I have written this book to be understandable to those who have done little or no financial planning in their lives. But I have also tried to include suggestions that readers who have already worked up plans may not yet have encountered. Please do not stop where an example seems inapplicable or incorrect, whatever the reason. Please, instead, read on and try to see where the truth of the lesson applies to your own life.

This request also applies to specifics of language. If you are married, for example, and a passage is addressed to singles, I would suggest that you read through the material, applying it where appropriate. If you are single or engaged and material is addressed to couples, why not read through it and see what it has to say to you? If you are not a parent, and the material is addressed to parents, there's no harm in giving it a chance! If you are not a Christian, or not "religious" or have resentment toward churches because of past experience and the material is about spiritual aspects of highest success, it certainly won't hurt you to read through it and ask whether faith in its purity is worth another look. Whatever the specific of a given passage, please don't let the fact that a passage is addressed to a person in a different state in life keep you from reaping the benefit of adding to your wisdom!

Because giving suggestions like the wisdom contained in this book can sound egotistical, I have tried to include some stories from my own successes and failures, so you will be reminded that I was once on the wrong path and my suggestions come from learning how *not* to walk through this life. That is why I take such joy in sharing the message of true wisdom.

I am a deeply committed Christian, and I have included much of God's wisdom in describing true prosperity. For readers who are not Christian, I have tried to keep my language as general as possible. But I state clearly my bias: It is only when we learn to put the Spirit of God and the wisdom, honor, and truth taught by Jesus Christ at the center of our lives that we will find fulfillment, for that is how we have been created. For that reason, let me suggest that you may have some thinking to do—perhaps even a whole lot of thinking—that brings you to a "mental and spiritual place" that is solid, true, and peaceful. The bottom line is that until we're okay with our Creator and with ourselves, there ain't no amount of money gonna make us truly joyful . . . or prosperous!

I believe we not only have to know God and how we as individuals fit into His creative plans, we've also got to know ourselves—what we fear, what we enjoy, what makes us the same as, or different from, others. It's the only way to understand our values, reactions, habits, and stumbling blocks. And it's the only way to figure out why we don't feel completely successful already (if we don't). For that reason, the first chapters in *Wisdom and Money* lay the spiritual and psychological groundwork for the financial skills in the later chapters. If your aim is to be prosperous, not just a person with more money, please work through these first chapters with open-mindedness, patience, and enthusiasm.

If you have not read *7 Laws of Highest Prosperity*, at the risk of sounding self-serving I suggest you borrow or buy a copy. In a simple, charming way, that fable will show you where you can be headed if you choose to walk the path of true prosperity. The story will make you more aware of what you are missing if you choose another way. The summary in this introduction and in chapter 3 cannot begin to give you a full feel for what it is like to strive for highest success.

After you have read *7 Laws*, begin to work through *Wisdom and Money*, praying as you do so for clarity of vision and for guidance on choosing the right financial adviser—assuming you feel you need one.

It is my heartfelt wish that you will use these two companion books to make the most of your money . . . and to bring yourself true success!

—Cecil O. Kemp Jr.
Franklin, Tennessee
February 2003

A NOTE ON PROCESS

For those of you who are married or contemplating marriage, working through the text of this book and its worksheets yields the best results when, at some point, the work becomes a shared process. When and how it becomes shared will depend on the particulars of your relationship. There are more guidelines on how best to work this material together in chapter 4. For those who are single, the process is simpler—they can work through the material alone and seek advice from mentors as needed.

If you are married or preparing for marriage, I suggest that each person work alone first, reading the text and answering questions fully and honestly. (You may find it helpful to keep a notebook handy as you work through the book.) It would be best if you and your partner each have your own copy of *Wisdom and Money*. (If you have only one copy for the two of you, you have my permission to photocopy the worksheets—for your use only—so your answers remain private until you are ready to share them.) Then, if your partner is cooperating in this endeavor, the two of you should compare notes on your worksheets. This sharing will mean revealing things about yourselves that you may not yet have shared with each other, but they are things that you need to understand about one another. Whether you work through one chapter before sharing, several chapters, or the whole book will depend on your relationship. Cautions on how to share, and how not to, are included below. A fuller explanation on how to share, and how not to share is given in chapter 4.

If you have a partner who does not want to cooperate yet, I suggest you work through the chapters alone and look for opportunities and safe ways to share a little of what you are learning. As I will say more than once, you are the only one you have the power to change. Taking the steps necessary to change yourself may bring the added benefit of stimulating a desire in your partner to change. Or it may not. Either way, have faith that, if you ask, God will work in your life in His way and His time. Ask, then, and watch for mentors He may send your way.

I cannot say it often enough: Money—the feelings each of us have about it, the way we handle it, our hopes and dreams about it—can be a huge source of conflict in a relationship. In sharing insights and answers with a partner, each member of a couple becomes vulnerable, so please be especially tender and gentle with one another. Discussions about money should be approached in a loving and cooperative spirit that is without hint or intent of deception.

Discuss openly, honestly, and candidly what each of you brings to this aspect of the marriage partnership.

Listen carefully and without making judgments. Allow your partner to speak without interruption.

When you do *respond*, do so in a gentle, unthreatening, and non-judgmental way, showing by a very brief comment or action that you are listening and interested. (For example, nod your head or say, "I see," or, "I understand," or, "Are you saying . . . ?" Do not, for example, say, "You ought to . . . " or, "I can't believe you . . . !" or, "How can you . . . ?")

You may find it helpful to practice this method of discussion on easier topics before trying it with money management.

Conflicts can also be avoided or amicably resolved and a happier marriage can result if a couple will spend dedicated time together, enjoying each other outside of the "big discussion(s)." And things will be easier, too, if you talked about money before you married. If it's too late for that, though, there's no time like the present! Thoroughly discuss marriage and money, with love and respect and the doses of humor that are inevitably needed.

I recommend that you plan to meet together several times for your ongoing discussions. This allows time to cover the broad range of topics that should be discussed and some "soaking time" between meetings. It will also allow you and your partner time to work through any differences (with or without advice on process or content).

If you are engaged and you believe that addressing money matters can wait until after you've tied the knot, my advice is: You are setting up your marriage for potential failure. It is wiser to take the time, *before* the rings are on the fingers, to discuss the quantitative *and* the qualitative aspects of money. For this reason, I strongly encourage you engaged couples to share deeply the concerns you have about money, success, security—all that you will learn about yourself in working through the text and worksheets of *Wisdom and Money.* You will not only learn more about whether your visions for your life match, but also what your strengths and weaknesses are when it comes to managing the "real" things of life. Knowledge like this helps you to grow in love and avoid surprises after the wedding, or it helps tell if the match was not, after all, "made in heaven."

TAKE NOTE OF
WHO AND WHERE YOU ARE

Money management. Two simple words for a difficult task. Two simple words that mean something different to each person who tackles the task.

There are probably hundreds of scenarios that call for varying approaches to money management—and even these can differ from one stage of life to the next.

The comfortable net worth (or income) ratios for someone who is thirty will differ considerably from the comfortable ratio for someone who is seventy-five.

Managing the household expenses at age forty with three teenage boys in the house will differ greatly from the household budgeting of a single twenty-one-year-old just starting out in a first apartment.

And the fifty-eight-year-old faces a completely different set of financial and personal needs from those mentioned above, needs that may include oncoming retirement and its challenges, possible college bills, and caring for aging parents.

Throw in second marriages, child support, job changes, unexpected medical expenses, fluctuating economic indicators and interest rates, and the scenarios become even more varied.

Of all the factors that deter successful money management, however, the most derailing is materialism and the great value we place on tangible consumable products. When it comes right down to it, if you want to achieve true prosperity, you've got to place a higher value on who you are and what you are becoming than on the things you own in life. You've got to value those things that are eternal, worthwhile, and truly real.

I propose that there are two constants in successful money management

—no matter the era, no matter the economic climate, no matter the financial status.

1. Your primary, real person is spiritual, not physical. Recognize this, walk with God, learn His thoughts, emulate Him, and work with a heart He leads.

2. Your net outflow needs to be less than your net income.

There. Simple, right?

I know. It's not so easy. But it *is* simple, as I will show you.

Believe me, I've been there and I know how it is to be brainwashed into thinking that this material, physical life is everything—that possessions count, that status and appearances matter more than a positive cash flow. I know how hard it is to let go of that self-serving mindset. But as I said, it *is* simple: The way to end up materially wealthy is simply to spend less than you earn each and every month. Simple to say. Certainly not always easy to do. But it *can* be done—and an adventurous, joy-filled, and prosperous destiny awaits you if you make up your mind to live through God and follow the wise rules of life and money management that lead to highest prosperity.

To begin your journey toward highest prosperity, you've got to know where you are—emotionally, financially, and spiritually. The text of this book and its companion worksheets cannot encompass every specific area and every question that you may need to answer. Every person is unique with a specific set of experiences, talents, areas to improve on, and needs. *Wisdom and Money* does provide a good basic framework for personal and financial exploration, however. Part I is foundational to the rest of the money management suggestions. Please don't skip it. Part II has as many specific guidelines as can be given for general readership. Taken as a whole, *Wisdom and Money* will help you write down your vision for your own definition of true prosperity. Then it will help you translate that vision into dreams and goals that can be achieved.

The text and the worksheets don't have a time frame—work at your own pace, but remember, *procrastination can be costly!*

You may want to revisit the exercises in the worksheets from time to time. Staying on the path is just as crucial as getting on the path in the first place. I invite you to do so.

Ready? Let's get started!

7 Laws
of Highest Prosperity

1. **The Law of Wisdom**
   Highest wisdom resides in God's supreme thought and love.

2. **The Law of Priority**
   Success that lasts can only be achieved when one prioritizes in accordance with divine instruction—at all levels, including financial matters.

3. **The Law of Motive**
   Meaningful work and living are motivated by unconditional love for God, others, and self.

4. **The Law of Generosity**
   Service and giving create abundance, for others and ourselves.

5. **The Law of Understanding**
   To love with God's heart, see through His eyes, and think His thoughts are the ultimate goals for the truly enlightened spirit.

6. **The Law of Preparation**
   Being responsible with and wisely managing life resources requires commitment to truly important purpose and careful planning.

7. **The Law of Preservation**
   Wise stewardship ensures that money, principles, values, and spiritual guidance can be passed from one generation to the next.

PART I

Groundwork

1

Money Personality
and Prosperity

No one can tell whether they are rich or poor by turning to their ledger. It is the heart that makes one rich. One is rich according to what one is, not according to what one has.

—Henry Ward Beecher

THE CONCEPT OF MONEY PERSONALITY

Over the years, it has been my observation that one of the most sensitive nerves in the human body is the one that leads to the pocketbook. That is because our attitude toward money is deeply interwoven with the more personal attitudes we hold toward life and try to keep to ourselves. The truth is, how we see money—which is what I call our money personality—is simply an extension of our overall personality. And understanding this money personality is essential to our financial success.

Our money situation is not, as some believe, a result of uncontrollable forces. Like most situations in life our money situation grows out of how we have reacted—and acted (or not acted) in regard to finances. These reactions and actions are chosen (however consciously or subconsciously) in accordance with our money personality. Therefore, understanding our money personality—and changing it if needed—is essential if we want to make the most of our lives and of our money.

The first step in doing so is not unlike how we try to understand the other aspects of our makeup. We need to look at where our own money personality comes from and what the different aspects of it are. We need to understand what its strengths may be and we've got to recognize the pitfalls in the particular money personality that "has our name on it." I bet you already know this from experience, as do the rest of us. . . .

Since the way we view money can be a touchy subject, even touchier than our opinions on politics and religion, and since it is one our society gives us tacit permission to avoid understanding, I suggest that you step back and take a deep breath. Get ready to investigate your money personality, which, I've learned through personal experience as well as through observation of others, will be a reflection of your character.

For courage, consider these quotes:

Return to the root and you will find the meaning.

—Sengstan

What happens to us is less significant than what happens within us.

—Louis Mann

If the going gets tough, remind yourself that when we want to change *any* aspect of our lives that's not going well, it's not a bad idea to pray first for keen insight and wisdom in both mind and heart. Then we are more ready to take a good hard look at what makes us tick.

It may be that, after you learn about your money personality, you will decide to seek an adviser of the right sort (a doctor, social worker, counselor, religious expert) to help investigate some aspect of your situation. It is my hope that your understanding your money personality will make it easier to understand how you have come to the particular financial situation you're in now—and how to change it.

You may decide to share your insights with those close to you. If you do, you will be giving them at least tacit permission to study their own money personalities. You will also probably receive a new level of love and support as a reward.

However you proceed, remember this: Since habits are one of the most important results of any given money personality, the point of understanding that personality is to begin to make changes in behavior. To pursue true prosperity, we must be ready to stop acting on our unwise habits and begin replacing them with wise ones.

WHERE MONEY PERSONALITY COMES FROM

Most of us already know that our personality is the totality of characteristics that distinguish us as individuals. Personality traits determine behavior—for example, how we handle success, difficulties, happiness, and stress.

And behaviors repeated over time become habits. Personality and its habits reflect genetic predisposition, body chemistry, and learned behavior. Other influences on our personality and habits include the level of our peer support and education, the extent to which we consciously choose to allow God to work in our lives, and the degree to which we are willing to change.

So it is with the way we handle money—yes, money! We each enter adulthood with a different set of givens and experiences that tend to condition our reactions to money—either negatively or positively or a combination of the two. These givens and experiences are responsible for our money personality. And they are important to understand. Money personality can change. After studying it, if we decide some aspect of it is not helpful as we would like, we can map out a path for changing it and our financial habits.

WHY MONEY PERSONALITY IS IMPORTANT

As we grow to maturity we find ourselves asking things like: What does money mean? How much do I deserve? How can I earn it? What should I do with it? How much should I save? How much should I give? How does my use of money define me as an individual? How does my need for money fit with what Divine Wisdom tells me? These are all useful questions. And how we answer them gives us a clue to our money personality.

Having been in the business of helping people make the most of their lives and money, I've learned how powerful our money personality can be. It can drive us to financial success or failure, and while doing so, it can either help or hurt people along the way. I've learned that one of the most foolproof indicators of whether or not a person will achieve true prosperity is that person's money personality.

Our money personality is seen in how we express our beliefs—our values and the priorities we set because of them—in regard to money, possessions, and other financial matters. It becomes evident when we look at the mix of our financial and life priorities, motives, attitudes, choices, and actions.

In this land of opportunity that has an economy based almost exclusively on money, the answer to "Why do you want to be prosperous?" can be found only by investigating our *true* beliefs (not the ones we think we have but don't act upon, and therefore don't have), and then by relating those beliefs to money. I encourage you to refuse to avoid this investigation. As difficult as it may be at times, it will teach you about a major aspect of your overall personality, one that you may have ignored or missed until now. The worksheets at the end of this chapter will help with this investigation.

THE HEART PULLS A LOT OF PURSE STRINGS

Anyone who has read my previous books, especially *Wisdom Honor & Hope* and *7 Laws of Highest Prosperity,* will not be surprised at this next statement: The heart and its source of inspiration and knowledge are crucial to the formulation and maintenance of our money personality.

I see the heart as the core of our character and personality—the reservoir of our dreams, hopes, and expectations, and the inner conductor through which our inspiration flows. The heart, not the mind, then, is really the center of our thinking. The heart ultimately controls our decision making and the actions we take and the habits we form. Hence, if we look at our attitudes, actions, and habits, we will learn a lot about where our heart is truly centered.

For example: You may intellectually know that helping the poor is a worthy use of some of your money, but unless your heart actually leads you to do so, I guarantee you will never donate willingly—let alone without hesitation—to any charitable cause.

TRUE PROSPERITY

It is a shortcut to sure failure to mistakenly believe that financial success comes only from an intellectual understanding of certain principles and an application of the right formulas, the saving strategies, and the wisest maneuverings within one's career. *Approaching a life of true prosperity without involving our hearts is like building a home without a foundation.* No structure, of course, will stand the test of time without a sound foundation. Since actions speak louder than words or thoughts, we must be brave enough to look at what our actions tell us about our hearts. This will lead to a true understanding of our money personality and thus to true prosperity.

The building blocks of the sound foundation needed for success in life and with material resources are solid heart-held values and priorities. These beliefs and habits are expressed in our money personality as well as in the parts of our personality that guide other aspects of life. Our money habits are formed by repeated actions (or failure to take action), based on models we've used, especially on the example and advice of mentors like our parents and other childhood and adult influences. They are also created by our personal interpretations of our own experiences and philosophies, and those of others.

EXPLORING THE MONEY PERSONALITY

As you explore the aspects of your money personality, keep in mind that the psychology of money is quite tricky, even for the experts. I am hopeful, however, that you will find the exploration of the source and nature of your money personality enlightening and productive. You may find that this journey helps you begin to conquer unfounded fears or concerns you have with or about money and material resources. Just knowing that there are different types of money personality should help allay unspoken fears: We are all in the same boat; we just have different ways of rowing.

I forewarn you: This journey may also suggest changes you might best make in your heart, to bring out better emotions, feelings, attitudes, behaviors, and habits.

After reading this chapter and completing its worksheet assignments, you should have come to a better understanding of your own money personality—especially your financial habits. This will better equip you to handle your finances wisely and thereby enhance your opportunities for life and financial prosperity—whether you manage money on your own or with a mate, whether with or without the help of a financial adviser.

Acknowledging the views of others should also have become much easier, as should wise communication. We all have standards for money behavior that we expect others to be aware of. So, regardless of income, age, race, or education, difficulties with and arguments about money are common among family members, friends, acquaintances, and associates in business relationships. The ability to communicate better that comes with understanding our money personality can help with all of this.

The process of financial planning put forth in *Wisdom and Money* strongly advocates discussing what you are learning and wanting to change with those close to you. Once you are aware of your money personality, it should be easier to hold these discussions. And after you understand your partner's money personality, it should become even easier. Please be sure to read the discussion guidelines in "A Note on Process" and in chapter 4 before you attempt these discussions.

If, after you study your money personality, you determine that you do not need to make any changes in your heart or life, you can still benefit from that study. You will be better equipped to understand and communicate wisely with those coming from a different perspective.

• Some Roots of the Money Argument Problem

Our attitudes about money often lead to argument. Money argument does not come only from whether or not we have a personality prone to flaring up at the slightest provocation. Nor does it come only from a lack of skill in how to hold a discussion. Understanding this will help us on the path to true success.

Sometimes inadequate income is the root cause. And frequently, quarrels are due to people's lack of understanding about why they feel the way they do. People will share their financial goals, but all too often, they are unwilling to share their fears and anxiety about money.

This is not just because they consider their ways of handling money private, although this is part of the problem. Some communicate so little about how they are handling their money that important others are left knowing virtually nothing about simple things like where the records are or what the names are of important financial contacts.

The truth is that, for many, money is an area of hidden, self-suspected incompetence.

None of us like the thought—or the reality—of being incompetent at anything. In other areas of our lives, when we feel incompetent, we recognize that folly can cause us to engage in unwise behaviors. For example, we may "sweep it all under the carpet" and pretend that the incompetence, problems, or quarrels don't exist. Or we may try to fake competency. We must also recognize that in the area of money denial is dangerous behavior. Faking it is also dangerous in any aspect of our lives, and a potentially destructive behavior.

Becoming competent with money and handling financial affairs is, for some, quite scary. To more than a few, it is so frightening that they never move out of their childhood dependence into financial adulthood.

I hope for better than that for you and all readers.

Here are a couple more observations from years of helping thousands handle their money more wisely. First, some who are quite rational in almost every area of life can be totally emotional, irrational, and careless with money. Second, it is common to see people who are inept at managing personal money, yet very effective at managing million-dollar budgets on the job.

Let's look at some common areas of differences in money personality.

• Gender Gaps in Money Personality

Looking at basic gender differences in money personality is enlightening.

Males tend to have money personalities that view money and material resources as status symbols. As a group, then, men tend to value the attainment of material goods for the illusion of power they see in them. They tend to believe that money brings with it success and prestige. Men tend to be impatient with slow, steady growth in investments and they therefore tend to take higher risks than women. Men will spend more, invest more, and borrow more.

When spending discipline breaks down in men, it's often for a few big toys. Using borrowed money, they may buy a lavish house or an expensive car or a showy boat, etc.

On the other hand, females as a group tend to have money personalities that view money and material possessions as providing security. As a group, women also tend to value material goods for the illusion they provide. But with women, the illusion tends to be that money can give them security. It *is* an illusion, since all the money in the world cannot protect from every calamity. Nevertheless, this love of security explains why women tend to be better savers, in general, than men, and why they are usually investors who are more patient with slower growth and who make fewer risky investments.

When their spending discipline breaks down, women tend to use borrowed money as men do, but the toys they buy are smaller—they just buy more of them.

Although there are clear gaps in how each gender tends to view the value of money and other material resources, the underlying source of problems is the same. Persons of either gender are looking for what is instinctively important to them. Problems come when the illusions intrinsic to one money personality or the other are not understood.

We follow illusion more easily when our priorities are in the wrong place. Any money personality that believes humanist philosophies will fall prey to the illusion that material goods can bring true prosperity. I do not believe they can guide you well because they teach that self-realization can be achieved by will and reason alone. I have found that the Philosophy of Wisdom, which is based on God's guidance, will keep you on the path to true prosperity. The Philosophy of Wisdom is explained in chapter 2.

• Generation Gaps

Now let's consider a difference in money personality based on generation gaps and the problems they may cause. The definition of success for the World War II generation was landing a good-paying job and providing the family with an easy life. For their children, the baby boomers—I include myself here—the definition of success remained the same, but the good life we were trying to reach was ratcheted up a few notches. Whereas our parents were thrilled to have a modest—and paid for—home, a television, a car, etc., and one parent at home to care for the children, we baby boomers sought more: more TVs, more cars, computers, a bigger and probably a heavily mortgaged home, etc. and no one at home with the kids. Forging this new kind of family with no role model for dealing with the new problems arising out of such change, we didn't always succeed at filling the emotional needs of our children.

Many of those born to baby boomers—after 1970 or so—saw their parents as not placing enough importance on family relationships. Like my children, they saw their parents as working long hours to provide good *houses*, for example, instead of good *homes* for their families. Taking this approach in my twenties nearly cost me my marriage and family, but I took full advantage of my second chance at valuing life's greatest riches as I should. Both sets of experiences have fashioned much of what I share herein.

The "flower children"—as some baby boomers were called—who discarded these materialistic values were a small segment. Many of them later sought success through money (though, perhaps, from less traditional kinds of jobs) and encountered some of the same dangers noted above. Others labeled material success as "bad" and chose not to earn enough to care for themselves later in life and perhaps not enough to fill the emotional needs of their families. Children of these kinds of baby boomers saw their parents as not giving money enough importance.

Regardless of which of these scenarios they experienced, post–baby boom children came into adulthood with the view that many of their parents had mismanaged the material aspects of life and, consequently, failed in their personal or business relationships. This generation has tended to see this failure as rooted in money and, in response, to base its own values, and thus its career choices, on aptitude and passion, not money. Some even have a "mortal fear" of money and its trappings.

• Mentors and Money Personality

Success or failure with finances depends a great deal on what we learn from our mentors. Parents are most often the mentors with greatest influence on us. We see how they have handled their lives and finances. Our success or difficulty or conflict with money can often be traced back to our views of the models we saw them use, however wise or flawed those financial and parental paradigms were (or are). In order to understand the strengths and weaknesses of our own money personality, we need to look at how our parents' approach influenced our philosophies and behavior.

At sixteen, were you like me? I thought my parents were living in the dark ages. But after I got married, finished college, started a family, launched a career, and barely survived a decade of living my philosophies of humanist nonsense, I was amazed at how wise my parents had been all along!

Let's take a look at gaps created by mentoring differences in childhood and the initial problems they may have left us with.

Some may have grown up in an environment where our parents lived and died financially poor. Those who have experienced this type of upbringing may fear poverty and be prone to work very hard. They may believe that hard work is the cure for poverty.

They may even make money and the knowledge of how to gain money their gods—that is, they may spend essentially all their energy on trying to obtain wealth, possessions, know-how for getting money, and the security they believe will follow. As I foolishly did, they frequently place a very high priority on career, which may lead to their neglecting their family's well-being or their own spiritual development.

Consider an opposite mentoring scenario but one with essentially the same result—the person raised in a family environment where money always seemed abundant, where it seemed to "grow on trees." These folks may enter adulthood underappreciating what poverty feels like but may also hold a high value on having money and its trappings. Much like those in the first example, they make career a high priority, since it seems the means of achieving what they think they desire—maintaining an economic level similar to that of their parents. These people find they cannot have the lifestyle they enjoyed growing up because their income (perhaps coupled with a different economic era) does not support such a lifestyle. They may become resentful and demanding of what they perceive as their "rights." They may then respond by overspending and using credit, both personally and in their business roles, to create money to maintain their accustomed lifestyle.

The illustrations I use here are merely examples. There are, of course, many differing scenarios . . . and not enough space and time to cover them all. There is not a specific subsection of the worksheet on the above-mentioned gaps aspect of your money personality, but many of the questions are about the same issues. I encourage you to think about gaps and make notes on your worksheet space about which areas apply to you and how they have affected you, for better or worse. If you believe in prayer, praying for enlightenment will help this process.

• Identify Your Landmarks

Every person, whether meaning to or not, creates landmarks in his or her life. These mark the end or the beginning of significant beliefs and habits. Negative landmarks indicate places where we've taken on unwise and destructive beliefs and habits. Positive landmarks shine on the turning points in our lives where we take on the new beliefs or habits that will lead us to true prosperity. Most of us agree that we would rather have more of the positive landmarks to characterize our life than negatives ones.

Directly or indirectly, the beliefs and habits we've taken on in the past are what lead to these landmark events and influence our subsequent behavior—including how we handle money. It's a good idea to look at our present behavior, and our past behavior too, in light of these landmarks.

To know and understand why we think, feel, and behave as we do with money, it is only appropriate that we go back to our beginnings and search for our landmarks. This method of examining some of the roots of our beliefs and habits about money will shed light on our present attitudes and behavior.

As hard as it may be to face, it is true that these root beliefs and habits come from our heart-held values. Let's abandon the idea that any past unwise behavior is a good excuse for some current unwise behavior with money. Instead, let's face the positive reality that we can change; we can pursue the wise and better way of handling our lives and material resources. There is not a specific subsection of the worksheet on understanding the landmarks of your money personality, but some of the questions are about landmark issues. I encourage you to think back and make notes on your worksheet space about which landmarks you remember and how they have affected you, for better or worse. If you believe in prayer, praying for enlightenment will help this process.

The foundation of that wise and better way of handling our lives and material resources is harmony in life's most important relationship—our relationship with God. If you haven't already, this is a good time to make a landmark commitment or recommitment to deepening that relationship. When asked, God always shows us what we have to know and do to improve our lives. How we respond is up to us. A closer relationship with God will help keep us from getting stuck in frustration, blame, or inaction. He will give us the courage and wisdom to use the knowledge of our past mismanagement of our life and resources to serve as a map of the paths to avoid as we journey toward sound judgment and true prosperity.

A SLICE OF MY STORY . . .

• How I Gained Some Financial Wisdom

My parents held beliefs that created and nurtured in them the values, priorities, motives, and thinking necessary for wise decisions in life and with money. They lived and worked according to a philosophy that places the spiritual connection to God at the center of thought, emotion, and decision making. They possessed the wisdom, honor, and hope that comes from loving and being aware of being loved by God, by allowing the indwelling Spirit of God to shape and guide them in every facet of life. Their passion in life, financial and otherwise, was serving Him by helping others.

In addition to their words, which they spoke in answer to my questions, their actions and their refusals to take action expressed a genuine belief in the need to continuously love and deeply respect each other, their four children, and all others. This love and respect were always evident in the twinkle in their eyes and the joy on their faces. Discipline and sacrifice were also as natural as breathing to my parents. This way of approaching life led them to continuously practice three very good money habits—saving, avoiding debt, and preparing for the future.

Their consistent practice of these beliefs and habits created in me the same landmark beliefs and habits, even the money habits they had. I didn't know it at first. *Though I ignored my landmark money habits right after I graduated from college, I returned to them about a decade later.* Over twenty years ago I committed to their wisdom, and have since followed them—with great success in every life dimension.

The values my parents prized were the source of their money habits. These values included honesty, courage, perseverance, faith, sacrifice, self-discipline, responsibility, fidelity, and loyalty.

They lived with justice and compassion. They worked hard, always sought the truth, never shirked their duty or forgot their friendships. My parents respected their employer and friends, always giving above what was expected or required. They were respectful of all and, though always eager and willing to help, never intruded. Both practiced such a strong work ethic that I can easily say they were the hardest workers I have ever known.

They were not driven by greed or the desire to accumulate excessive money or to spend what they had solely on themselves; rather, they were motivated to be a blessing to others. With their time, skill, and money, they were givers, not takers. Without fanfare, they often used those God-given blessings to do kind things for those who could not do for themselves. They knew that Love helps those who cannot help themselves and that the most rewarding Love is the Love you give.

When they made a promise, they kept it. Their character and integrity silently manifested every day. They let their conduct do the talking. Ben Franklin could have been describing them when he said, *"Well done is better than well said."*

My parents' Spirit-led character, willpower, and minds worked together to make them persons with great inner prudence and discretion in all their dealings. One of the facets of my dad's personality that impressed me the most was mentioned by one of his sons-in-law at my father's funeral: It was his ability to reduce something to its lowest common denominator. His genius for pinpointing the essentials proved him a very wise thinker. I believe this was a result of his mind and thinking being controlled by his wise heart.

My parents taught their children well. They did not pay us for picking cotton grown on our farm, or for doing our daily chores. They felt this work presented opportunities for my siblings and me to learn responsibility and accountability. They believed there were lessons within the work that provided a reward better than money—namely, helping others as we sought to do our best.

My mother and father demanded the best each of us kids was capable of. Excuses were not in their vocabulary. Excellence was the only standard by which they measured themselves . . . and us. Yet they instilled confidence by example and nurtured it with constant encouragement.

3 HABITS

1. *Saving.* My parents first set aside a percentage of every dollar earned, before any of the household income was spent.

2. *Avoiding Debt.* Except for one minor exception, my parents never used installment accounts, credit cards, or any form of debt to buy consumable goods and services *(things you use up quickly)*. The story is too long to repeat here. Suffice it to say, that exception was costly and they and I learned the lesson well. Even when they had to use debt to buy an

appreciating investment asset like a home, they paid the debt as soon as possible. They wanted the peace of mind and the savings on interest. They paid off their home mortgage in thirteen years!

3. *Preparation.* Sometimes I think my parents invented details. They were always advance-preparation addicts. They were the most skilled planners I've ever known.

With these three simple but very profound habits, my parents created positive landmarks and powerful life and financial results. As a result of these habits, my father retired when he was fifty and my mother retired when she was forty. For over a quarter century after that, they had the financial resources to do what they wanted, whenever they wanted.

Were they able to achieve this because they had been making huge salaries? Not by a long shot! The *most* my parents ever earned—together—in one year was about $60,000 in gross income. (This is their largest annual gross income adjusted to the spending power of today's dollar.) Out of this they tithed to the church plus gave to other worthy causes, paid taxes, and supported four children. Yet still they were prosperous and enjoyed an early retirement.

So . . . what do you plan on accomplishing with your life, your income, your assets? What philosophy will guide you to reach those goals? What heart-held beliefs will the habits of your life and finances express?

As we move forward in your reading and working on your finances, please try to remember:

> *A sound philosophy of life and money expressed in wise habits is the bridge from poverty or false success to highest prosperity.*
>
> —Cecil O. Kemp Jr.

WISDOM AND TRUTH ARE NEVER OUT OF DATE

Few would argue against my parents' qualities as good models for our personal lives today. But models for money management?

Some will guffaw over the supposition that their example is legitimate for financial decisions. They will exclaim that we cannot adapt such patterns to today's high-tech, fast-paced world.

Consider the undercurrents giving rise to these questions and doubts.

We have come to the point in our society, especially in regard to material resources, where pretentiousness, shallowness, and selfishness cause us to overlook the beautiful, enduring value of simplicity. Thus, we incorrectly believe that those who have achieved real success are only those who have a remarkable, even phenomenal, quantity of dollars, possessions, or intellect.

We have come to a superficial, false perception of real success. Many even think that success can be achieved only by super persons who are either so charismatic, visionary, creative, or skilled—physically or mentally—that the rest of us cannot even attempt to attain their success. This explains why there are two common complexes: the superiority and the inferiority complex.

In our careers, in our families . . . and with money management . . . we usually adopt as role models those who are physically, intellectually, and materially gifted. The truth is, these are not the most important models, although some are good.

I see my parents as excellent models for all facets of our lives, including how they put money in its proper perspective and wisely handled it and the other material blessings of their lives accordingly. Because they were not unusually gifted but simply lived according to hard-won convictions that bred wisdom, honor, and love, they are more easily imitated than "superpersons."

I repeat again. The models most of us adopt are people whose example has been lived out in front of us. We follow those who have had the most time, power, and opportunity to influence us. From the outside looking in, my parents may seem quite unremarkable. They were a simple, hardworking couple who held three full-time jobs—proudly being excellent parents, factory workers, and farmers of forty acres of less than choice land.

But if you stop and consider how they moved from financial poverty to spiritual riches and then to retiring early—in a house they owned, without hurting anyone "on the way up" but, indeed, while helping those they encountered on their path through life—I believe you will agree they were very remarkable. Perhaps even, in a more real sense than is normally spoken of, phenomenal.

The landmark life and financial habits of my parents were shaped largely on the beliefs and habits of their generation. Their money personality was a successful application of values that many in their generation shared. These values, and the money habits, especially, are rarely seen in practice—or taught—today in such detail. They are a crucial foundation that is lacking in today's culture—a foundation that should be instilling positive landmarks in our children.

I may have veered big-time from my parents' teachings in my post-college attempt to find a shortcut to prosperity and fulfillment, but it was the landmarks established in my heart, based on the bedrock of my parents' beliefs and actions, that gave me a place to return to when I failed. I had principles to guide me when I committed to regaining my spiritual and financial footing. It was the combination of their influence, my own good and bad experiences with money, and my personal relationship with God that led me to the 7 Laws of Highest Prosperity (learned the hard way) and allowed me to fill the pages of this and previous books.

I encourage you to review and possibly to rethink your definitions of success and wealth, your values, and your priorities. Take a soul-searching look at your own money personality. I encourage you to honestly answer this question: "Who am I, anyway? And why do I want to be prosperous?"

And I encourage you to take a hard look at the "old-fashioned" wisdom of Scripture and my parents and figure out why it may still work well for you.

Before proceeding to the next chapter, please consider and record your thoughts on the following worksheet, Exploring My Money Personality.

WORKSHEET 1

Exploring My Money Personality

NOTES FROM READING THIS CHAPTER

PART I
MY BASIC MONEY PERSONALITY

Now you can begin to explore your money personality through a three-step process of self-examination.

1. Examine your overall personality.
Are you a giver or a taker, cautious or rash, moderate or whole-hog wild, secure inside or in need of outside affirmation?

Are you disciplined or not? Do you follow through on your resolutions? Or do you procrastinate? If you procrastinate, do you want to follow through? If so, what helps you to follow through most consistently? What keeps you from doing so? How do you feel about that?

Do you avoid what hurts? If so, how do you feel about this quality in yourself? How do you feel about how it affects those close to you, those who pick up the burdens you avoid owning as yours?

2. Examine the roots of your personality.
    Determine what your parents or caregivers (or other mentors on money) taught you about handling money, since this is an important influence.

3. Identify the driving force behind how you handle money.
Are your spiritual or ethical values reflected in how you choose to spend or save money? Or do you separate your spiritual life from your economic life? Do God and goodness even come into the picture when you're reviewing your budget? If so, how is this so? And how might it be more fully so? If not, how can that change? Note below at least one thing you could do to begin this change.

PART II
MORE ABOUT MY MONEY PERSONALITY
    The following exercises will help you explore and learn more about your money personality. Please be completely candid in your answers to the questions. If a question isn't phrased in financial terminology, assume it is about life in general. I encourage you to approach and complete this exercise soberly and thoroughly, because of its enormous potential value to your life, relationships, and finances.

List the five top blessings in your life.
    1.
    2.
    3.
    4.
    5.
List your three best money habits.
    1.
    2.
    3.
List your three worst money habits.
    1.
    2.
    3.

Record images from the past.
    Think a moment and then record one incident that typifies your father's style of spending and saving. Then do the same with your mother's spending

and saving styles. Record the images you see when you think of these things and comment on how your financial style matches that of your father or your mother.

Repeat the above process for anyone who you feel has been a significant mentor or influence on you to this point in your life.

List the past decisions you've made at the most important landmarks in your life—both in the area of your life's guiding philosophy and of how you manage your finances. List only those that you see as guiding your current thinking and behavior. After listing them, ponder each for a few minutes and record your feelings and thoughts.

Identify various personality characteristics about yourself.
Do you know how to spend and enjoy money, or are you a compulsive saver?

Is risk a blind spot for you?

Do you feel guilty making a lot of money?

Do you view money as your security or merely as a tool to achieve concrete, rewarding goals?

Do you trust or distrust others with your money?

Do you take criticism personally, even if true and regardless of how constructively shared?

Are you a worrywart? Would others agree, except that they might characterize you as a "control freak"?

When someone in a position of power tries to manipulate you into taking an action you strongly disagree with, do you tend to take the action out of fear, but fume and fuss to yourself (or someone close to you) without voicing your concerns to the person applying the pressure? If not, how do you react?

What is the process you go through in asking for forgiveness or forgiving someone?

Are you typically indecisive? Or, if you are typically decisive, do you ever regret your decisions?

When not knowledgeable, do you simply avoid dealing with things no matter how important? Or do you seek information and advice?

Are you a do-it-yourselfer, a self-teacher? Or do you prefer to be taught in a step-by-step way?

Do you do what you say you'll do, or do you procrastinate?

Examine some of your money habits.
Out of each dollar of after-tax income, what are your percentages for giving and saving?

What is your current savings system?

What is the most important thing you want to teach your children about money?

Have you ever spent excessively on a gift for someone, in order to impress them?

Have you taken "shopping sprees" to reward yourself? Did you use credit to pay for it?

What are the names of your current creditors? What did you buy and why? How much do you currently owe and what is your target date to pay off?

How would you describe your spouse's (or intended spouse's) spending behavior?

Has financial wastefulness and/or procrastination affected you and your family? How?

Which of the following phrases best describes *your* investment philosophy? (Circle one.)

Very conservative	Middle of the road
Conservative	High risk taker

Which of the following phrases best describes your *spouse's* investment philosophy? (Circle one.)

Very conservative	Middle of the road
Conservative	High risk taker

How diversified are your investments, both in terms of type of investment and companies you have shares in?

Examine some of your feelings about money.
What is the worst conflict you and your spouse (throughout this book, substitute the appropriate word for *spouse*: intended spouse, partner, etc.) have over money?

What is your greatest fear about money?

What are your financial and life priorities?

What are the financial temptations you face? Why? How are you currently managing them?

Have the desire for the approval of others and for power negatively affected your life and finances?

Have you ever used money as a substitute for other ways of expressing your love? If so, why?

What are the sources of your negative feelings about money? How do you cope with them?

What does the word *generous* mean to you?

What is your attitude about paying income taxes? What are the motives behind that attitude?

Have overreactive emotions caused you heartache, sorrow, and regret in the past? How?

Note your concluding thoughts on your money personality.

Having gone through all these questions, what conclusions have you drawn about your particular money personality? Note as many important points as you wish to remember. Then circle the ones you would like to keep in mind when you begin to share your discoveries and visions with your partner (so the sharing will be more successful). Underline the ones you want to tell your partner about.

Share your discoveries with your partner.

If you feel you are ready to share these discoveries with your partner, please be sure to reread the cautions in the text of chapter 1 about why people argue about money. Then go over the guidelines in "A Note on Process" and in chapter 4.

You may find it better to wait until you've worked through all of part I of *Wisdom and Money* before you set up a time to share your thoughts.

Whichever method you choose, good luck in your sharing!

2

THINKING LIKE SAM

We have two lives. There's the one we learn with and the one we live after that.
　　　　　　　　　　　　　　　　　　　　　　　　　—Bernard Malamud

Before moving further into the financial food for thought that is the real nitty-gritty of this book, let me spend a little more time on what may, at this point, seem to be a digression. I believe what I am about to share is the essential ingredient to the formula for financial success that you seek. And I believe that, by the time you have finished working through this book, you will believe that too.

THE PHILOSOPHY OF WISDOM

True happiness—this is what you seek, is it not?

To find it, keep in mind the following statement by a famous mathematician and philosopher:

Happiness is neither within us only, or without us; it is in union of ourselves with God.

　　　　　　　　　　　　　　　　　　　　　　　　　—Blaise Pascal

There are skills and habits essential to attaining and maintaining the personality, the character that will bring you highest prosperity, which I define as well-being in every dimension of life, not just the accumulation of material wealth. The skill of heart-based thinking and the wise habits that come from that way of thinking are the visible signs of the soul-spark at the center of a life guided by the Philosophy of Wisdom. Their importance to bringing you fulfillment is shown in the companion to this book, the fable *7 Laws of Highest Prosperity.*

• Back to Sam

Let me summarize from *7 Laws* how important it is to live by the Philosophy of Wisdom. This summary is a poor substitute for reading the book itself, but it will help those who haven't read it until they get the chance to do so. And it will remind those who read it awhile back of how the story develops.

Sam the wood gatherer (in the book *7 Laws*) sought happiness. He was a questioning sort of fellow and he began as a youth to wonder if there was a better way to live his life. Soon circumstances dictated that he make his first visit to the big city just beyond the small village where he was brought up. There his eyes were opened to material wealth and he met a man named Menro. This Menro saw the signs of Sam's restless search. Subtly, he began to suggest to Sam that there was indeed a better way to live life; it was a way where he would always do the best work he possibly could. Menro promised Sam that if he followed this way, he would not only be able to earn a better living, he would always feel good about himself and what he did.

Although Sam misconstrued most of what wise Menro was advising, Sam listened. As a result of their meeting, he moved from his village into the neighboring big city that seemed to be filled with all the good things he'd longed for. Sam began a new life there.

At first he enjoyed what most would view as enormous success. He married Suzette, the woman of his dreams. Together they had three beautiful daughters. And as Suzette raised them and quietly pursued her own career, Sam worked day and night to become a man who appeared to be successful.

But somewhere along the way, Sam put aside the values and priorities of a wise man. As a result, he forgot what had been so truly important to him, and he missed out on enjoying life's greatest riches. As the years passed, he began to focus more and more on money, possessions, and status until, in the blindness of his ambition, he made some very unwise choices that led to near financial collapse.

Sam almost despaired as he faced the results of his unwise actions. Fortunately, though, he did find the path to a better way of life—after he began to listen to the wise mentors God put in his path. The story helps the reader to see, step by step, how Sam's mentors helped him get onto the road of atonement, heart-based thinking, and wise habit, and in the end, find the true happiness that he had sought from the beginning.

Because you have picked up this copy of *Wisdom and Money*, I assume you—like Sam—are looking for a better way to live your life. A way you hope will lead to true happiness. And I, like Magowin the cobbler, am going to tell you right here, right up front, that the better way is not simply a plan for creating a budget or for finding good places to invest your money or save for college or retirement—although those are important and I will address them and much more. The better way must begin, as it did for Sam, with a careful examination not just of your finances but also of your whole way of thinking —of what matters most to you. I would request that you ask yourself what your actions say about what you value, what you hope to get out of life. When you leave out your *if only*'s, are the values your actions show the values you mean to express with your life? Believe me, I know this way of thinking can be a challenge, at first. I ask you to dare to take that challenge!

As you consider my challenge, please read what a famous physicist once said:

Some things you can count don't really count; some things you cannot count really do count!

—Albert Einstein

And think about the truth of what my father once told me:

A person with an experience is never at the mercy of a person with a theory.

—Cecil Kemp Sr.

I have observed thousands of people in the successful financial planning and investment advisory business my wife, Patty, and I operated for over sixteen years. I can say that I know Einstein and my father hit the jackpot of life wisdom! The intangibles are what people find to be most important to them in the end. If you use only the chapters of *Wisdom and Money* that speak of budgeting, saving, and investing, you will probably improve your finances, but you will not become wise. So please take up my challenge, which is based on over thirty years of personal experience.

FINDING LIFE'S GREATEST RICHES

Life's greatest riches, then, are what matter most, what are valued the highest. They are not mere money or even relationship with family, though these are wonderful and in this book I will help you strive for them in the right ways. Life's greatest riches are what bring us true happiness and they are found in only one place. That place is the same as the source of wise money management. It is the Source of all wisdom.

Although many think that, if they just do things a certain way, they will "get it right," I have to say that it is my experience that striving to do right on the human level alone is a setup for failure. It has been my experience that the insight we need to see what changes we should make to improve our lives flows out of an interactive partnership with the indwelling Spirit of God. That is the wellspring of the power to make the personality changes required to possess the desire, discipline, and heart-based thinking and habits to manage our life and finances wisely. When you let God help you, you will develop wise habits and find the wisdom you need to accomplish whatever, deep down inside, you long to accomplish.

Hard to believe? You can use *Wisdom and Money* without God. But if you do so, you will miss most of the wisdom it contains. Let me remind you of something else that famous physicist once correctly said:

> *Problems cannot be solved with the same level of thinking that created them.*
>
> —Albert Einstein

The higher level of heart-based thinking that Sam the wood gatherer had to reach, and that I encourage you to reach by applying the contents of *all* of this book, will lead you to true happiness. Maintaining heart-based thinking requires listening to the indwelling Spirit and responding. Most likely, the response will require that (1) you learn to habitually occupy your mind with the right things and that (2) you busy yourself with the right activities. I have found that, as we do so, we too begin to experience what Sam experienced—the lasting peace, joy, and happiness that this heart-based living brings. And we come to consider the discipline needed to live this way immeasurably worthwhile.

Where does this higher level of thinking come from?

HEART-BASED THINKING

> *Character passes into thought—not vice versa.*
>
> —Ralph Waldo Emerson

Most people will agree with Einstein and Emerson. Higher-level thinking requires getting out of your rut. It comes *from* better character, it doesn't *cause* better character. So what is the cause of better character (which is related to the personality concepts of the last chapter)?

I believe that better character is something we humans cannot produce by ourselves. Highest character (in its superlative form) is God-like character that can result only when we choose to let the Spirit of God that lives within work through our human spirit—Blaise Pascal's union of ourselves with God. When we allow this, we are freely given three qualities of right thinking (gifts, if you prefer). Those qualities are wisdom (spiritual knowledge), honor (spiritual ethic) and hope (spiritual inspiration). How this heart-change occurs is metaphorically described by Jesus in the fifteenth chapter of John. In paraphrase, He said, *"I am the vine; you are the branches. Whoever lives in Me and I in him bears much fruit. And apart from Me you can do nothing."* Keep this beautiful picture of the union of the strong grapevine and its leafy branches laden with grapes in mind as we work together to help you become more highly productive in your life.

Through the Spirit of God's active presence in us, our character and personality—our very heart—is transformed and we are filled with a vitality that produces heart-based thinking, which will bear much good fruit. The presence of God within purifies our hearts and gives us the better way of thinking that will lead to better character. We begin to live more fully by the five core beliefs of the Philosophy of Wisdom: (1) the power Source for a life built on the Philosophy of Wisdom is God; (2) true wisdom, purpose, and joy come from loving God, listening to God, allowing God to love you, and serving others; (3) we are a combination of the physical and the spiritual, and we must acknowledge and experience both to live fully; (4) the life-changing power of prayer is real; (5) we are assured of guidance and help.

As we become transformed, we will find it easier to live by the 7 Laws of Highest Prosperity that are a key component of the Philosophy of Wisdom. They are based on Psalm 19, verses 7 through 11. They are printed opposite the first page of chapter 1 in this book.

TRUE PROSPERITY

What is the payoff for all this initial extra effort to change our way of thinking? The payoff is true prosperity as opposed to mere material wealth. When we ask the Spirit to tell us how to think and act, when we ask Him to send us mentors, when we ask for the ability to discipline our life, when we ask for the help to see what needs to be changed so that our character and personality will be more godly—more generous, hardworking, and joyous— we are living by what I call the Philosophy of Wisdom. Our resulting new God-like character will be driven by true inner prosperity—peace, joy, integrity, and real hope, a confident expectation and certainty about the future.

This new inner state of ours, filled with these new qualities, leads to higher-level thinking and to habits of thought and action that result in true outward excellence. Best inner being produces highest prosperity—a state of living that is marked outwardly by gracious goodness and noble conduct with money and every facet of daily life. Again I say: Those outward expressions come from having an inner person guided by eternal priorities, unconditional love, and generosity. I have never, in my experience, seen life excellence come *before* eternal priorities were taken to heart.

The Spirit's presence is, in essence, the medicine that heals our unenlightened moral nature, making us intellectually, morally, and spiritually sound and healthy—able to measure up to divine standards in how we live our lives and handle material resources. This is the foundation of higher-level heart-based thinking.

With this foundation in place, I promise that you will be able to develop and apply the life and financial habits that are at the heart of true greatness and genuine success with money. These habits, discussed in the next chapter of this book, are the same habits Sam of *7 Laws* learned from his mentors, the most important of whom was his wise wife, Suzette. Sam learned to always do his very best work, to set his feet on the right and wise path, and to pass along his gifts and knowledge to others. You can do this too. Attaining heart-based thinking and habits is indeed possible in real life, too—not just in fiction.

If you choose to attain them, you will no longer describe your life in these ways: You will no longer:

- go too fast in important facets of your life;
- let money, possessions, power, or other false status symbols call your name and divert your attention from your true priorities;
- live your life foolishly and recklessly;
- experience anxiety and fear about events you cannot control;
- have trouble sustaining meaningful relationships with the important people in your life;
- commit foolish actions that put your valuable relationships or anyone's life—including your own—at great risk;
- find your life unfulfilling or unsatisfying for reasons you can't define;
- enjoy your life, but feel it could be better somehow.

When you apply the heart-based thinking and wise habits that come from the Philosophy of Wisdom to your life, you will begin *immediately* to feel the fruits of following the philosophy's wonderful inner spiritual path.

But to do so, you have to make a choice. Choice is an awesome privilege and power, regardless of how it is exercised. If you choose to live by the Philosophy of Wisdom, true and lasting success will be the result in every aspect of your life—from the sphere of personal peace and joy, to that of your relationships, to that of leadership wherever you live and work and to your finances—as it has for millions of people over the course of thousands of years of history.

If you do not agree with this declaration after you have read this book and applied its principles to your life, if this book does not pay its way after you have finished applying it to your life, write to me. *I will be glad to give you a full refund of what you paid for it.*

This promise comes from my own heart-felt experience. Like Sam, I once blindsided myself with folly, compromise, and the empty promises of materialism. But almost two decades ago I dusted myself off, turned back onto the right road, and with my family, began again my life's journey along the spiritual path to wisdom, honor, and hope. I have since walked the inner path to true greatness. On it, I have made the most of my life and money, making both count for what really counts.

It is my hope that *Wisdom and Money,* with God's help, will teach you to do the same.

Before proceeding to the next chapter, please consider and record your thoughts on the following worksheet, Food for Thought.

WORKSHEET 2

Food for Thought

NOTES FROM READING THIS CHAPTER

FOOD FOR THOUGHT

Pause and read these inspirational quotes before going on to the next chapter. Then record your thoughts in spaces provided.

Keep this in mind: To know the better way, the most important suggestion I can make is that you partner with the Creator. To do so, you may want to consult the Scriptures and find appropriate mentors.

Thoughts of Others

For the sake of getting a living we forget to live.

—Margaret Fuller

One who loves is a participant in the being of God.
—Martin Luther King Jr. (paraphrase)

What happens to a man is less significant than what happens within him.
—Louis L. Mann

My Thoughts of Note

Lasting joy is found in pursuing higher purpose, doing the greater good.

Motive and desire are the on ramps to the path of life we follow.

Personal choice is the entrance and exit.

Record your thoughts in the space provided.
 Use this space for notes, after considering the words above and those below.

Thoughts of Others

Nurture your mind with great thoughts. To believe in the heroic makes heroes.
—Benjamin Disraeli

It's not how much we do, but how much love we put into doing.
—Mother Teresa

My Thoughts of Note

The mighty tree yielding the fruit of success began as a seedling of hope.

New strengths and future blessings are very often discovered in the middle of life's greatest adversities.

Record your thoughts in the space provided.
 Use this space for notes, after considering the words above and those below.

Thoughts of Others

I live my life in God, in the mysterious ethical divine personality which I cannot discover in the world, but only experience in myself as a mysterious impulse.

Out of the depths of my feeling of happiness, there gradually grew up within me an understanding of the saying of Jesus that we must not treat our lives as being for ourselves alone.

The tragedy of man is what dies inside himself while he still lives.
—Albert Schweitzer (all three quotes)

My Thoughts of Note

Look up to find the missing piece of the inner puzzle.

We're either driving away from or toward the Divine.

There are no parking spaces, rest stops, or time-outs in between.

Record your thoughts in the space provided.

Use this space for notes, after considering the words above and those below.

3

Wise Habits

We make our habits, then they make us. Wise habits are a servant, while unwise habits can be a slave master and your worst nightmare!

—Cecil O. Kemp Jr.

I want to share the most important habits you can foster in order to achieve financial success. We are all creatures of habit—and habits direct our daily living and working. Some of our habits are good and some bad. It is those bad habits that we need to get rid of in order to achieve our financial goals, and then we need to establish some good new habits in their place.

The secret to breaking unwise habits and forming (or retaining) ones that lead to highest prosperity is shared in chapter 2. In a nutshell, the secret is to develop heart-based thinking. We do this by listening to the still small voice of the Spirit of God. When we listen and respond, we allow our Spirit-led heart to rule our ego, mind, and body.

WHY ARE WISE HABITS IMPORTANT?

Every habit begins, is maintained, or is changed by exercising our power of choice. With each choice we choose to concentrate on something or someone we consider more desirable than something or someone else. If you want to achieve true excellence in life and with money (and in so doing, secure enduring benefits for yourself and leave valuable footprints for others to follow), then you must appreciate the importance of habit and begin to develop wise, lifelong ones. You probably already know this, but just in case you are not convinced, here are some inspirational quotes:

Habit is stronger than reason.

—Santayana

Every habit, good or bad, is acquired and learned in the same way, by finding that it is a means of satisfaction. We allow [habits] to persist by not seeking any better form of satisfying the same needs.

—Juliene Berk

We become what our most dominant thoughts are.

—Earl Nightingale (philosopher)

• Thinking in "3-D"

As you probably know, unwise habits can endanger the length as well as the quality of our lives and the results we attain with money. Happily, we can learn to recognize and adjust our unwise habits in time to delay or reverse their effects. Consider the three *d*'s of moving from unwise to wise habits:

1. *Desire*—really wanting to adjust unwise habits;
2. *Determination*—willing to put in the effort needed to change for the better; and
3. *Discipline*—making a heart commitment to take responsibility for our habits, even when our minds and bodies rebel.

Habits, both positive and negative, are powerful. Even if you allow your heart to be Spirit-led as I recommended in the last chapter, breaking negative habits can be difficult. To break the unwise habits you have fallen into and to substitute wise habits that are spiritually motivated and that offer substantially better results, you will need resolve.

Let me tell you a story, which I hope will fix in your mind the importance of listening to that voice if you wish to succeed in any aspect of life—personal, financial, or business.

• The Wise Woman's Success

A wise woman who was traveling in the mountains found a precious stone in a stream. The next day she met another traveler who was hungry, and the wise woman opened her bag to share her food. The hungry traveler saw the stone and, forgetting his hunger, asked the woman to give it to him. She did so without hesitation.

The traveler left, rejoicing in his good fortune. He knew the stone was worth enough to give him security for a lifetime.

But a few days later he came back to the wise woman. He told her he'd been thinking. Even though he knew the stone had great value, he was giving it back. He was hopeful she would give him something far more precious instead.

"What is it you want?" she asked him.

He replied, "Please give me what you have inside you. Tell me about the treasure that enabled you to give me the stone."

What treasure did the wise woman possess? In our society, especially in business circles, the word *successful* has been reserved for those who seem remarkable when measured by inferior standards like money, possessions, title, and physical and intellectual prowess. This is a superficial, false perception of success.

You probably have figured out by now that I use the word *successful* to describe those who are remarkable because, by measuring themselves with God's higher standards, they listen to His guidance and they become enabled to do ordinary things extraordinarily well! And how do they get that way? Like the wise woman, they all possess the habits of inner greatness.

Are they religious people, with superhuman ability?

No, yes, and yes.

No, they are not what many call religious; they do not live solely from the "outside," by religious regulations.

Yes, they are truly religious in that they are at peace with the God within and therefore with everyone and everything in their lives. Guided by heart-level thinking and wise habits, they love, laugh, and add soul-spark to the lives they touch. They are sound in all ways because they are spiritually centered.

And yes, they do have superhuman ability, but it does not come from their own human nature.

TAKING UP THE WISE WOMAN'S CARGO

The wise woman in the story possessed habits that made her far more wealthy than if she'd had only material wealth, financial skill, or any other such resource (like her precious stone). She had these habits because she cooperated with Someone who possessed her. I like to think of God as the precious living stone or jewel in my heart. If we allow Him to do so, He will transform our thinking and our habits so that we change from earthbound caterpillars to soaring, heaven-bound butterflies! To be truly great, we must use His indwelling Spirit as the power that guides our habits in this earthly life.

I didn't always think this way. It took me years before that lightbulb came on—the one that informed me that I was carrying around the most precious treasure on earth—and in heaven! Rather than treating the Spirit within me as a precious living jewel, I had been acting as if He were a cold, dead rock—a piece of worthless baggage I had to carry around! Like Sam the wood gatherer, I waited until I had learned my lesson the hard, expensive way before

I decided to backtrack and rediscover my inner treasure. Let me tell you: Material wealth, accolades, or high-energy success are wonderful; but I can say from experience that none of them compare to the inner greatness He creates when we allow Him to change our personality and, in turn, lead us to higher-level thinking and wiser habits. This inner greatness cannot come about just from following an intellectual idea. We cannot inherit it from wise parents. Neither can it be realized simply by being born again, attending church, or playing by religious rules. In keeping with Blaise Pascal's advice quoted in the last chapter, if we want this inner greatness, we must make a big-time, life-changing, conscious choice to allow the Spirit to guide us. And we must remain faithful to that choice.

For it takes a union of our spirit and the Spirit of God—what I refer to it as connection at the heart—to form and continually live the habits of true greatness. In this union, our personality will change and our heart-based thinking will grow. We will then be able to live wise habits based on the nine gifts of the Spirit: love, joy, peace, long-suffering, gentleness, goodness, faith, meekness, and self-control.

It would be easier if knowing this in itself were enough, wouldn't it?

But the facts are that the principles, values, and priorities of any philosophy become effective in our everyday living and working only when they literally become the fabric of our whole being. Through habitually applying any inspired truths, our spirit becomes a mirror image of whoever or whatever our source of inspiration is. So, as with the body, if we want to keep our spirit healthy, we need to choose a wise source of fuel, of inspiration. This will lead us to happiness, and to true greatness.

TRUE GREATNESS

While it is important we be well rounded, I believe *spiritual* greatness (excellence) is what true greatness is all about. It is the beginning point of well-being on all levels. It is indeed the secret to genuine and lasting success with life and finances.

So I encourage you to be spiritually minded. When spiritual matters take priority in our thinking over all other things, excellence in every way will become our priority. And this is a prerequisite to becoming successful with money. As we pursue material wealth, we need to be careful that nothing replaces our central focus on the pursuit of spiritual excellence. The soul-spark that comes from living this Philosophy of Wisdom will help you live a better way. As you work through material in *Wisdom and Money,* your heart-based thinking and heartfelt wise habits will, among other things, help you communicate with your partner about your discoveries and resolutions. These habits are the secret to genuine, lasting success in all aspects of your life as well as in terms of financial wealth. (Remember Sam? His first taste of this excellence was his awakening pleasure in a job well done. He was beginning to live by wise habits.) Heart-based thinking and heartfelt wise habits will ensure that true greatness remains your goal.

• An Example of True Greatness

My parents were what some might call common people, but they succeeded in an uncommon way. They had more at the end of their life than would be expected of "common" people. They retired earlier. They gave more away. And they did so because all their lives they practiced wise habits —habits of true greatness.

HABITS 1–6: HABITS OF TRUE GREATNESS

There are more than six of these habits, but I will briefly share the six that I feel are key to making the most of your life and money. Then I'll suggest four others that will help bring about true prosperity.

• Habit 1: Read and live by Scripture

• Habit 2: Pray about everything

Twins, these two spiritual habits teach us God's perspective so that we can have God's effectiveness in our decision making. Practicing these habits ensures that we grow deep spiritual roots and are equipped with the wings of faith in God.

As Sam the wood gatherer discovered when he was driven to the woods in search of the firewood he could no longer afford to buy, when we need answers about money and material resources, or any other aspect of life, we need to seek out our Maker. Like Sam, once we begin to practice this habit, whenever we are in need we will automatically go to the thing and the person we love most—Scripture and the Man Upstairs.

I encourage you to find a quiet place to meet with God and read at least one chapter of Scripture a day. As you read, make your reading a conversation with God—"O Father, I see that I have failed You like this person I am reading about; forgive me!" Or, "O my God, I want to be like this person; please help me!" and so on. Keep a journal of your thoughts. Then, in your secret meeting place with God, allow His Spirit to help you internalize what you have learned and live it out in daily conduct.

In the mad rush of modern life, our strength ebbs and we lose focus. Prayer is an interlude where our eyes turn upward, for answers to the demands that overwhelm. Alone with God, we have opportunity to both speak and listen. As we pour out our heart, He embraces us and listens. Secure in His love, we wait, giving space for His Spirit to refresh, renew, and impart wisdom and power for the journey.

Pay special attention to these truths:

- Prayer is your invisible tool that can make a very visible difference.
- Always—all day long—stay in a prayerful attitude.
- Listening to God should take priority over talking.
- Prayer changes things when nothing else will or can. As more and more health care professionals and scientists now acknowledge, the power of prayer to change your life, your financial situation, or your physical or emotional health is real!

• Habit 3: Worship regularly with like-minded believers

Worshiping in a group environment is essential to spiritual refreshment and growth. As God said, He is present in a place where His followers pray together. Therefore, group worship is a wonderful time to experience Him in a very real and renewing way.

In addition, we are nurtured by our church community in ways we are not nurtured elsewhere. When we become active members of a church, we join a unique and essential extended family, opening ourselves to the warmth and strengthening power of that fellowship.

• Habit 4: Practice the Golden Rule

Treat others as you would like to be treated if roles were reversed: Before acting, think, *How would I want the person I love most in the world to be treated by a stranger?* Then treat this person in that same way.

This is a life truth and a financial truth as well!

• Habit 5: Make the things of God the focus of your thought life

I can paraphrase Philippians, chapter four, to say: Whatever things are true, honest, just, pure, lovely, or of good report, whatever has virtue or praiseworthiness, these are the things that should be your inward food for thought. When faced with financial choices or difficulties, thinking this way is vitally important to wise decision making and to having the faith and courage that ultimately lead to life and financial success.

• Habit 6: Trust God in all things, at all times

Faith and worry are incompatible. Worry breaks the single-minded concentration on following Jesus' teachings about faith, prayer, and making wise choices. Release the cares of life to God, including those involving your finances. In faith, rely on God's promise that *all* things work together for good for the children of God. Look through the eyes of faith and unwaveringly stand on that promise.

I believe these six habits of true greatness are at the heart of spiritual and financial excellence and also at the heart of a life of humility and service.

Their source is the Spirit of God—the precious living cornerstone who, if allowed, will create the inner greatness that is the foundation of masterpiece lives. The Spirit of God is the supernatural power source for enjoying the better life of abundance in the here and now—on this side of heaven!

HABITS 7–10: FINANCIAL HABITS WORTH NOTING

These six habits of true greatness and the following four financial habits have helped millions of people throughout history achieve highest prosperity. Some readers will probably agree that the next four habits are orthodox when discussing financial success, but may find the first six to be quite unorthodox. Nevertheless, I state from experience, if you try them all, I promise you will be very pleased with the result.

These four habits help you stick to your financial plan and budget. There will be much more discussion on each of them in coming chapters.

• Habit 7: Set up a system of discipline and follow it

Someone once observed that the successful person has the habit of doing things that those who fail do not like to do. It is worth noting that successful people do not like doing those things either, but their dislike is subordinated to the strength of their purpose. A system of wise and reasonable rules to govern conduct in money matters is essential. This includes budgeting, saving, investing, and spending systems. (Habits and methods for establishing these systems are discussed in upcoming chapters.)

Success with money does occasionally occur without the use of personal discipline. But more often, success with money requires discipline. History is full of examples of personal, family, and business distress that was caused by lack of discipline in finances, passions, and appetites. But it is also full of examples in which discipline has led to enormous life and financial success.

• Habit 8: Do not procrastinate—take action after appropriate planning and preparation

Goethe said, *"Things which matter most must never be at the mercy of things which matter least."* To me this means we are to quit dawdling and procrastinating and take charge! We are each responsible for our own life. There is no one else who is. Each of us makes the choice to act or not to act. If we are prone to the self-serving attitude of letting others take care of our responsibilities, we need to change that attitude. All of us should dream, set goals, and then take the initiative. More than just taking the initiative, we should be proactive: We should seek out our course of action to make our dreams and goals a reality. (Congratulations! That is what you are doing by reading this book—seeking solutions. I will encourage you to act on what you find here.)

Earlier, I recommended that this process of preparation and planning begin by your studying Scripture and asking God for direction. At this point, let me suggest that, as you read *Wisdom and Money*, you resolve now to form new habits of dreaming, setting goals, preparing, planning, executing, assessing, and adjusting, in that order. We will look into the specifics of how to implement these habits in more depth in following chapters.

• Habit 9: Keep your promises

A financial plan and budget, prepared according to my recommended steps, means you are making explicit promises to yourself and often to others as well. When you make and keep promises, you strengthen your willpower. Each time you keep a promise, you increase the amount of trust you have in yourself, to walk the talk with God's ongoing help. And keeping promises can help overcome procrastination!

I suggest you start with small steps and work your way up. For example, if you have a problem with overspending, make yourself a promise that the very next time you are offered the opportunity to get another credit card, open another installment account, or buy something with an existing credit card, you will simply say "No" and stand firm.

• Habit 10: Develop a long-term perspective

Remember Aesop's fable "The Goose That Laid the Golden Egg"? A goose had faithfully served his owner by laying one plain old egg a day. One day, to his amazement, the farmer discovered a golden egg—and each day thereafter the goose continued to supply him with a golden egg! Eventually, pleasure got the best of him. Growing greedy, and anxious to speed up the process of attaining wealth, the farmer killed the goose in an attempt to remove all the golden eggs at once—but, of course, the eggs he expected to find had not yet been formed. Now he had no goose and no more golden eggs.

In the book of Proverbs, Solomon taught that steady, diligent labor brings prosperity; hasty speculation brings poverty. I agree! Slow and steady is better. Evaluate your progress often and remember: *"Inch-by-inch, it's a cinch."*

INSIGHTS

- Loyalty to truth is a prerequisite for receiving more.
- Greater abundance begins with a better, higher perspective.
- The wisest habit is the habit of listening for and to the still small voice of God within.
- Routine is the time interval between inspiration and results.
- Where you choose to place your attention defines and directs your life.

Before proceeding to the next chapter, please consider and record your thoughts and work through the exercises on the following worksheet, Brainstorming My Habits and Visions.

WORKSHEET 3

Brainstorming My Habits and Vision

NOTES FROM READING THIS CHAPTER

There are two parts of this worksheet. The first part helps you look at some of your habits of thought. The second part helps you change those habits by asking you to brainstorm on the possibilities of your life. Enjoy working through them!

PART I
BRAINSTORMING MY HABITS

As you did with the advice in the last chapter, please pause and read these inspirational quotes before going on to the next chapter. Then record your thoughts in spaces provided. This foundation to heartfelt habits of thinking and acting are what will help you stay the course!

Thoughts of Others

Wise people, even though all laws were abolished, would still lead the same life.
—Aristophanes

We are all happy if we only knew it.
—Fyodor Dostoevsky

Neither shall you allege the example of the many as an excuse for doing wrong.
—Moses (paraphrase)

My Thoughts of Note
The wellspring of true service to others is love of God.

Life walking with the Divine is a grand adventure, a thrilling and exciting daily journey full of highest rewards.

Record your thoughts in the space provided.

Use this space for notes, after considering the words above and those below.

Thoughts of Others

This, then, is held to be the duty of the man of wealth: First, to set an example of modest, unostentatious living . . . to provide moderately for the immediate wants of those dependent upon him; and after doing so to consider all surplus revenues which come to him simply as trust funds, which he is called upon to administer . . . in the manner which, in his judgment, is best calculated to produce the most beneficial results for the community—the man of wealth thus becoming the mere agent and trustee for the poorer brethren. . . .

—Andrew Carnegie

My Thoughts of Note

Soul health is the individual's and the world's major health care need.

The highest pursuit of life is discovery of the Divine and then who we are in Him.

Record your thoughts in the space provided.

Use this space for notes, after considering the words above and those below.

Thoughts of Others

You cannot serve the Divine and money. Choose the Divine, money matters will then be taken care of.

—Jesus (paraphrase)

Wisdom is more profitable than silver and gold, and more precious than rubies. Long life is in its right hand and riches and honor in its left hand.

—Solomon (paraphrase)

Be not made a beggar by banqueting upon borrowing.

—Ecclesiastes

My Thoughts of Note

Become exceptional at the ordinary.

Discipline is God-given inspiration wisely controlled as He leads.

Record your thoughts in the space provided.

Use this space for notes, after considering the words above and those below.

PART II

BRAINSTORMING MY VISION

We often live life habitually, driven by immediate need, without taking the time to look at what could be. Understanding our vision and our dreams is critical to a life of true success. I encourage you to begin to form a new vision with new habits of thinking and action.

I hope you enjoy the exercises below.

• Scenario 1: Imagine . . .

You have no bills, no financial worries, and no barriers in your way. You have permission to pursue the work that brings you the greatest joy, peace, excitement, and adventure.

A. Describe three visions.

Write three activities, tasks, causes, or careers you can envision yourself doing or experiencing or empowering. These may be things you already are doing, or they can be activities or jobs you've dreamed of doing or of enabling others to do with your assistance. Just answer honestly and listen to your real voice telling you what truly does or would make you "feel alive." (If you would actually love to be running a business or creating artwork, say so, and describe the business or the artwork. Don't answer what you think you *should* want, answer what you really would *prefer* to be pursuing.)

Vision 1: I picture myself . . .

Vision 2: I picture myself . . .

Vision 3: I picture myself . . .

B. Review your visions.

Now go back and reread your visions. Below, in the three spaces provided for each "vision" on the right, write down three words or phrases that describe how you *feel* while you're pursuing these envisioned activities, tasks, causes, or careers in your imagination.

Vision 1:

This makes me feel . . .

Vision 2:

This makes me feel . . .

_____

_____

_____

Vision 3:

This makes me feel . . .

_____

_____

_____

C. Note how you answered.

If, for example, you noted that all the activities make you feel *peaceful*, then your inner person—your unique self—values peace. Or if you wrote down *powerful* twice, then your inner person values power. These are clues to your money personality. Bear in mind that no value should be labeled as "good" or "wise" or "bad" or "unwise." (Perhaps you were born to harness power and will use it to help mankind!) The point is, you need to come to an understanding of what you *do* value—and what your heart yearns for.

Note here what you see about yourself from this envisioning.

D. Expand your vision.

Write down what your envisioning shows you about who would benefit from each dream.

Okay. You're still imagining—no worries, no bills, no barriers. You are still pursuing these three dream activities. Keep envisioning, but this time examine the desire and motive behind each wish, goal, or vision.

Are you the only one who would benefit if you could make this happen?

Who else would benefit?

How would they benefit if you were pursuing your dream or if you achieved it?

You don't have to be specific about the "who." Perhaps you'll conclude that you are the only one who will benefit. In that case, give yourself the permission to expand this vision to include others. Is your dream activity directed to others—for example, something like "saving a community landmark"? Examine your motives to see if this is for selfish reasons, or if there are others who would benefit if you carried your dream into reality.

Is your dream activity "to learn and start organic gardening?" Brainstorm on how this could benefit others. Would you produce more than you need and share or sell to others? Would your spouse benefit because you would be fulfilled? Would the community benefit because you have a yearning to develop new hardy crops?

Close your eyes and really envision how this particular dream of yours would actually impact others. Then write it down on the left-hand side of each section below (leaving the right-hand section for the next stage of work.)

Vision 1: Others will benefit because . . .

This makes me feel . . .

_____

_____

_____

Vision 2: Others will benefit because . . .

This makes me feel . . .

_____

_____

_____

Vision 3: Others will benefit because . . .

This makes me feel . . .

_____

_____

_____

E. Note how you feel about these visions.

In the spaces on the right-hand side of the above section, add three words or phrases that describe how you feel when picturing the ripple effect or benefit that will come about because of your chosen activities, tasks, causes, or careers.

• Scenario 2: Now Imagine . . .

You *do* have mounting bills and debts and schedules to keep. Your inner dreams and spiritual life have been put on hold while you try to succeed at this "physical realm gig." Your busy life is directed by immediate needs and fueled by a desire for more possessions or higher status to fill an emptiness you feel. All this leads to greater dependence on a steady paycheck and more stress from more bills. For the rest of your life you remain blocked by financial hurdles, ongoing emergencies, doubts, fears, or a lack of conviction to pursue your real desires.

You had promised yourself you would get to those dreams; you had told yourself you'd get out of debt; you had told yourself that having a fancy car or big house would make up for never getting around to launching your own small business.

You had even told yourself that maybe when you retired you would finally get to those personal dreams—but now your grown children are in debt and in need (they learned from you . . .) and you're too busy working a part-time job and helping with children and grandchildren to see beyond the next month.

The book that may have touched another heart never got written.

The leadership qualities you knew would be a positive influence on others never got put into action.

The photographs of children that would have lit up their parents' faces never were taken.

The invention never got marketed.

The travel diaries never got written.

The scholarships you always wanted to fund never got funded.

The light you were meant to shine got hidden under a bushel basket.

The restaurant you envisioned all your life never became real.

The nurse you knew was within you never had her chance.

Your knack for mechanical ingenuity was never utilized.

The small house in the country was "never meant to be."

A. Describe three alternative visions.

For each of the visions in scenario 1, use the space below to fill in the essence of the dream that, in scenario 2, will not be fulfilled. Then describe how you feel about the possibility of never fulfilling that dream.

Vision 1: I may never fulfill this . . .

                                                                    This makes me feel . . .

_____

_____

_____

Vision 2: I may never fulfill this . . .

                                                                    This makes me feel . . .

_____

_____

_____

Vision 3: I may never fulfill this . . .

                                                                    This makes me feel . . .

_____

_____

_____

_____

B. Note what will be missed.

For each of the visions in scenario 2, describe what the rest of us would miss out on because you did not fulfill this dream. Then list three words or phrases that describe how this loss to others makes you feel.

What creation or song or benefit—that only you could have achieved—would die with you, never to be realized, if this scenario were to come true?

Vision 1: If I never fulfill this dream, others will miss out on . . .

This makes me feel . . .

_____

_____

_____

Vision 2: If I never fulfill this dream, others will miss out on . . .

This makes me feel . . . .

_____

_____

_____

Vision 3: If I never fulfill this dream, others will miss out on . . .

This makes me feel . . .

_____

_____

_____

Puts a new light on things, doesn't it?

• What if . . .

What if the still, small voice within you—that disquieting, inner voice that rules your heart—what if that voice is God tugging at your soul saying, *"Use the talents and passions I gave you. You were created to create with Me. You are my beloved child. Your dreams and visions are the prayers we send to each other."*

What if one of these personal dreams of yours—maybe two of them—maybe all three—could give joy not only to you, but some form of happiness or relief or wisdom or help to someone else—perhaps to many, many people?

If you have a wish, a heart's desire, a vision of yourself doing or manifesting or being something that suits your talent, listen to it very closely. If that same dream would help others and if your main motivation in achieving this dream is to somehow be of service to others, then the Creator has a mission for you.

Can you imagine turning down a call—a call specifically for you—to do meaningful, significant work that benefits others and also provides you with an income?

People turn down this kind of calling every day. Worse yet, they repeatedly turn it down throughout their lives. They get to the end of their life and say they did not do what they thought they really were created to do.

I encourage you to dream big, dream wisely, set goals that reflect your most important dreams, develop an action plan based on those goals, and work that plan with God's great help!

There is more on the goal-setting process in chapter 5.

4

RELATIONSHIPS AND MONEY

Love does not consist in gazing at each other but in looking outward in the same direction.

—Antoine de Saint-Exupéry

I hope that you have read 7 *Laws of Highest Prosperity* by now. If so, do you remember Suzette and Sam's fireside talk in chapter 8? I encourage you to re-read that husband and wife chat before reading this chapter.

If you are not married or considering marriage, you might be tempted to skip this chapter. But there is quite a lot of good advice here that applies to everyone, especially in the areas of respect and love for others and in the area of communication. I promise you, no matter what your state in life, reading this chapter will be profitable.

If as you read you find yourself thinking, *This sounds great, but I'd need a new partner to make it work*, then know that in a marriage as in everything else, change must begin with you. You are never alone when you walk with God. He will help you make the changes you need to make and He will bless you for having a willing heart. He will also bless you for working on yourself instead of trying to change your spouse. That is the way God works—person to person. Simply pray for your own guidance, and speak only when He prompts you to. Pray for your spouse too, remembering your own weaknesses and trusting that the Spirit will be working in your spouse's heart (whether it seems obvious to you or not!) in the same way He works in yours. Trust Him and obey Him as He whispers to you, and remember that it was a *fictional* Sam who started his journey to highest prosperity alone and found a wise, supportive wife already ahead of him in that journey.

In real life it isn't always that simple. If your spouse is not yet perfect (!), begin your journey alone as Sam did, and patiently wait to see what develops. Be strong and courageous. Read this chapter for the knowledge of how a couple can work together, and—who knows?—perhaps one day the two of you will sit down together just as Sam and Suzette finally did, to set out on your journey. Whatever happens, I predict that you will be glad you worked through *Wisdom and Money,* and your spouse will be thrilled with the changes in you. He or she may even be inspired to make some changes too.

TALKING ABOUT MONEY

How does a couple talk about finances? My suggestion to couples is that both partners work through this book, chapter by chapter, first individually. Then, if the relationship is ready, go over your worksheets together. This is especially true of the first five chapters. When you get to the later sections of the book on budgeting, saving, investing, etc., it might be best to go through the exercises together.

When you do get together to have your discussions, set aside enough uninterrupted time to be able to sit down alone and talk freely about your dreams, your goals, your vision for the family, and your finances. This will probably take several sessions and a commitment of several weeks. In order for the dreaming process to be productive, all your sessions, especially the ones on what you discovered about your money personalities (worksheet 1) and the ones about your personal dreams and those for your family vision (see worksheets 3 and 4), should be characterized by openness, with each person encouraged to express his or her innermost dreams and desires without value judgments. There will be time down the road to evaluate which of the dreams should become goals, and which goals are worth developing action plans and working toward. The conversations about money should openly examine and clarify what each of you brings to the financial table in the marriage partnership and how financial matters will be handled. As a couple, your goal in this book will be to write down your family vision and the mutual agreements and the money-management ground rules by which you hope to fulfill that vision.

I suggest taking time *before* you marry to create this family vision and to review and clarify financial issues and roles. But even if you haven't had the chance to do that before marriage, I suggest you begin it now, then review your visions and how they are being met (or not)—as well as your financial role assignments and how they are working—routinely and regularly during married life. (I recommend this be done at least once a year, preferably every six months.) This process will make for greater financial security and a far happier relationship.

• Honesty

Open and honest conversation (no confrontational methods allowed!) is essential to discussing and establishing written ground rules for money management. Honesty supports an approach to handling money which helps avoid serious disagreements later. As I suggested above, before you talk together, you should separately examine your own views toward money. Remember that men and women tend to hold significantly different views. (See chapter 1.) It is important not only to understand these differences but to talk about them and to work together to establish a mutually agreed upon protocol for handling money within the marriage relationship. To ensure that you establish as comprehensive a protocol as possible, first consider this entire chapter on your own. While reading, think about the process of discussing the material about what will make it easier for you to speak honestly with your partner and about what will make it easier for your partner to speak honestly with you. Then together, work the exercises (in the worksheet to this chapter) to help you come up with guidelines for your discussion. When you are ready to begin your talks, identify each major step of how money should be handled in the marriage and mutually agree on who will be responsible for each. I urge that each partner take on significant roles and not assign the handling of money to one person.

• Money Personality and Marriage

If you haven't already, share the results of your money personality worksheets with one another, and discuss all your views concerning money —your values, priorities, motives, and mental attitudes. When you discuss these, always be sure to explore why your spouse or spouse-to-be answers a particular question in a particular way—without being confrontational. Understanding another person for who they are (as opposed to who you thought they were or who you would like them to be) is an art!

Sharing your worksheets from chapter 1 ("Exploring My Money Personality") should be a considerable subject of the conversation. Enjoy it!

MAKING A PLAN

The soul-searching discussions of these first four chapters should lead into earnest and practical discussion on very important topics. The worksheet for this chapter will ask you to begin to make a financial plan for your life. Frequently, different attitudes about the level of money earned, assets held, and how money should be handled can cause conflict when discussion is attempted. There are guidelines for dealing with this potential for conflict in several topics of this chapter.

If you are prudent enough to be working through this book together prior to marriage, and if you both approach these issues humbly and with prayer, many of your differences can be amicably resolved before the wedding, thus making for a much happier marriage.

(Bear in mind that attitudes reveal a lot about a person—how they feel about tithing, saving, and spending says volumes about their mindset, spiritual direction, and self-discipline. If these differences lead to a decision not to marry, then I am going to go out on a limb and say that this is probably a divinely led conclusion. Also bear in mind that marriage—according to Scripture, God's divinely ordained institution on earth to represent His relationship with His people—is a growth process. It cannot *start out* perfect because the two partners are not perfect. Individually and together, with God's help, you will work a lifetime on becoming less selfish and more centered on the needs of others—your partner first, then your children if you have them, and then the rest of humanity. And it doesn't *end up* perfect either, not in this life! There will always be room for improvement for you both. So adjust your expectations and ask God for help in becoming the person He has in mind for you to be and get ready for a very fulfilling life with the one you love.)

Whether you are considering marriage or are already married, the planning session I have suggested will help you establish a protocol of how finances are to be handled within the marriage relationship. This session should also include discussion and agreement on:

- careers and their impact on the marriage, family, spiritual matters, and finances;
- who will work outside the home if and when children enter the picture;
- who will keep the household checkbook and pay household bills;
- percentages of earnings to be set aside for giving, saving, and spending;
- budgets, setting expenditure goals, investment approach, and so on;
- joint ownership of property (advantages and disadvantages);
- wills (be sure you are in agreement about what you both want, in case you both pass away at the same time. If either of you dies without a will, your spouse may receive only a portion of your separate property. The rest may be split among minor children or relatives, depending on laws in your state—see chapter 14, "Preserving Your Estate");
- medical coverage and beneficiaries of life insurance policies and retirement assets;
- other items you or your partner feel important to discuss and reach agreement on.

SEPARATE FINANCES?

Some, including financial professionals, advise that assets, liabilities, and incomes—those brought to the marriage and even those established individually within the marriage—should be kept separate. *I do not agree with that at all.* Though this may sound like simple financial common sense, it is normally a self-serving jackhammer of folly pounding away at the emotional and spiritual foundation of the marriage and the lives of all affected.

In marriage, two become one—that's the wonderful, empowering thing about marriage! Marriage is about joining together for support, comfort, and realizing lifelong goals—not about individuals with two separate lives. Financial resources are an energy source that the two individuals share to accomplish joint goals. Does that mean that the Mr. has all the same goals as the Mrs.? No, but together they each have the separate goal of helping the other to achieve their singular dreams, raise a family perhaps, support a philanthropic cause, and so forth. Becoming one is a spiritual function. Separating financial resources is a self-serving and, in my view, dangerous way of entering a marriage relationship. Even if one is wealthier than the other, or makes more income from working outside the home, my view is still the same: *When you marry you become one. If you are not willing to do this, you are undercutting your marriage from the start.*

For most rules there are exceptions, of course. I do think there are certain times when the couple can mutually agree that certain assets and liabilities should be legally separate for the purpose of maximizing the family's assets and income and minimizing taxes and other liabilities. But even then, always check with each other on the motives behind the decision. It might also be wise for each to have a separate checking account if—and I emphasize the *if*—they are used to deposit and disburse mutually agreed-upon budgeted spending sums. It is also wise for each to establish credit in his or her own name. But I am not thereby suggesting that either of you use that as justification to ignore the guidelines I share in other chapters about spending, consumer debt, and use of credit. With these exceptions noted, I do not recommend the common practice of the separation of assets.

What is my response to some who do not share this united-front approach to marriage and money? Who think it outmoded, old-fashioned, or even ignorant!? I can only warn you that over thirty years of personal and professional experience have demonstrated to me that when spouses aren't united on money matters, they are more likely to have destructive conflict over them!

Disagreements about money are the number one cause for quarrels between spouses and a leading cause of divorce. If you are committed to walking with God in your own life and in your marriage, then I recommend you trust the divine wisdom that teaches the sanctity and oneness of marriage—in all matters.

THE BASICS ON HOW TO APPROACH DISCUSSING MONEY

• With Love

The first law of highest prosperity is the law of Wisdom—the wisdom to let God guide you and fill you with unconditional love, patience, understanding, and the passion to serve others. When you have a financial discussion, bring God into the conversation—not in a doctrinal or judgmental sense, but in a very real spiritual sense. Try praying together. Then you will approach the money issues with the attitude that money is an energy source that can help sustain and support you and serve others.

Spouses who get real satisfaction and ultimate fulfillment are the ones who reach out beyond themselves to demonstrate real love, real caring, real concern for their spouse. As we are able to do this, a style of giving and sharing to help the partner build and reach his or her dreams becomes more and more natural to us. Let me emphasize: *These are not natural attitudes.* Self-sacrificial love does not come naturally. My experience has been that it results only when we allow the indwelling Spirit of God to give us the desire to please God above all. Only His Spirit can give us that desire. But if we ask Him for it, He will gladly give us our request and more—more than we ever imagined!

Remember too what I said at the beginning of this chapter: Let the changing begin with you. As I said, you have no control over your spouse. But you do have the power to seek God's help in changing yourself. This is the place to start. This is the place to continue. Let God do the work in the heart of your beloved. Only He can make the transformation necessary there. As only He can make that transformation within you.

Being the best spouse you can be and having a successful marriage is an ever continuing journey of attending to the needs of your spouse. The indwelling Spirit of God empowers and teaches you along this path. If you have been, as we all tend to be, pretty seriously focused on yourself and your needs, this may sound not only impossible but unpleasant to attempt. Believe me, it's the means to a journey of great joy and happiness, and *it is indeed possible!*

• With Cooperation

Unconditional love leads us to the desire to share our responsibilities equally—and to share the credit too. Work together toward common goals. Create an environment that gives your spouse the opportunity to demonstrate his or her talents with money, a sense that you are willing to be part of a team, that you are willing to make the necessary sacrifices, that you are ready to realistically evaluate your list of needs and decide that maybe some of them are actually wants that you can do without or wait until later to possess. Support each other in working toward those dreams. Help each other along the path. Do not take each other for granted. Take time to talk, take time to be together and nourish your relationship—take the time to plant some roses and come back often to water them.

• With Elephant Ears and Powder Puffs

We all need wise listening and speaking skills to communicate effectively, especially about money and its trappings. Those skills must be more than theoretical constructs in a marriage—we must demonstrate them in our personal examples. Put on your "elephant ears"—a pair of big, big, big ears, long on listening. Listening tells others you really care about their feelings, thoughts, and views about money. Money matters are often difficult to discuss. People quarrel easily about finances, especially when sacrifice is involved, and these quarrels arise even more easily where poor listening skills and ineffective or overemotional communication is a habit. It helps to recognize that what we are seeking when we jump in, interrupt, and give inappropriate or inappropriately timed advice is a false sense of power. This is hardly the environment for excellence and success.

Practice "powder puff" communication—tone of voice, body language, timing, appropriate silence, and soft, gentle, encouraging, uplifting, and positively affirming words that convey thoughtfulness, wisdom, appreciation, and praise.

Good listening and speaking skills produce a lasting and positive impact on your marriage as well as on other relationships. They also help bring good results from your financial dreams and expectations.

• With Thought and Sometimes With Silence

Consider whether now, later, or perhaps never is the right time to express yourself. Timing matters! Think before you speak or write anything. If we want to communicate so that our spouse understands, the beginning point is not opening the mouth too soon or picking up the pen to write a flood of words. Think about what you want to express, then think about how it will be received if said in a certain way. If the point of communication is to be heard, you the communicator need to take into account not just the intended meaning but also how it will sound to your partner.

HOW *NOT* TO DISCUSS THE SUBJECT OF MONEY

• With Blame

We are all tempted to assign blame. Self-righteous indignation lets us off the hook—we feel we don't have to take responsibility if someone else is to blame—right? And therefore we don't have to do anything to fix the problem.

On the other hand, it is honorable to accept responsibility for our own attitudes and choices regarding money and material resources, whatever they may be and wherever they have led us and our relationship. So in discussing your financial plans with your partner, be honorable!

Instead of casting blame on your partner, be wise and learn all you can from each failure as well as each success. Look hard at your own part in the problem. If you have little responsibility in one particular situation, remind yourself of your failures in other areas and how you want(ed) to be treated about them. (If your spouse can love you despite them, you can love your spouse as he or she works through this imperfection.) Ask the Spirit within to help you with the heart-skill of forgiveness.

Remember, you are responsible for your part of your relationship with your partner. You already know that an attitude of love and acceptance from one we love fosters in us the ability to remember that we can choose more wisely the next time. So give that love and acceptance to your partner. You will find that the air is cleared once blame is removed—or even just lessened, for a start! Hope will bloom and the discussion will continue.

You will both be encouraged as you come to see that you truly *do* have the power to change your marriage and your money management for the better.

• With Guilt

As you turn your focus from your spouse and onto yourself, remember that the point of doing so is to fix the problem. Wallowing in guilt leads only to failure. Dwelling on your own guilt in a lengthy way sidetracks the discussion, focusing it on you instead of on the problem. Do all you can to avoid such sidetracks in your discussions.

When you are alone, look for symptoms of guilt: It is often a hidden burden (often not admitted even to yourself). If you find it, let it go. If appropriate to the relationship, ask for, and *take* forgiveness. Doing so will give you the energy to talk with your partner and map out a plan for action. (If not appropriate to the relationship at the present time, ask for and take forgiveness from God, and proceed to making amends. Use a mentor if you need one. Then get back to the part of the conversation that *is* currently appropriate to your relationship.)

Don't forget that we all experience guilt at some time in our lives, either because we did something we perceived as wrong, or failed to do something we should have done. It is good to remember that, like blame, guilt is a symptom of not yet having taken responsibility for our actions, not yet having asked for forgiveness (from God, others, or ourselves), not yet having made amends to those we've hurt. If you feel guilt over something, treat it like a red light at an intersection: It is a sign that something needs to stop so that something else can take its place. Whatever you have unwisely done with money (or anything else), you now have the chance to change it. So accept responsibility for your mistake, ask for and receive forgiveness (letting go of guilt), make amends, and go on from there. Praying for the heart-skill to do all this well will help immensely. Praying to be reminded to put new habits into action will help your discussions. You will find you can use your heart-based thinking and wise habits sooner than you thought! Don't be afraid to give a smile or a hug.

Now return to the discussion with your partner. Talk about what you are both trying to resolve: how best to make changes.

HOW TO PREPARE FOR CONFLICT IN DISCUSSIONS

Blame and guilt are the major players in any discussion that ends fruitlessly in unresolved conflict. We are all human: One way or another, conflict may arise in your efforts to discuss money management. Please do not fail to overcome that conflict.

Failure to resolve conflict is the biggest obstacle to keeping marriage partners on the path toward achieving their life and relationship purposes, as well as highest prosperity. Wise partners are those who take the time *before* conflict arises to have in place an effective means of ensuring that the conflict is promptly and wisely resolved. Otherwise, the couple cannot achieve desired results. Unresolved conflict over money will ultimately cause strife and division, adversely affecting your unity and commitment to each other. I urge you to approach money in the marriage in ways that move away from conflict, toward peace and security.

You might start by agreeing on how you will proceed if conflict arises. Some couples give each other the right to end the discussion when things get out of hand. Either partner can say at any time something like, "This is getting off track. Let's stop for now and start again after we've had time to think about what's going wrong in this attempt to discuss our finances."

If this happens, do not blame your partner for calling the discussion to a halt. Have faith that he or she has the best interest of the relationship at heart. Pray for help, if you need it. Seek a mentor if you need one, but please don't let yourselves get stuck in a cycle of bitterness that leads to failure.

Because it is such an obstacle to so many, I repeat: If you're in the habit of carrying a grudge against your spouse over money or anything else, get over it the biblical way! Ask the indwelling Spirit for the heart-skill to forgive. Ask yourself bluntly, *Which would you rather have—the right to carry a grudge or a positive, loving relationship with your spouse?* Remind yourself that unresolved conflict brings destructive complexity to our lives. Remind yourself that resolving conflict is as simple as making the choice to let our spouse off the hook and work out a way to get along. Remind yourself how much more with our life—and finances—we can accomplish with a spirit of love and an attitude of forgiveness. Then ask God again to instill His motives into your heart: Ask for the gift of unconditional love so that your relationship can be healed of this conflict, the discussions on money management can continue, and your life can become one filled with success.

In summary, if you want to move forward, past conflict, to marital and financial success: When you say you forgive, truly release your spouse or another from further obligation. And when you ask for forgiveness, be sure to receive it fully.

For readers who don't have the blessing of having come from backgrounds that have taught them the basics of positive relationship skills (and many don't have that blessing!), I list some below. I encourage all readers to read them, and pray for guidance on which they need yet to develop. Then move forward with new heart-based thinking and wise habits of action.

MOVING FORWARD
• A Few Simple Relationship and Money Rules
- Ask nicely.
- If your spouse is doing well, say so privately and publicly; give heartfelt praise to your partner every opportunity you get. I find that expressing gratitude and respect toward people is very helpful, as is showing them your acceptance, approval, and appreciation. This is not always easy, but it's always rewarding.
- If either of you makes mistakes or fails, discuss it pleasantly and lovingly and move on.
- Do not expect your spouse, or yourself, to be perfect.
- Promote the end goal of the marriage and don't limit yourself or others when it comes to setting your sights on your overall financial goals. Having faith in one another's abilities and working together is essential in marriage, family, and finances.

• Key Lessons From More Than Thirty Years of Marriage
Marriage can be a big, delicious slice of heaven on earth. It requires that each partner give attention to detail, demonstrate willingness to compromise selfish interests, respect the other's differences without criticism, and make the effort to create an atmosphere that encourages and allows the other to grow as the marriage grows.

Most importantly, marital excellence requires that we come to understand the true meaning of love. Excellent marriages are created, not merely born. Recognizing and taking care of the little things that add up to big things is a key to happiness in marriage. Live without regrets. Every day, in thoughtful, sincere ways, make sure your life partner knows the depth of your love. Put your arms around each other or take one another's hands and say, "I love you." "Thank you." "I appreciate you. I don't take you for granted."

"Together we can make it." "Forgive me, and please, let's move past anger and forget each others' mistakes and shortcomings." "This is the best part of my day, coming home and being with you."

Marriages flourish when both partners do more than they bargained for, always looking for the good in things and in their spouse, keeping uppermost in their minds that it takes years to build trust and only seconds to destroy it. Marriage is about being the person we strive to be, the life partner we can indeed be, with God's great help. Marriage requires making spirituality the priority in the personal life of each mate, in the marriage relationship, and in the family relationships. This is the foundation of marital excellence: Two must stand together, form a circle of love, stay together, and fail, grow, and succeed together. Unconditional love in the marriage relationship is experienced only when God is in the relationship as the head of the household, at the heart of each partner's being.

MONEY AND YOUR CHILDREN

Children have never been good at listening to their elders, but they have never failed to imitate them.

—James Baldwin

All parents want their children to become shining stars. The question is how to wisely launch those little stars into life's firmament and teach them to let their lights shine. Children who see their parents spending time with their Creator every day—listening to Him, trying to obey Him, and apologizing when they fail—are learning the most important requirement for becoming a shining star. Wise parental modeling continues as you live, work, and handle everything you put your hands to, with wisdom, honor, and hope.

These same concepts apply to teaching our children financial responsibility. We teach them much more with our actions than we ever could with words. The old adage *"Actions speak louder than words"* definitely applies. For instance, wise parents who live caring for others, caring for themselves, and caring enough to be wise stewards of all that has been entrusted to them, including their children and material resources, receive a double benefit. Besides contributing to their own true prosperity, they point their children toward a hopeful future. Wise parents who live the importance of accepting responsibility for their personal well-being and for handling money wisely demonstrate to their children that living this way leads to excellence and lasting success. When parents set and keep within boundaries themselves, they show their children how to set their own boundaries in a reasonable way and how effective it is to do so.

Setting appropriate financial boundaries, of course, teaches our children financial discipline. If we have, instead, taught our children how to spend money but not how to save it, we need to take responsibility for our over-sight. A situation like this calls for humble discussion and new action.

Studies show that the average American child or teenager influences or directly spends several thousand consumer dollars a year. If you are parents who have neglected to train your children properly through your example or words, you will most likely find they have little concept of how money is earned or saved—or for that matter, how it is properly spent. Do not criticize and blame! Remind yourself that if you have taught them to be financially incompetent, it should not be a surprise that they have ended up incompe-tent. Then remind yourself (and them, when appropriate) that we all have two choices concerning money: Either money controls us, or we control money. The wise choice is for us to control money and teach that principle to our children.

• 7 Do's

Almost anything we dream for our children is possible if we and our children are living in harmonious relationship and active partnership with God. We choose the seeds we plant in their lives, and one day those seeds will come to fruition. Here are seven suggestions you can use to help your children become wise stewards of financial resources:

1. Do as you tell your children to do. Set a good example of wise tithing, saving, and spending. They will learn from, and copy, your example anyway. "Do what I say, not what I do" is not a very powerful injunc-tion.

2. Teach your children the value of money early. Give them a regular al-lowance as part of their share of the family income and for performing well their designated chores. Use the allowance to teach them responsi-bility and accountability. Too many parents make every decision for their children and then wonder why their children don't learn to make wise decisions when they get out on their own! Let them make their own choices, rather than making every choice for them. Allow them appropriate space to learn and practice responsible decision making by neither stepping in too soon nor coming in too late. Give them the op-portunity to learn by the natural consequences of their actions. Conse-quences—positive or negative—are often far more effective teachers than restrictions or other punishments that, in the end, tend only to make parents the bad guys.

3. Encourage your children to earn extra money working odd jobs for people you know and trust.

4. Establish checking accounts in the names of children old enough to use them. (You may have to be listed on the account, depending on the rules of the financial institution involved.) And open separate savings

accounts for them too, to help them learn to make choices about their savings.

5. Encourage your children to save for specific purposes, such as toys, entertainment, or college. Teach them the concept of how interest is earned and how it is compounded, using the information about this in chapter 8, "Forced Saving."

6. Hold your children responsible for paying for their own expenses—such as school supplies—from their accounts.

7. Teach your children to pay cash or not to buy. Teach them the dangers of buying on credit, and when doing so is appropriate. Don't allow affection to suspend your good judgment when teaching thrift.

• Roots, Wings, and Marks of Greatness

There are two lasting bequests we can give our children: One is roots. The other is wings.

—Hodding Carter

Wise, honorable, and hopeful parents work to build a foundation of strong ethically- and spiritually-based roots for their children (which will become a heritage to pass along to their children's children). The following "three *r*'s" are some of the best roots we can give our kids—for life as well as for financial management:

- Respect for others;
- Respect for one's self;
- Responsibility for one's choices.

As parents, we should teach our children the importance of individual responsibility and accountability.

Money habits can be established at an early age and the personal and monetary examples we set for our children will influence their future financial choices. Many parents give the responsibility of daily chores to their children—such as making a bed, putting away clothes, and taking trash to the curb. They also may offer an allowance, particularly for special chores or extra help they offer other family members. An allowance that recognizes the child's contribution to the family and the home offers lessons in responsibility, accountability, and rewarded compensation—as well as opportunity for lessons on good spending and saving habits.

Teach your children that along with earning and spending money comes decision making. With decision making comes responsibility. Help them see that responsibility—knowing they've done their best and served others—is a better reward than money.

Let me emphasize again that personal models are the best way to ensure that children will gain a sound spiritual and financial foundation, a foundation based on the roots of eternal truth and the wings of faith in God. With such a basis, the probability becomes very high that our children will become shining stars who become difference makers with their lives and finances. I believe in the unqualified uniqueness and nearly limitless potential that lives in every child.

Our purpose as parents should be marking our children for greatness by helping them to light their small lanterns with the Spirit within so that they can become bright lights illuminating the world with the fruits of the Spirit: the virtues of love, joy, peace, patience, kindness, goodness, benevolence, faithfulness, gentleness, and self-control. They will then be better equipped to dream big and dream wisely, to land safely in the inevitably stormy times life has in store for them, and to achieve their highest potential.

INSIGHTS

- When we make wise choices, we can look back to see a tree where we left a seed.
- Modeling wise behavior helps our children find a hopeful future.

Before proceeding to the next chapter, please consider and record your thoughts and work through the exercises on the following worksheet, My Initial Money-management Ground Rules.

WORKSHEET 4
My Initial
Money-management Ground Rules

NOTES FROM READING THIS CHAPTER

PART I
IMPROVING SENSITIVE COMMUNICATION

As before, work these exercises on your own, then, if you are in a relationship, share them as seems appropriate for your relationship.

• **Scenario 3: Imagine . . .**

Begin to imagine scenarios for you as a couple. You may wish to include communication visioning as well as life-dream visioning. Use some of the format you used in the Imagine scenarios in worksheet 3. Note some of these dreams below.

• **Scenario 4: Imagine . . .**

Begin to imagine scenarios for your family. Use some of the format you used in the Imagine scenarios in worksheet 3. Note some of these dreams below.

PART II
FORMING INITIAL MONEY-MANAGEMENT GROUND RULES

Now you are ready to write your initial money-management ground rules. These will change as you learn more, but I suggest you begin now. For now, they may include only how and when you will share your dreams, and how you will deal with conflict when your discussions become difficult. They may also include how you wish to pray to together.

If at all possible, whether you are married or engaged, both you and your partner should sit down, go through your answers together, and talk privately about money. If you have not already done so, discuss your differing money personalities; then discuss how, together, you can approach money decisions *with grace and mutual agreement.* (Remember, no one approach to life or money is right or wrong.) To discuss these things, use the guidelines for discussion given in "A Note on Process" at the front of this book and the more detailed guidelines in chapter 4, "Relationships and Money." Pledge to each other that you will keep the conversation honest and open (no confrontational methods allowed).

Note below any discussion rules you decide upon, so that you will not forget them!

Include time, place, and what you intend to do to keep the conversation positive as well as what you intend to do if conflict arises. Don't forget to agree on how you want to pray for your sessions and what times you want to schedule to do more fun things together. Both of these last two suggestions will help alleviate conflict.

If these conversations go well, you may want to venture on, to openly examine and clarify what each of you brings to the financial table of the marriage partnership. Then you may talk about what each of you wants to get out of this study of finances, and perhaps also make an agreement on how financial matters will be handled. For example, you may decide which areas will be handled jointly, which separately (and why—see comments on this in chapter 4), and how the cyclical tasks of handling your finances will be shared (again see comments on the importance of this in chapter 4). You may go so far as to include how long you think you want to keep this arrangement, and when you will review it for possible change. You may also decide to go through the list of topics given in the "Making a Plan" section of chapter 4.

Write down your resulting mutual agreements. They are the initial money-management ground rules of your marriage.

Taking time to review and clarify financial issues and roles before you marry, and repeating the process routinely and regularly during married life, will make for greater financial security and a far happier relationship.

If you are not married or your relationship is not yet ready for such a discussion, think about all that you have learned so far. Decide which ground rules you want to apply to your money management from now on. Write them down and review them periodically in the future. Use a mentor, if appropriate.

Do you need a reminder to review your ground rules? Try putting a note to review them on the last day of your annual appointment calendar, or use your computer reminder program, if you have one, or put your written ground rules in a place where you'll find them unexpectedly, or use some other method that you think will work for you. Don't let "forgetting" be an obstacle to your continued success.

Congratulations on working this chapter!

• **Notes on my/our money-management ground rules**

PART II

Digging In

5

Setting Goals

Without vision, we perish.

—Solomon (paraphrase)

According to some studies, only about one in four people have written financial goals. Many people, it seems, spend more time planning their next vacation than they spend planning their financial destiny. This is not only sad, it is frightening. An important step in achieving financial success lies in setting financial goals with specific action plans and then executing them.

I encourage you to always dream big dreams inspired by divine connection. And always convert those dreams into a few specific written goals, together as a family if appropriate. Then regularly monitor your progress and adjust your dreams and goals accordingly.

Since you are reading this book, I assume you agree that your financial future is worth the effort to learn to plan with those close to you. I hope you are excited about getting to work on your more detailed written plan for your financial future. This is where the groundwork I have shared—the examination of money personality, and the encouragement to use heart-based thinking and wise habits, both spiritual and financial—will help you begin to achieve your personal vision for your (and your family's) future. Now that you and your partner have agreed upon rules for discussion and joint prayer before your talks, and then practiced them so that you can share your discoveries and hopes and dreams and attitudes about money; now that you have also looked at how to help your children establish good habits, both spiritual and financial, by directly guiding them and by your example; now that you have written some basic money-management ground rules about what you want from this study of finances and who will handle what for the next period of time . . . now let's get to the work of breaking down your vision into dreams and goals that will help you reach that vision.

SETTING GOALS TO REACH YOUR DREAMS

As you study and seek to apply the material in this chapter, please don't confuse vision, dreams, and goals. I use them to mean three completely different things. *Vision* is the totality of our dreams—what we desire and see in our mind's eye for every facet of our lives. It is what you have been working on in the first part of this book. *Dreams* are (often) vague notions of specific things we desire for the future. They are good to have, but to be realized, dreams need to be translated to goals. *Goals* are the concrete ends for achieving those dreams, for which we have developed specific action plans with timetables.

As you consider the dreams and goals I recommend in this chapter, you may be tempted to think some of them do not fit this definition of goals but are, instead, mere dreams. Let me assure you: They are not dreams. Many use the word *goal* only for achievements that can be measured quantitatively. I believe a goal has to be measurable by more than objective, quantitative standards. Indeed, life's most important goals are measured by subjective, qualitative standards. We are about to examine a simple system for setting, evaluating, and adjusting financial goals—short-term or long-term. Before you set your initial financial goals, though, let's examine five overall goals that everyone should have.

RECOMMENDED OVERALL GOALS

• Goal 1: Genuine Contentment With Life

Strengthen yourself with contentment, for it is an impregnable fortress.
—Epictetus (c. 55–c.135 A.D.)

Contentment should be the most important goal of personal financial planning. Being content with life is not a matter of having a certain quantity of possessions or money. Nor is it being resigned to our situation or circumstances. It comes from knowing the Divine's plan for our life, accepting it, and cheerfully and joyfully working by that plan.

Contentment is related to obtaining love, security, and self-esteem; and material possessions and recognition *are* part of feeling secure. But people who make the accumulation of possessions or rewards their number one goal do not end up feeling satisfied in life; instead they find themselves on an ever increasing drive for "success" that leaves them feeling empty and perhaps even deceived and angry.

I am horrified that so many chase money, possessions, power, pleasure, knowledge, and education as though these things will make them happy. I have seen the resulting depression, frustration, and hardness of heart that can result. I find it immensely sad that, over the past fifty years in our country, these potentially good things have come to be seen as goals that measure the "quality" of life.

History has proven that, for most people, a satisfying career and the ability to earn a good living are important contributors to contentment. When kept within the boundaries that a priority of achieving contentment provides, these companion goals do help us maintain warm, loving relationships with family and friends and a sense of fulfillment. When we focus on contentment as our goal, directly or indirectly we make wise critical choices relating to money—for example, our choice of career, where we will live, how much we will spend, how much we'll save and how we will invest our savings, how much we will give away and to whom, and in the case of couples, the goal of contentment affects such issues as which spouse(s) will work outside the home and how, in the process, the family will be protected, and whether or not to have children and if so when and how many.

In my view, financial success is one among *many* means for improving the contentment in our lives. It is certainly not the only means—or even necessarily the most important one. It is also my view that financial success is nothing more than a means to the end of soul improvement, because such continual heart improvement is where contentment is truly found. That is why having a personal, harmonious relationship with the Divine is the end toward which wise people work. They recognize that being in harmony with the Divine is how we are created, and therefore we cannot be content without it. They think with wise motives and apply wise methods to their decision making. When contentment is a higher priority than being financially successful, when contentment is our number one goal and therefore our guiding principle, we will find both personal fulfillment and true success.

• Goal 2: Maximized Earnings Through Right Livelihood

I'd rather be a failure in something I love than a success in something that I don't.

—George Burns

You have probably heard someone or other recommend that people pursue careers offering the highest earning possibilities. On the contrary, I recommend that potential earnings should not be the dominant factor in making a career choice. When we make career choices based only on the possibility of a high income, we will likely end up sacrificing satisfaction. As the old adage says, *Money can't buy happiness.*

The wise way to maximize earnings is to pursue a career that suits your passions and aptitudes and that serves others—this method of earning your living is sometimes referred to as "right livelihood." Do whatever you do well and do it because you want to, not just because you want status, money, or material possessions. Choose work that you can throw your whole heart into, work that will make a difference by serving others in some way, now and in eternity! I guarantee that doing what you love with a professional attitude will lead to a sense of satisfaction about what you have done with your life. You will be earning more than money!

Your children, too, will be positively affected by your example. Your contentment will be augmented by seeing them learn that they can derive satisfaction from a career that is truly successful, that is, a career that has sprung from the passions of the heart rather than from the love of money or prestige.

Please don't assume that right livelihood must be obtained with a college degree, I might add. In my opinion, a college education as a means to financial success is stressed too much. Even though statistics indicate that the person who obtains such a degree has the highest potential for lifetime earnings, and I agree that it is preferable to a high school diploma for some people, I am not one who clings to the notion that a college degree is a must for everyone. Our society has thousands of success stories of people who have demonstrated common sense, wisdom, training, and the ability to find contentment with little or no formal education. (Perhaps the reasons for going to college might be examined: Are you going for job training or to build contacts in a field that interests you? Or are you going to expand your capacity to reason wisely and to appreciate other points of view while gaining improved ability to argue your own views in new contexts?)

We have all heard that money cannot buy real happiness or love. It therefore makes sense that our career choices, and those we encourage in our children, should be based on right livelihood, on pursuing our passions in life. Doing the work for which we have aptitude and serving others through our work will not only support us but also maximize our earnings potential. Whether we earn a lot of money or not (and we probably will), we will certainly end up more content than those who chase after empty dreams. And since content people do better at their jobs, they are more likely to succeed in the material sense.

• Goal 3: Financial Security Through Provision

This, then, is held to be the duty of the man of wealth: First, to set an example of modest, unostentatious living [and] to provide moderately for the immediate wants of those dependent upon him; and after doing so to consider all surplus revenues which come to him simply as trust funds, which he is called upon to administer . . . in the manner which, in his judgment, is best calculated to produce the most beneficial results for the community—the man of wealth thus becoming the mere agent and trustee for the poorer brethren.

—Andrew Carnegie

Financial security is often defined as the comfortable feeling, the peace of mind we have when we know our financial resources will be sufficient to fulfill our needs—and of our appropriate desires. Provision—providing for present and future needs and being sure that a given dream is a need and not an empty desire—is indeed a wise goal.

The feeling of financial security brings with it a feeling of confidence that comes with the sense that we have succeeded in putting our current and future finances in a good state. We are therefore unlikely to be anxious, worried, or afraid about this crucial area of life.

I urge you to aim for financial security through provision, not maximization (a pursuit of wealth for its own sake). Providing for your present and future needs is wise, but spending every waking moment plotting and scheming to make absolutely the very most money you can (maximization) make is an unhealthy approach to managing finances. Greed—striving to acquire wealth for its own sake—is a destructive motive and it cannot lead to contentment.

When you stick to the time-tested 7 Laws of Highest Prosperity, which are printed facing the first page of chapter 1 in this book, you gain true prosperity and security. (If you haven't already, please read them and think about them, particularly laws six and seven, the laws of Preparation and Preservation. More detailed information on these laws is given in later chapters of *Wisdom and Money*.) This wise approach to handling money and material resources ensures that you are able to provide for your loved ones and yourself and also reach out to others in need and support the causes that share your values.

• Goal 4: Moderate Consumption and Efficient Spending

Things which matter most must never be at the mercy of things which matter least.

—Goethe

According to the quote I gave earlier from Andrew Carnegie, the first duty of a man of wealth is to *"set an example of modest, unostentatious living. . . ."* Such a man will most likely become truly prosperous. As you consider the goals of genuine contentment, right livelihood, and wise provision, consider also the goal of moderate consumption, which includes the goal of efficient spending.

Money can be used for two purposes only: spending and saving. When you wisely choose to be moderate in consumption, you are spending your money efficiently and you are beginning to amass money that you will be able to wisely save for the future, to invest with discretion and prudence. I believe we all have deep in our hearts a yearning for a simpler, more deliberate life, a life like the one my parents lived. There is more detail in later chapters on how to spend moderately and efficiently, and on how to save and invest prudently.

- **Goal 5: Accumulation of Assets for Specific Needs**
Bridge the gap which exists between where you are and the goal you intend to reach.

—Earl Nightingale

In order to manage your money wisely, you need to anticipate specific events likely to occur in your life—both short-term and long-term—and accumulate assets to meet them. This will be easier to do if you have adopted the previous four goals, especially goal 4. If you are spending efficiently and consuming moderately, you will accumulate assets to meet needs. I encourage you: Do not be afraid to reject our society's pressure to go into debt so that you can have what you want now, without waiting until you can afford it.

Be one of those people who *do* set aside money each month, for example, to pay for an upcoming vacation trip. It's absolutely okay—indeed desirable—to come back from a vacation or get through the Christmas season without debt!

When you contemplate going into debt, be sure it is necessary and appropriate to the dreams and visions you have set out for yourself and for your family. And, when appropriate, before you take on a burden of debt, discuss the pros and cons with those you love or with your chosen mentor(s).

The goal of always having the assets to meet need when it arises will help you set more specific goals for fulfilling your vision.

THE SHORT AND LONG OF IT

Specific financial needs and goals come with two labels: short-term and long-term. Some experts use the term *short-term* to refer to needs that will arise or goals that will be met within a year, using the term *intermediate* for those that will occur in years two through five. When I speak of financial needs and goals, I follow the lead of the experts who don't break things down so minutely. I use *short-term* to mean financial needs of less than five years.

Regardless of how you choose to slice it or dice it, short-term and intermediate goals are those coming up soon. They may include such decisions as a down payment on a home, buying a new car or computer, or paying for a wedding. A short-term goal that almost all money professionals recommend is accumulating an emergency fund as soon as possible. This pool of readily accessible cash will help out with such unexpected events as a large car repair, a legal bill, or a stint of unemployment or disability. An emergency fund helps avoid the excuse that "there's never any money left to save or invest for long-term goals."

Some goals may be short- or long-term depending on the situation. For example, if you are saving college money for a child who is only five years old, that is a long-term savings goal. On the other hand, if the child is seventeen, that goal is definitely a short-term one.

Long-term goals (typically those more than three to five years away) should include planning for retirement and building an estate. These goals are considered long-term for two reasons: The pool of money you need to achieve the goals is large, so you'll need time to build it; and the types of investments you will need to make in order to reach these goals are typically riskier over the short term, but historically, have had better long-term returns.

Knowing which type of goal your goal is will help you choose how to accumulate the assets for it. For example, while you can save for long-term goals in traditional short-term investments (like money market savings accounts), in general these types of investments will not allow your money to grow as fast as long-term alternatives, such as stocks and longer-term bonds. I recommend you buy stocks and bonds only through mutual fund investments.

Such investments—stocks, for example—have averaged over 10 percent or so annual returns for the last sixty years—far better than cash equivalents such as treasury bills (under 4 percent). In any given year (like 2002), or even for several years in a row, stocks might not do well. You would not want to invest in stocks to buy a new car in two years, but they can be excellent for building a sufficient retirement nest egg. (Much more on saving, investing, and retirement planning in coming chapters.)

SYSTEM FOR SETTING GOALS

What must you do to turn your ideals and your financial dreams into reality?

The first step is dreaming. I recommend you dream with prayerful communication between your true inner spirit and God. This life of awareness of God's love for you will give you the conviction to live your destiny—and this will help you set appropriate goals. If you have worked through part I of this book, you have already begun to examine your dreams.

The second step is to become aware of how to tell if your dreams are realistic and what to do if what you see as important dreams, or goals needed for fulfillment of those dreams, conflict with what others close to you see as important.

After you and those important to you do worksheet 5, "Setting My Goals," consider these guidelines for the second step:

- **Setting Goals Guidelines**
  - Set aside a convenient time just for the purpose of discussing dreams and goals with those who are important to you. (If you are alone at this time in your life, choose a mentor.)
  - Choose a comfortable place; ask the family to talk openly and honestly without confrontation. (Use the guidelines in "A Note on Process" in

the front of *Wisdom and Money* and the more detailed guidelines in chapter 4.)

- Share the dreams and goals you've written down; ask family members to share theirs.
- Consider and discuss the values, priorities, motives, and attitudes of the dreams and goals that are being shared.
- Decide which goals are short-term (those taking less than five years to achieve) and which are long-term.
- Examine each dream carefully: Can it be made into a positive goal for you? For the whole family?
- Is the time frame you've assigned to each dream reasonable? Are difficult steps needed to achieve them? Are the sacrifices needed to meet them appropriate? Is everyone willing to make them? If everyone in the family is willing to work toward the dream, write it down as a goal. If the group is not willing to take any difficult steps that would be necessary to realize the dream, move on to examine the next dream. (You may decide to seek an appropriate mentor to help wrestle with a dream or goal that seems too difficult at this time. Or you may decide to bring it back to discussion at another session.)
- Focus on what you can do and are willing to do, together if you have a family involved.
- Plan and execute agreed-upon goals. Set up a reminder system to see how you are doing.
- Set up a schedule for further discussions, so that you can monitor and adjust the agreed-upon goals as needed.

INSIGHTS

- There are no limits to your dreams when God is your source and guide.
- Take the first step—create goals and write them down to express your dreams more concretely.
- Blossoms may become tattered or torn, but the seeds of real hope and new life are within each flower.
- Goals are the fuel of forward momentum.
- God gives His children the strength, faith, and courage to be content, regardless of circumstances.

Before proceeding to the next chapter, please consider and record your thoughts and work through the exercises on the following worksheet, Setting My Goals.

WORKSHEET 5

Setting My Goals

NOTES FROM READING THIS CHAPTER

PART I
DREAMS I WANT TO SET GOALS FOR

Now you are ready to begin setting your goals!

A. Choose a dream to explore.

Using the exercises in the previous chapters, choose a dream or a few dreams or several dreams that you want to explore goals for achieving. I have left room here for five dreams you may think you are ready to set goals for. You may want to brainstorm fewer dreams or more dreams.

1.

2.

3.

4.

5.

B. Choose a dream to work on.

After you brainstorm your dreams, I caution you to settle on just one for your first discussion, probably a dream for the family, not just for yourself. Change is difficult and you and/or your loved ones will probably become overwhelmed if you try to achieve too many dreams at once. The wise path to success is taking things a step at a time. Listen to the one dream he or she has brought to the discussion. Choose one dream you each agree to work on first. Write it down in the space below.

PART II
MY PRELIMINARY GOALS

Congratulations on choosing your first dream to commit to!

Write down your goals.
Write at least three personal or financial goals that will help you achieve that dream.

1.

2.

3.

4.

5.

6.

7.

8.

9.

10.

When do you think you should achieve each goal?
List here the ones that are short-term goals (1–5 years).

List here the ones that are long-term goals (6–20 or more years).

Now try to break down the goals further. Go back and place beside each goal a number that indicates the number of years within which you wish to achieve each goal.

To further break things down, please underline any goals that have a one-year notation.

Using the space below, write at least one sentence for each one-year goal that tells why you are committed to achieving these one-year goals.

Think about who will do each task for each goal. Be ready to discuss this at the appropriate time.

PART III
DISCUSSION AND AGREEMENT

Use the guidelines at the end of chapter 5 and those in "A Note on Process" in the front of this book and the more detailed guidelines in chapter 4, and discuss your chosen dreams and goals with the appropriate person(s) close to you. Don't forget to pray together and to break the discussion down into several sessions if necessary. Note that this will be a different discussion from the ones before. They were focused on simply sharing your visions and your dreams. This discussion will be focused on why you want to pursue this dream together. Taking the differences in your approaches to life and money into account, gracefully listen and decide which dream and which goals you will pursue. Agree on which category these goals belong in (short- or long-term) and write down a timetable for realizing the goals needed to attain your dream. Don't forget to map out who will handle what task associated with these goals. Agree on when and where you will meet again to see how your plans are going.

PART IV
OUR DREAM AND OUR GOALS

Note the dream you will work on.

This is the dream we agree on:

Note the goals to achieve this dream.

After you have labeled them "S" or "L" and given them a number for the number of years you think they will take to achieve, write them below in the order of the number of years you've assigned them, smallest number first. Underline the one-year goals. Write the tasks needed to meet the one-year goals and the name of the person who will take on responsibility for that task. The detail of this time frame and organization structure is what will enable you to follow through on your plan. If you are already working on goals that will take longer than one year, do the same for those.

Note the time and place where you will review your progress.

We will meet at _____ on _____
to review how we are doing.

PART V
REMINDERS

Make a copy of these goals and hang them up on your bathroom mirror!

6

Managing the Financial Cycles of Life

What will be has already been.

—Solomon (paraphrase)

Understanding your vision for your life and understanding your strengths and weaknesses and other givens in your money personality are important first steps in finding contentment. Choosing a dream to pursue, and writing out a time frame and organizational structure for achieving the goals, both short-term and long-term, that will lead to that dream's fulfillment are good next steps in gaining financial security.

Part of fulfilling your dream is understanding where you are at present and watching that situation change—for the better, of course! These changes do not occur in a static environment. You will be growing older and your types of income and expenses will change along with you.

CYCLES: HOW TO PLAN AND PREPARE FOR THEM

Typically, there are four cycles of financial life. These cycles will interrupt your plans or interfere with your confidence if you don't take them into account in setting your goals. Your action plan should take into account the cycle you are in now, those yet to come, and your present and desired financial profile. (See the last topics in this chapter, "Finding Your Net Worth" and "Using Your Net Worth to Increase Your Wealth.") The more you adapt your preparation, planning, saving, investment, and spending strategies to the stage of life you are in now and the ones you have yet to encounter, the more successful you will be.

Some strategies that are appropriate when you are single and twenty-five are often not appropriate when you are married and fifty-five or when you are *not* married and fifty-five! Some factors other than age and marital status that help point to the appropriate financial strategies are: Current and desired housing scenario; preferred age to retire and any money already in place to fund that objective; number of children, their ages, plans for them to attend college, and any money already in place to fund that objective.

An outline of cycle-by-cycle basic conservative financial objectives for saving, giving away, spending, and investing is given below. By conservative I mean planning that takes into account only what you believe will happen in all likelihood. It treats any other income as a bonus. I argue strongly on the side of such conservative planning!

Since some investment suggestions are included, it will help to explain two categories of investments here. More suggestions on investing are given in chapter 13, "Investment Wisdom."

When investments are looked at by objective, they are referred to as either growth investments or income investments. A *growth* investment is made primarily to increase the value of that investment asset. The growth investments' income—interest, dividends, capital gains—is usually allowed to compound (it is automatically reinvested) so that the investment grows as quickly as possible. This type of investment might be purchased for the long term or the short term, but normally it's bought for the long term. It is usually more aggressive than an income investment, and therefore can be more risky.

An *income* investment is made primarily to provide regular payouts to the buyer. The investment's income—interest, dividends—is paid out automatically, either to a separate account or by check to the buyer. This type of investment might be purchased for the long term or the short term, but normally it's bought for the short term. It is usually less aggressive than a growth investment, and therefore usually less risky.

More details on the objectives outlined below can be found in the chapters that follow.

CYCLE 1: EARLY ADULTHOOD TO AGE 29
Primary Suggested Objectives

Concentrate on developing good saving, investment, and spending habits. Develop these basic habits for financial success before you leave your twenties:

- *4 Habits for Financial Success*

1. *Give* a tithe of 10 percent of your after-tax income to the church you attend. In addition, I encourage you to give generously to people and other worthy causes, as your finances allow.

   As the laws of Wisdom, Priority, Motive, and Generosity promise, when you give, you will be applying higher wisdom, making first things first, living divine motive, and creating abundance for others while receiving back more than you give. If you cannot see how to tithe this much at first, start with a smaller percentage, then increase annually until you reach that 10 percent.

2. *Save* at least 20 percent of your post-tax income for future needs. This is the law of Preparation in action. The 20 percent includes, but isn't limited to, accumulating an emergency cash reserve; capital to fund college for children and personal retirement; a separate savings account that will be used to make longer-term investments.

   If you have debt that is not related to an investment asset (an asset that typically retains or increases in value), allocate some of this 20 percent toward paying off this debt. Examples of such debt are balances due on credit cards, installment accounts, and education or vehicle loans. With the remaining portion of the 20 percent, begin accumulating savings earmarked as recommended above.

   I realize that 20 percent sounds like too much when you first think about it. In chapter 8, "Forced Saving," there is more detail on why 20 percent is my recommended saving level. But right now let me suggest that you *not* put off the saving habit. If you're having an allergic reaction to 20 percent, begin with a lower percentage—at 5 percent or 10 percent—and work toward the point where you will be able to suck it up, bite the bullet, and save 20 percent!

3. *Spend* moderately and efficiently—live on 70 percent of your after-tax income.

   Avoid using debt to increase your consumer spending capacity. Spending discipline, together with wise investing and seeking to minimize taxes, is an example of the law of Preservation in action. (There are times when using debt for investment purposes is wise, but using debt to buy consumable goods and services is never wise. See chapter 9, "Spending Wisdom" for more detail.)

4. *Invest* by following a reasonably conservative strategy that is well-defined and saves on taxes. Chapters 12 and 13 give details on the positive impact that wise investing, including investing with tax advantages in mind, can have on your financial profile.

Whether you are single or married, if you cultivate these four habits early, prior to age thirty, you will have laid a solid foundation for a lifetime of success with money. That foundation should be built upon throughout the four cycles as appropriate, by continuing to apply the 7 Laws of Highest Prosperity that are evident in these four habits and other financial strategies shared in earlier and coming chapters of *Wisdom and Money.*

If you are already past thirty and you are just starting to look for and apply wisdom to your finances, don't be discouraged. Start where you are now, with what you have now. Make gradual, small changes. Success in little things will encourage you to make bigger changes later.

And if you are among the many—in any of the four cycles—who don't overspend but still struggle to make ends meet financially, then don't throw up your hands and say, "No way can I apply these concepts or ever hope to achieve true prosperity!" Start by counting your blessings. To a much greater degree than perhaps you have realized—be you single parent or hourly laborer or widow or other—you are already richer than many will ever be. Use the spiritual and emotional wealth from your relationship with God— your faith, courage, and sheer determination—to dwell on what you have, not on what you don't. Then put your energy into creating a better financial life by wisely managing your giving, saving, spending, and investing as best you can, according to the guidelines in *Wisdom and Money*!

Other Suggestions

- As yet another example of the law of Preservation in action be sure to use these early years to teach your children good habits with money. Continue this parenting wisdom into their teens.

- Don't buy too much house! Don't imitate the many who, in cycle one, buy excessively expensive homes, then use the high mortgage payment as an excuse for not saving and for ignoring other important financial principles (like giving) and important financial objectives (like college funding for children and saving for personal retirement). Your house is an investment too. But too much house violates the principle of diversi- fication of investments discussed in chapter 13, "Investment Wisdom."

  It is my recommendation that you look for a house that you can afford to pay off in eight to twelve years without giving up on the above percent- ages of your income (single income, if you decide to have only one working parent for a number of years).

- Use caution when picking mutual funds to invest in. Some savers under the age of thirty may feel they can take greater risk in investments, buy- ing, for example, aggressive-growth stock (sometimes referred to in this book as equities) mutual funds. I do not disagree with this approach as long as prudence is exercised. Think carefully about how much of your overall portfolio will be at risk. Talk with those close to you and use mentors if appropriate. Pick a risk level that both you and your partner are comfortable with. (See chapter 13, "Investment Wisdom.")

- If you are married with two incomes (and if you can afford it), consider living on one salary; save and invest your partner's total income. Besides the obvious advantage of accumulating savings quickly, this has the added advantage of avoiding dependency on that second salary. Then, when children come along, you will be able to let go of the second income and have someone at home with the children full-time. Please be sure to review suggestions regarding career, children, and family, and dreaming and goal setting in chapter 5, "Setting Goals."

- Be sure to put a good insurance strategy in place. Cover major risks. One risk to insure is loss of valuable assets to peril (fire, hurricane, etc). Another is loss of income due to the death or disability of the major wage earner. You will want to maintain insurance during all four cycles to cover peril, life, and disability at least until you have accumulated enough assets to replace what you are insuring. As you accumulate more assets, therefore, the amount of insurance coverage should decline.

CYCLE 2: AGE 30 TO 49

If in this cycle you are just beginning to apply wise financial planning and preparation concepts and principles, be sure to adopt the guidelines given for the first cycle. Work as quickly as possible toward implementation of the strategies for both cycles.

Primary Suggested Objectives

- Pay off your home mortgage, if possible, by the time you are forty.

- Keep yourself as debt free as possible for consumable items (items like clothes, household goods, and other items that we use quickly; credit card and education and vehicle loans, and installment payment accounts).

These two strategies are the most important financial objectives to reach —before forty, if possible. Indeed, the sooner you achieve both of these, the more money you will have available to fund other key needs like college for the kids and personal retirement.

- If you haven't yet attained your savings goal of 20 percent of post-tax income, increase the percentage of your income that you save during this cycle. The more years you have to save at this level, the more assets you will have to meet needs of the coming years.

- Continue other first-cycle habits and guidelines, including giving at least 10 percent, reserving 20 percent for saving and for eliminating any consumable-item debt, limiting spending to 70 percent of after-tax income, and maintaining an appropriate insurance strategy.
- If a housing purchase is made in cycle two, it is wise to apply the same guidelines as given in cycle one.
- Continue to invest your savings wisely for future need. Work hard to minimize your taxes through sound strategies found within the clear black-and-white of the tax code. No "gray area" stuff! For example, start funding a 401(k) plan to the max if such a retirement savings plan is available with your employer. If you are self-employed, you will want to consider a SEP (Simplified Employee Pension). Regardless of your employment status, IRAs are an option worth considering. (See especially, chapters 11, 12, and 13.)

Other Suggestions

- During this cycle some of your investments can still be as speculative as in the first cycle; you still have time before retirement to recover from any setbacks. As you move into your forties, however, start shifting your investments to more conservative mutual funds. It's still okay to have the investment portfolio skewed toward equities, but do have a good percentage of bond mutual funds.
- If you must borrow at any time during this stage of life, be sure it is for investment assets, not for fast-depreciating consumable goods like cars, boats, overly expensive vacations. When you borrow, be certain you are borrowing because of absolute need—not frivolous, expensive desire. *Pay back loans ASAP.*

CYCLE 3: AGE 50 TO FORMAL RETIREMENT

Even if in this cycle you are just beginning to apply wise financial planning and preparation concepts and principles, don't lose heart and don't fall prey to the notion that it's too late. Instead, adopt a can-do attitude and the habits and guidelines given for the first and second cycles. Work as quickly as possible toward implementation of the strategies given for those cycles as well as for this cycle.

Primary Suggested Objectives

- Save.
- Save.
- Save some more.

Why is the emphasis on saving so important during this cycle? Retirement is looming on your horizon. "Make hay while the sun shines," as my dad was fond of saying. As family expenses decline, put your money away for retirement.

- Do not overcelebrate with the extra cash flow you find you have when your children finish college and you become empty nesters.
- Continue the habits and strategies from earlier cycles, including the giving, spending, insurance, and debt habits and guidelines.

Other Suggestions

- If a housing purchase is made in cycle three, it is wise to apply the same guidelines as given in cycle one.
- Keep a good mix of equities and bonds in your mutual fund portfolio and keep on pursuing solid tax saving strategies. (See chapters 12 and 13.)

CYCLE 4: RETIREMENT

If you are beginning wise financial planning in this cycle of life, adopt the guidelines given in the first three cycles, but work as quickly as possible toward the priorities listed in this cycle as well.

Primary Suggested Objectives

This is where the applied habits and guidelines of earlier cycles begin to pay off.

- Make sound tax and investment decisions with your distributions from a formal retirement plan.
- When you formally retire:
  - Draw first on your investments that have not been tax-deferred;
  - Postpone drawing on accumulated earnings in IRA accounts, since you will have to pay taxes on them;
  - Transfer your 401(k) and other retirement distributions into an IRA to delay taxes;
  - Invest in mutual funds made up of safe, shorter maturity bonds;
  - Shift your equities to more conservative stock mutual funds;
  - Remember: Income, not growth, is most important now, but keep some growth stock mutual funds in your portfolio to offset the effect

of inflation and taxes. (See chapters 11, 12 and 13, for more details on each of the above strategies.)

- Have fun. If applicable, work to avoid getting in your spouse's hair. And give more of your time, money, and skill to serve God by loving and caring for others.

Other Suggestions

- If a housing purchase is made in cycle four, I recommend paying cash for it (unlike my recommendation for such purchases in the previous three cycles).
- Continue to plan, save, and invest with your tax-deferred monies. (See "Keeping More of Your Bread" in chapter 12.) Taxes do not stop when you retire. The need for sound tax planning may never be greater than during your golden years.

FINDING YOUR NET WORTH

A key point of the cycle-by-cycle strategies of financial planning is, of course, to increase your overall wealth. Since financial wealth involves so many factors, you should measure its changes with the tool accountants call your net worth. This is very similar to what businesses do when they create their balance sheets.

Knowing your net worth and your cash flow (which is a tool explained in the next chapter) will give you a clearer picture of what is affecting your wealth building and what may be eating away at the progress you're making. These tools will also make you more aware of options you otherwise might miss and of how options change over time.

If you have a computer and already track all your finances on it, it may calculate your net worth for you. (Since these programs depend on your input in terms of assets and liabilities as well as income and expenses, I recommend that you check the program's net worth statement against the one given in the worksheet to this chapter, to be sure all aspects of your net worth are included.) If you use such a program and you have only *some* of your finances entered in it (like checking and savings accounts and stock holdings), those numbers can be easily plugged into the form given in the worksheet for this chapter. If you do not use a computer program to track your finances, you can choose to calculate your net worth as of the date of your last statements from banks and other institutions.

In looking for the values of your assets and liabilities, I encourage you to remember that the goal of finding your net worth is not to judge yourself, but to see where you really are, so you can change your situation: Be honest. Be thorough. Watch for the typical mistakes people make, so you can calculate your net worth accurately:

- Don't just assume your car is worth what you owe on it. Check the blue book value. This can easily be done online if you have access to the internet or for no charge by asking your bank or banker. (See Appendix.)

- Check the current stock prices of any securities. (If you don't have an online method for doing this, you might calculate your net worth as of the date of your last statements.)

- If you own a house, find out this year's market value. This can be done inexpensively by checking with a friend or associate who works in residential real estate sales in your area. Alternatively, check with the appropriate local governmental agency for recent sales of residences in your and immediately surrounding neighborhoods. Be sure to obtain applicable square footage and amount of land involved in those sales. Use the information obtained to calculate average sales price per square foot and per acre. Apply those averages to your scenario.

- If you plan to include a potential inheritance, do so only if it is already in your name or provided for in a written will of someone who is already deceased.

- When you list liabilities, don't forget the loans you might have against the cash surrender value of any whole life insurance policies you may own. Cash surrender value is the cash the insurance company would pay you if you canceled the policy and physically surrendered the written agreement you have with them.

- List *all* your personal loans, including credit cards, installment accounts, and vehicle or education loans not paid off.

- List as a debt any debts of other people or organizations that you have guaranteed and are likely to have to pay.

Finding all this information may entail some homework on your part, but you owe it to yourself to know exactly where you stand financially. After you've found all the numbers you need the first time, it will be easier to do it the next time. If you find yourself lacking the courage to admit to some of your actual numbers, pray for guidance and strength.

USING YOUR NET WORTH TO INCREASE YOUR WEALTH

Once you learn to calculate your net worth, you will want to schedule times to recalculate it regularly. I recommend you do it monthly at first, then at least once a year. This regular check-in will help you see what's going well and what isn't. It will also make you more aware of options for the cycle of life you're in that you may have missed, and alert you to options for cycles you have not yet grown into.

Don't forget to use all your discussion skills when you meet with your partner or mentor to share your findings!

Remember: The mathematical value of the number you get when you calculate your net worth is not the most important thing. It's what you do to make it change in your favor that counts!

INSIGHTS

- Each of us comes to every phase of life a novice. Begin each phase with the goal of becoming even more wise (becoming aware of your changing financial situation and future needs), ASAP!

- What is to be has already been. Look for the best footprints to follow: Look carefully for God's, then follow them.

Before proceeding to the next chapter, please consider and record your thoughts and work through the exercises on the following worksheet, Finding My Net Worth.

WORKSHEET 6
Finding My Net Worth
(My Balance Sheet)

NOTES FROM READING THIS CHAPTER

FINDING MY NET WORTH

A. Calculate your net worth.

If applicable, begin by dividing up the research with your partner or mentors.

Existing Assets

Checking accounts   _____

Savings accounts   _____

IRAs   _____

Certificates of Deposit   _____

Savings bonds (current value)   _____

Life insurance (cash value only)   _____

Securities (market value)   _____

Annuities (surrender value)   _____

Automobiles (blue book value)   _____

Residence (market value)   _____

Other real estate (market value)   _____

Pension (value of vested interest)   _____

Household furnishings/jewelry   _____
    (current market value)

Other   _____

Other   _____

Other   _____

TOTAL ASSETS   _____

Existing Liabilities

Mortgages (balance)   _____

Equity line/2nd Mortgage (balance)   _____

Car note/lease (balance)   _____

Charge account balances   _____

School loan balances   _____

Other Debt   _____

Other Debt   _____

Other Debt   _____

Taxes owed   _____

Charitable pledges   _____

Other   _____

Other   _____

TOTAL LIABILITIES   _____

Subtract total liabilities from total assets:

Total Assets _____

Total Liabilities − _____

TOTAL NET WORTH = _____

B. Evaluate your net worth.

How did you do? Do you have a positive number?

Would you like to see it go up each year? Good. You have a new goal! Your goal is:

I want to be the kind of saver and investor who achieves an increase in net worth every year.

Note anything you learned or decided you wish to track in more detail between now and the next time you calculate your net worth.

C. Share your net worth calculation with your partner or mentor.

Use your discussions skills to do so. Schedule the next time you will calculate your net worth and write that time here. Use your reminder system to remind you to do so.

For the first year I recommend that you evaluate your net worth every month so that you have a very clear picture of what is affecting your net worth. Some items, like cars for instance, wreak havoc on your net worth, especially if they are new. Their value goes way down and your car note may not go down much at all. The aim is to continually increase your net worth and to acquire as little debt as possible. Wouldn't that be a great feeling? Then go for it!

7

Forward Budgeting

Things which matter most must never be at the mercy of things which matter least.

—Goethe

Once net worth is known and the cycles of life are understood in terms of financial needs, you are ready to start working on the specifics of your financial plan. Budgeting is the first tool to use to help you meet your goals and realize your dreams. I recommend that you choose forward budgeting (setting aside an amount for giving away and for saving *before* you set amounts to spend), not backward budgeting (starting with amounts you think you need to spend and hoping there will be something left over for giving and saving).

As you begin to work on your budget, arm yourself with courage and determination. What seems difficult at first will soon become familiar to you, and then will become, I hope, a routine in your life. This chapter gives you all the basics you need to complete the worksheet that follows it. But saving and spending have so many intricacies that I've given more detail on them in the two following chapters. As you work through chapter 7 and its worksheet to come up with your first forward budget, stop and read chapters 8 and 9 if you feel a need for more detail. They will give you more of the why's and how's of making your budget work for you. If you don't feel a need, just glance at them to see what they cover, and then decide whether you want to learn about them *before* you work on your first forward budget, *as* you map your budget out, or *after* you've given that first budget a try.

As your forward budget begins to pay off, you can use the suggestions in the rest of the chapters of *Wisdom and Money* to use the money you accumulate. Those chapters will help you choose your investments, save taxes, and plan for the time when your estate will be passed on to heirs you designate.

In all this financial planning it helps to keep Sam the wood gatherer, from *7 Laws of Highest Prosperity*, in mind. He made progress only after he began to live by most of the following spiritually based rules of thumb. These are the rules I have based my own success on. They come, too, from my twenty-five years of watching thousands I have advised—individuals and businesses—try to institute good financial practices. These rules are the essence of *Wisdom and Money*. I promise you that they will head you down the road to financial security.

7 FINANCIAL RULES OF THUMB

Employ:

1. Forward budgeting: Budget so that you will be able to give and save before you spend. (Don't budget only what you intend to spend.)

2. Forced saving: Make saving and becoming debt free your priority, equally and simultaneously.

3. Wise moderate and efficient spending: Live beneath your means and avoid debt, especially for consumable goods and services (those that are used up quickly or that lose their value quickly). Especially refrain from financing this kind of spending with credit card or other forms of debt—pay cash instead.

4. Wise liquid assets: Keep a reasonable amount of cash accessible at all times.

5. Realistic retirement funding: Make it your aim to have 100 percent of your present income to live on after you retire. Be safe, not sorry.

6. Wise insurance: Let your heart (the Spirit within) guide you. Buy life insurance in an amount that, together with your net assets, would provide as you wish for those you love in the event of your death.

7. Wise investing: Make return *of* capital a priority over return *on* capital in your investment decisions.

These simple rules, when applied, can have a profound impact on your life and finances.

FORWARD BUDGETING

Budgeting in its strictest sense is *the* essential tool for planning and preparing to preserve your finances in the short term (one to five years). Such a budget should be written down so that it can be referred to. It should include both income and expenses. In its broader sense budgeting encompasses the whole financial plan, which is essential to planning and preparing to pre-serve your finances in the long term (over five years). In either sense, the point of wise budgeting is to gain more than mere financial health. Done properly, budgeting will help you arrive at true prosperity.

If you want to arrive at such true success, I recommend that you begin to write a forward budget, not just a budget focused on spending. When you use the essential tool of forward budgeting (budgeting so that you plan to give and save before you spend), when you see forward budgeting as your friend and not some arbitrary tyrant telling you what you cannot do, your budget-ing efforts will move you toward true success. Even if you've never been able to put a budget down on paper or set aside savings consistently, you will find that creating a forward budget is not as difficult as you probably thought. It will quickly give you a sense of control over your whole life, not just your spending. And that's what you're looking for, right?

THE HEART OF THE FORWARD BUDGET—IN 5 EASY STEPS

As you create your forward budget, you will be following this outline of budgeting wisdom, which repeats some of the four habits for financial suc-cess listed in the first cycle of life in the previous chapter. These guidelines are so important to achieving true prosperity that I want you to return to them again and again until they have become second nature to you.

1. Project your realistic income, after taxes, for the next fifty-two weeks (one year). This will help you budget wisely.

2. Earmark the first 10 percent of your net (after-tax) income for a mini-mum amount to give away. Give it off the top every week (or each time you receive your income, if it's not weekly) to your church and to oth-ers in need. *Off the top* means *before* you spend *any* of that money! As you become used to this budget structure, increase to a higher percent-age.

3. Earmark the next 20 percent of net income as savings for future needs. Save this forced saving amount every week, or as often as you receive your income. As noted in chapter 6, if you have debt for consumable items, apply part of the 20 percent to pay off that debt and build your way to a savings of 20 percent over time. Don't let debt discourage you. Just bite the bullet and begin immediately to set aside—not spend—that next 20 percent of your net income for either paying debt or saving. You'll be surprised how quickly this saving habit will feel good!

4. Limit spending to the moderate, efficient amount of 70 percent of your net income. That is what will be left after you give away the first 10 per-cent and save the next 20 percent. No fudging (borrowing) allowed!

5. If cuts are needed to pay your bills and keep this breakdown of your income, get serious and cut!

LIVING BUDGETING WISDOM

Knowing your assets and liabilities, which you discovered when you found your net worth, will help you track your progress toward financial success. Knowing your income and expenses, and writing them into a budget, will help you create that progress. You will project (estimate with as much knowledge as possible) your income and expenses over the next year to create your budget.

If you cannot yet project your income for the coming year because of changing circumstances, begin by working on a budget for the past year. Look at the income you had, and how it was spent. This is not a bad beginning to learning how to budget.

Projecting sounds like an intimidating task, doesn't it? Let me tell you: It can actually be fun! Once you have your first budget, you might change the projections for all kinds of dreams and goals and eventualities. Doing so will tell you the consequences of choosing this or that.

But first, let's talk about the steps in shaping your first budget.

EXAMINING INCOME

Each time Patty and I go through the forward budgeting process, we are always reminded of how blessed we are to have the income we have. So . . . pause and say a prayer of thanks for your current income, whatever the level may be. After you've lived with your first forward budget for a year, begin to look ahead to the potential wealth that can be built as income increases. Or if you're married and have a two-income household, dream about the day when your assets will be sufficient to allow one of you to stay at home full-time, if that is a goal.

GIVING AND SAVING FIRST

• Why Budget Forward, Not Backward?

Most believe that developing a spending budget is the first step in becoming a good manager of your personal finances and money. A spending budget is one focused on how much you can use to spend on things you desire. If anything is left after spending, spending budgeters then consider giving and saving. I disagree with this approach.

Over my many years of helping people and organizations shape their finances to attain prosperity, I have noticed that living by a spending budget empowers the one category of finance management that causes the most problems—spending. At the same time, it neglects to develop the two financial disciplines that lead to highest prosperity and financial security—giving and saving.

Some of you may remember Foghorn Leghorn (an old cartoon rooster) watching a pint-sized chicken hawk drag a fox—the chicken's natural enemy—into a hen house and saying, *"I say—I say there—I think you're confused."* Let Foghorn help me clear up some confusion you might have.

Budgeting your spending first is the backward way to go about budgeting because it brings the fox of overspending into the hen house of financial health. As Foghorn would say, "You do know—I say—you do know that the fox eats the hens, don't you? Spending eats the successful budget, son! Wise up!"

A backward budget approach—one from the "what can I buy" viewpoint—establishes behavior that dooms giving and saving before they ever have an opportunity to get out of the starting blocks. And giving and saving are what will feed you physically, and your spirit-person as well, over the years. Instead of budgeting backward, give and save first. This forward budgeting approach not only will make you happy, it will keep spending in its proper place: Forward budgeting disempowers the overspending monster.

• Let's Talk Tithing and Giving!

We make a living by what we get, but we make a life by what we give.
—Norman MacEwan

Tithing. The very word sends chills down the spines of many, but that's because those people don't understand the higher laws governing the road to a happy life. All through history the happiest, wisest, and most truly prosperous repeatedly tell us how important and fulfilling it is to faithfully tithe and give.

When you do, I promise that you will end up experiencing just the opposite of resignation to live with less. I promise that you will awaken your soul and your heart to the realization that you have wealth in your life, and that you are truly blessed to be in the position to share.

Why? Because it is already in your heart to share. Haven't we all said at some time or other, "Gee, I'd like to have a million bucks so I could give money to . . ." I urge you not to wait until you have a million to have the fun of giving. Start now!

The reason so many of us find the suggestion to tithe so difficult is that we think of giving as a loss to us. The more we give, the less we have, right? . . .

Wrong. As those who have discovered its blessing know full well, giving fills you with a great sense of abundance. It also helps you to feel that, in a small way, you are changing the world for the better.

Traditionally one tithes 10 percent—the word *tithe,* in fact, means one-tenth—to one's church. I recommend, if at all possible, that you begin by distributing your 10 percent giving budget to your church and to people in need or to other worthy causes.

If you cannot give a full 10 percent, start with a smaller percentage of your net income. This will establish the habit of giving, which will help you feel better about your life and finances while it helps others as well. As you become able, give away more than 10 percent. Aim for tithing at least 10 percent to your church and then giving other substantial amounts to people and to organizations in need.

As you decide how much to give away and to whom you will give it, don't forget to decide how often you will give your budgeted amount, and what the logistics of your giving will be. Some people give anonymously; others use their names. Some put their giving budget in a special bank account as they receive their paychecks and distribute it as it seems appropriate; others give in lump sums. An automated system of setting money aside, like the one described in "How Best to Implement Forced Saving" in chapter 8, can be a good way of ensuring that your giving remains funded as planned.

Don't give because you expect to receive something in return. Don't give out of guilt. Give because it will bring joy to your life as well as to those who benefit from your gift. Riding a roller coaster is thrilling. Dancing till dawn is fun. But you will find that heart-based tithing and giving are the blasts of a lifetime!

I guarantee that you will find giving to be the most rewarding way to invest your money. Do not miss out on the wealth that will come into your life once you become a giver. Step back from any mindset programmed by our materialistic society and say to yourself, *"Okay, this is the amount of money I get to give away! What a great feeling! I won't miss it because I've budgeted to give it. So, what super things can I do with it this year?"*

• Saving—The Discipline Must Be Built In

After you budget giving, pay yourself (and your family) next. What I mean is set aside 20 percent of your income after taxes and earmark it for savings. Budgeting this so-called forced savings before you begin to spend will help you zoom along to financial success. How you organize putting your forced savings into your savings account may vary. It helps many people to deposit their budged amounts as they receive their paychecks—weekly, twice a month, or monthly. Others find that an automatic withdrawal or deposit system keeps them honest. (There is more detail on such a system in the "How Best to Implement Forced Saving" section of chapter 8.)

At first, you may have to use some of this savings budget to pay off debt. Doing so is another part of forward budgeting. There is more about this in the

"Avoid Debt for Consumable Goods and Services" section below, and also in chapter 8.

Then you should project (estimate as best you can) what you need for an emergency fund and begin to fill it to that level. This rainy day fund should include the amount you need to live on for at least six months, in case of a drop in income. (You will find this amount when you work on worksheet 8.) It may also be used for emergencies that will inevitably crop up, like unexpected large medical bills. Your emergency fund might also be budgeted to include those large annual expenses that are hard to save for, like tuition and home and/or automobile insurance premiums. The annual deductible amount on your insurance policies should also be in this fund. Place this money into a savings storehouse that is easily converted to cash on short notice. (There is more explanation on this type of account in the "How Best to Implement Forced Saving" section of chapter 8.) Once you have budgeted the goal amount of your emergency fund, keep adding to it until it is at that goal. Then replace whatever you take out with part of your 20 percent savings.

As your emergency fund grows, you will be able to really see how your disciplined savings habits are paying off. You will also be ready to start rolling money from your 20 percent savings budget into investments and other savings vehicles. Returns on investments will help pay for longer-term goals such as college for your children and retirement for yourself and your partner.

As mentioned earlier, I realize that 20 percent sounds like too much when you first think about it. In the next chapter, "Forced Saving," I go into more detail on why 20 percent is my recommended saving level. But right now let me suggest that if you're having an allergic reaction to 20 percent, begin with a lower percentage and work your way up. I highly recommend that you not put off the saving habit. If necessary, start smaller—at 5 percent or 10 percent—and work toward the point where you will be able to suck it up, bite the bullet, and save 20 percent! Don't cheat yourself by saying you'll never live by forced saving.

Forced saving puts financial discipline up front, where it will do the most good. It doesn't require a prophet to predict that, without the discipline of giving and saving up front, you are destined to fail. Why? We're all human, and although we have good intentions we all are prone to take the road paved with good intentions. . . .

If you want to accumulate material wealth, please give to others and then to your own savings before you spend. This will take away the power spending will constantly try to exert over your life. Quit borrowing to buy consumable goods and services like clothes, vacations, gifts, etc. Live *below* your means so that you can give and save! If you don't want to accumulate money, remember that not doing these things may well lead to your being a burden on others at some later time. I feel confident you are an industrious and just person, preferring to be proactive so that has little likelihood of happening.

When we use our money wisely we discover true significance, satisfaction, security, and sanity. Practicing deferred gratification by living within the guidelines I have recommended for giving and saving is the only way to attain the highest and lasting prosperity. Why not let the wisdom of God lead you toward this wise, pressure-free life?

MODERATE, EFFICIENT SPENDING

Finally, you are ready to look at spending! What is the easiest way to control the spending part of a forward budget? Most people spend more than they need to. To them I say cut up your credit cards—and then cut your discretionary spending (spending that is not essential to your life, spending for goods or services you choose to have or choose to have a higher quality or quantity of)! Even if you are not overspending, overindulging, or under-saving, you probably have room for improvement in this area. I urge you to cut up your credit cards—literally. Don't use an installment credit account or a credit card ever again, unless you vow to pay them in full every month—and follow through!

There are some people who underspend. To them I say: Look at the effects of defining basic need too narrowly. Are those close to you defensive, unable to pursue dreams they have a right to, not able to open up and share simple pleasures with you? There is something better than control: It is that feeling of pride you get from doing well by those close to you, that feeling of uninhibited affection that grows from a relationship shared with equal respect for each other and based on the Love within. If you are missing these things, I urge you to pray for and choose an appropriate mentor.

• Avoid Debt for Consumable Goods and Services

If you buy only what you can afford, you will save untold amounts of money and worry. If you already owe for purchasing goods and services that are to be either used up quickly (like groceries or gasoline) or that significantly decline in value immediately after purchase (like furniture or vehicles) or that lose all their value over a short time (like the newest thing in clothing, which, if you think about it, you know will go out of style shortly), you need to honor that "last ever" debt for such items and pay it back (from your 20 percent savings budget) as soon as possible. Then refrain from ever going into debt for these things again.

Once you have paid off this unnecessary debt, you will see the benefits of moderate spending almost immediately: You will see your savings for your rainy day fund accumulate, and then your savings to put into investments. Why pay others for simply providing advance funds for things you don't need? Or for things you do need but that cost significantly more than they have to when you don't budget ahead for them? Doing so only robs you of money you can use for your own enrichment and for giving to others.

If the minimum required payments on your debt for consumable items amount to more than 20 percent of your net income, figure out how much you can pay each cycle, then allocate by percentage how much of this amount would go to each creditor. Then call your creditors. Tell them you need to reduce the amount of your regular payments and tell them how much you can afford to pay them. Make sure your proposed payment plan is realistic, or they will simply dismiss your request without serious consideration. Many creditors will work with you.

If they do not accept what you propose, send the lower repayment amount to your creditors anyway, and accept the consequent finance charges. Or cut your monthly outflow for other expenses, so that you can repay the larger amount without going further into debt.

Since most people will be paying for this consumable debt out of their savings budget, payments on such loans are not in the discretionary expense part of the budget worksheet in this book. If you are paying some of your debt down from the expense part of your budget, add that part as a discretionary expense category.

• Mental Blocks About Discretionary Spending

As you shape the spending part of your budget, you will do yourself the most good when you make yourself take a hard look at the most important category of spending: *discretionary spending.* Understanding what really is discretionary spending will help you make cuts in spending to fit your new forward budget.

Identifying discretionary spending can be difficult, at first. We all have mental blocks against letting go of what we value most. If you have not done the work of listening to the Spirit within as Sam the wood gatherer did in *7 Laws of Highest Prosperity,* if you have not yet developed his eventual mature level of heart-based thinking and wise habits of thought and action, if you have not yet become adequately skilled in discussing difficult subjects with those close to you and listening to their feedback, you may have trouble being honest even with yourself about which items on your spending list are discretionary and which are essential. Why not take a moment to review part I of this book, and pray for guidance? Two typical problem areas in regard to discretionary spending are (1) seeing too little as essential (nondiscretionary), or (2) seeing too much as essential. The latter is by far, of course, the most common problem.

I have seen some consider as *discretionary* (unessential) any spending other than the most basic food and shelter and clothes, leaving themselves and/or their families in true need. I have seen others consider anything they desire at the moment to be *non*discretionary (essential), simply because they think it will fill the void within. I urge you to listen to the Spirit within. When you are in balance with the Love and Light the Spirit brings, you will find it easier to be in balance with what is nondiscretionary and what is discretionary spending.

In deciding which is which, do not be afraid to toss ideas back and forth with those close to you and to use a mentor. Whether or not they end up taking it, everyone benefits from advice.

Do not get discouraged! It is normal to have to examine carefully the number and quality of discretionary spending items. It is normal, too, to have to take a hard look at these items in order to categorize them as needs or wants. Having the courage to do this will keep discretionary items from breaking your budget before your budget has had a chance to lead you to financial success.

• Where to Cut First

Cutting discretionary spending is at the heart of creating a forward budget. Go to work immediately, using the right instrument—a razor-edged axe!—for lopping off excessive spending. As my dad would say, "You have to mean business and you have to stick to your guns."

Nondiscretionary Spending

It is my personal opinion that *nondiscretionary* monthly expenses should include only what is needed to sustain a reasonable quality of life and fulfill obligations:

- mortgage or rent payments, including necessary insurance and taxes;
- utilities (electricity, heat, water, basic phone);
- basic groceries (cut out the smoked salmon, alcohol, and other luxuries!);
- basic transportation, including necessary insurance;
- basic clothing;
- required medications;
- child care (where husband and wife work outside the home and cannot arrange schedules or make alternative arrangements to handle this vital function);
- child-support payments, alimony, and other court-ordered payments;
- garnishments (amounts creditors are taking out of your accounts); and
- loan/debt payments for consumable items.

You may at first have to make your consumer loan/debt payments out of your 20 percent forced savings budget, so when you get to your budget worksheet, you won't want to list them under nondiscretionary expenses.

I categorize all disbursements other than those on the above list as discretionary because you either have a choice whether or not to buy them or a choice about the level or quality of your purchase. Remember: The term *discretionary* does not mean you cannot or should not buy these things, it means you need to buy them wisely, within the framework of your forward budget.

Discretionary Spending

Under *discretionary* items I include:

- vacations, second homes;
- extended utilities (gas for gas logs, etc.);
- extended phone service (extra phone lines, cell phones, internet, etc.);
- regular or enhanced TV (cable, satellite, etc.);
- expanded groceries (cigarettes, alcohol, specialty breads, meats, cheeses, etc.);
- extra vehicles and related operating costs, including insurance;
- clothing beyond basics;
- first-class medical care;
- child care (beyond requirements previously stated in nondiscretionary category);
- life insurance (I have recommended that it be in your plans, but it is not a necessity);
- household furnishings;
- personal care (items and services);
- entertainment;
- dining out;
- private or higher education;
- etc.

I know that many readers will, at first, view some of the above-listed items as necessities—but they are not. They are wonderful, life-enhancing items and services that we should enjoy only when and how we can afford them. If we fund them on credit, believing we deserve them, we will have borrowed from an even more precious commodity—a fulfilling, truly happy life with lowered anxiety and greater security.

Why do I categorize these items so harshly? The number and quality of discretionary purchases are the two things that break most people's budgets. I want you to budget with a disciplined attitude, so that it is easier to manage paying for your discretionary purchases. You must be willing to sacrifice a little today so you can achieve tomorrow's important dreams. And the first cuts in your new budget will come in the category of discretionary spending. I encourage you to look at this group of expenses with a fresh, objective eye. Then cut, cut, cut . . . and cut some more. The more you cut, the more you will realize you can do without. Get in the habit of thinking, Do I *really* need this? Remember the pitfalls of different money personalities and ask yourself if you are falling into one. Then look at both the number of your discretionary purchases and their quality as places in a budget that are easiest to cut.

A SLICE OF MY STORY . . .

• An Example of Budget Discipline

I remember fondly how my dad and mom would leave the farm every Friday to attend to various matters in Louisville (pronounced Lewisville), Mississippi (pronounced Missipy). While in town, my father would deposit a predetermined amount of their earnings into their savings account. The rest, less his share of the discretionary spending money, went into their joint checking account. Mom used that to run the household and cover her share of the discretionary spending. Dad would put his share of the discretionary spending money into a hidden compartment of his wallet.

When they got home, he would pull a chair up to the kitchen table, take out his wallet, and count his money (hidden compartment included). As my mother tells the story, Dad found it uncomfortable to sit on a wallet bulging with such a large stack of bills, so he would then put some of his money either in his shoebox "storehouse" or back into their savings account.

This kind of discipline may sound old-fashioned, but it's this very type of discipline you will need to commit yourself to in order to set up and follow your forward budget. Remember, you need to value your own vision and dreams and goals more than you value material possessions. You will be able to do this if you center your happiness on the Spirit within. As you budget, plan for this true prosperity, not just a temporary feeling of satisfaction based on the instant gratification of desires. And then get down to work!

The reason so many dreamers fail—they're not willing to come down out of the clouds and get to work at the things that turn their stomachs.

—Susan Glaspell

Enjoy making and sharing your forward budget. It will give you a sense of control over your whole life, not just your spending. And that's what you're looking for, right?

INSIGHTS

- Failing to plan is planning to fail.
- The important battles take place in the silent chambers of our hearts.
- Courage is the strength to eliminate the walls, visible and invisible, that confine us.
- Determination is the inner rope that keeps us hanging in there, taking us to the top of the mountain of success that others long ago quit climbing.
- Sharing and giving to others generously are the petals of the flower of God-like love.
- Generosity is a secure investment that endures and yields rich dividends.

Before proceeding to the next chapter, please consider and record your thoughts and work through the exercises on the following worksheet, My Cash Flow and Forward Budget.

WORKSHEET 7

My Cash Flow and Forward Budget

NOTES FROM READING THIS CHAPTER

CREATING MY FORWARD BUDGET

As you work on your forward budget, use chapters 8 and 9 as more detailed guidelines if that helps you make a better budget. "Forced Saving" and "Spending Wisdom" and their worksheets will give you more detailed information on how to set and live by wise savings and spending budgets.

A. Determine your gross income.

Find what your gross income (income *before* taxes) is likely to be for the next twelve months. (You will calculate your net income in part B of this worksheet.)

If you cannot do this because of changing circumstances, begin by tracking your gross income and net incomes from the last twelve months. Then you will be able to do a second budget by substituting anticipated (and, if applicable, necessary) changes.

Be totally realistic. Pie-in-the-sky income expectations usually turn out to be exactly that.

Income sources for purposes of budgeting could include:

$_____ Your wages and salaries

$_____ Spouse's wages and salaries

$_____ Tips, bonuses, and commissions

$_____ Child support, alimony, or other such allowances

$_____   Social security and retirement distributions

$_____   Grants, scholarships, public assistance, or tax refunds

$_____   Dividends and interest earned

$_____   Proceeds from sale of assets

$_____   Other items, such as rents, royalties, and gifts

$_____ TOTAL **GROSS INCOME** FOR THE YEAR

B. Determine your net income.

Determine your net income (income *after* taxes) for the same period of time.

First list how much of your gross income will go for taxes. (Use last year's records if taxation and income have not changed. Otherwise, do the figuring: Use tax tables for the current year, available by calling the IRS and your state and local tax agencies, or by downloading from the internet.)

Note that you may be paying property taxes along with your mortgage payments. Check your year-end statement for the final totals on property taxes paid. Sales tax should not be included here. It is budgeted as part of the cost of paying for expenses. If you are self-employed, do not include your business taxes here. Instead, use your business's net income (your business gross less business expenses less taxes on business income) as your gross income, and list your personal taxes here.

OUTFLOW in taxes for both you and your spouse (if applicable):

$_____   FICA

$_____   Federal income taxes

$_____   State and other local income taxes

$_____   County and city property taxes

$_____   Annual vehicle taxes

$_____   Personal property/fire/water taxes

$_____   TOTAL TAXES FOR THE YEAR

Now deduct taxes from your gross income.

$_____ Gross Yearly Income

– $_____ Total taxes

= $_____ TOTAL **NET INCOME** FOR THE YEAR

C. Earmark the first 10 percent of your net income for giving.

If you are tempted to shake your head and say, "You've got to be kidding," please reread the reasons for not skipping to step D. They are given in the "4 Habits for Financial Success" in the first cycle section of chapter 6 and in the "Let's Talk Tithing and Giving!" section of chapter 7 and also in previous chapters. Remember: You are creating a forward budget here, one that is in line with abundant living—so give first to God. Thank Him for His hand of blessing for giving you the 100 percent from which you can give the 10 percent and keep the remaining 90 percent to fund your saving and spending!

Figure the 10 percent of your net income for the year as follows. (Use the net income figure from step B.)

Net income for the year: $_____ (from step B)

× _____0.10__ (10%)

= $_____ TOTAL TITHE FOR THE YEAR

If you cannot give 10 percent to the church and others in need, start with a smaller amount and work up to it. Then try to surpass the percentage! Tithing 10 percent is a minimum, not a maximum. I recommend that you give your tithe to your church and additional offerings of money and goods to other worthy causes. Giving above 10 percent should come out of the 70 percent allocated to spending, and thus be treated as a discretionary item.

Dream a little. . . . What could you do with this wonderful sum of money? Tithe to your church? Support a foundation? Give to someone in need? Help send a young adult to college? Fund an outreach project? Support a missionary?

List five causes other than your church to give money to that would give your heart joy.

1. _____

2. _____

3. _____

4. _____

5. _____

As you dream, decide which giving style best suits your personality: One check per year according to a set pledge? Routine giving per month to one or more specific, predetermined charities? Use an automated system to put aside a set amount per month in a special account (similar to a savings account) and then giving as special needs become known to you? Giving individually or as a family? Giving anonymously?

Write how you will structure your giving below.

D. Figure your personal income for the year.

Your personal income is the portion of your net income to use for yourself (and your family).

Subtract the 10 percent tithe amount from your net income for the year.

$_____ Net income for the year

– $_____ Tithe (God's gift that I give back to the world)

= $_____ TOTAL INCOME I/WE WILL USE FOR THE YEAR
(Personal Income)

E. Pay yourself next.

Earmark the next 20 percent of your net income as forced saving.

That's right. Since this is a living, forward-thinking budget—a financial plan that's in line with highest spiritual values and offers ultimate freedom and prosperity—not a spending budget—you are still not ready to spend. First you must pay yourself (and your family) so that you will be able to in-crease your assets.

Remember: What you do with this 20 percent savings will differ accord-ing to which cycle of your personal and financial life you are in. If, for exam-ple, you have consumer debt to pay off, pay it out of this 20 percent before you pay yourself. If you have not yet established your emergency fund, there are more suggestions on that in worksheet 8. Then proceed to the savings strategy that fits your current situation. If you need a reminder about the savings strategy I recommend, please reread the section "4 Habits for Financial Success" in chapter 6 and the section "Saving—The Discipline Must Be Built In" in chapter 7 and all of chapter 8.

Figure the 20 percent of your net income for the year to earmark for savings as follows. (Use the net income from step B, not your personal income from step D.)

Net income for the year:

        $_____ (from step B)

    ×   _____0.20 (20%)

    = $_____ TOTAL SAVINGS AMOUNT FOR THE YEAR

I recommend that if you are paid regularly, you divide this budgeted savings amount by 52, 24, or 12, depending on whether you are paid weekly, twice a month, or monthly. Or use one of the automated withdrawal or deposit systems described in the "How Best to Implement Forced Saving" section of chapter 8. Then set that sum aside each payday, in your storehouse savings account!

F. Figure your net cash flow (spending budget).

Now subtract that 20 percent savings amount from your personal income from step D (not your net income from step B).

        $_____ Personal income for the year (from step D)

    – $_____ Forced savings I/we pay myself/ourselves

    = $_____ NET CASH FLOW FOR THE YEAR
                      (Amount I/we have to spend)

This net cash flow *is* the your budgeted allowance for spending. To be financially successful, you need to limit your spending to your net cash flow —or less. No padding that number with borrowed funds, using credit cards, installment accounts, or any form of debt!

G. Determine your current actual nondiscretionary and discretionary spending.

Now for the real challenge! See if your actual spending is equal to or less than your net cash flow or must be cut to match this spending allowance. The first step is to know how much you are spending now, and which categories that spending falls into.

Log a 3-month Record

This is the step in writing your budget that takes the most work and the most patience. It is also the step that will change your spending habits the most.

From a recent past three months' time frame, use your checkbook log, credit card statements, any receipts you may have, and your own memory of all the cash expenditures unaccounted for. Record every expense item for those past three months and put the totals of each subcategory into the appropriate chart in steps G-1 and G-2.

Please do not delay the budget development process, and thus delay any needed cutting of expenses, by waiting to track the next three months' expenses before beginning the spending part of your budget. I adamantly disagree with those who recommend budgeting by waiting.

It would probably be a good idea to review the text in the subsections of the "Moderate, Efficient Spending" section of chapter 7, especially "Where to Cut First," before you fill in the amounts for each category.

G-1: Nondiscretionary Expenditures

	Month 1	Month 2	Month 3	Total of 3 Months
Mortgage/rent/ insurance[a]	_____	_____	_____	_____
Electricity	_____	_____	_____	_____
Heat	_____	_____	_____	_____
Water	_____	_____	_____	_____
Basic phone	_____	_____	_____	_____

---

[a] Home insurance premiums are often paid with your mortgage payment. Check your statement to find out your monthly escrow payment.

Basic groceries _____ _____ _____ _____

Basic transportation/
insurance (car #1)[a] _____ _____ _____ _____

Basic clothing _____ _____ _____ _____

Required
    medications _____ _____ _____ _____

Required
    child care _____ _____ _____ _____

Court-ordered
    payments _____ _____ _____ _____
    (child-support, alimony, etc.)

Garnishments _____ _____ _____ _____

Loan/dept
    payments _____ _____ _____ _____

TOTAL _____ _____ _____ _____

The number on the bottom right of this chart is your total nondiscretionary spending for your chosen three months. Use the space below to find your average *monthly* spending amounts for nondiscretionary disbursements.

Take the total of all categories for all three months (the bottom right number) and divide by three.

$_____ 3-month total of nondiscretionary spending

÷ 3 = $ _____ Monthly nondiscretionary spending

My current monthly nondiscretionary spending is:

_____

[a] Car insurance premiums are usually hefty and may come due only once or twice a year. You will need to allocate an average monthly cost for these premiums into your budget.

G-2: Discretionary Expenditures

As you look for discretionary spending, be sure not to forget fast-food and beverage and auto fuel purchases if you routinely buy them. If you use credit card statements, log each charge but not the payment itself that you make—otherwise you'll be double logging. Even if you only sent in the minimum payment, still log every charge on the statement. (Just because you have not paid for these items yet does not exclude them from your purchases that month, right?) Be sure to log any interest or penalties you may have incurred.

To help you track all your discretionary spending, here is a list of sample discretionary spending categories. See also the discretionary spending subsection of "Where to Cut First" in chapter 7:

- retirement contributions, life insurance,[a] home repairs;
- car #2 loan/lease, car insurance;[b]
- gas, parking, tolls, transportation costs, car upkeep;
- health insurance, out-of-pocket medical costs, dental care, eye care;
- child care, education, student loans
- dining out, vacation, travel, other recreation and entertainment;
- clothing beyond the basics, personal care, household furnishings, storage fees;
- hobbies, clubs, magazines, gifts;
- cigarettes, alcohol, and gambling
- credit card late fees/penalties (avoid these by understanding the terms of your cards and paying on time!);
- loans not covered in any category above or in nondiscretionary categories;
- any other outflow particular to your financial situation.

Not all the above spending categories will apply to you, of course. For this reason, please label your own headings for discretionary spending, plug in your category expenditure totals for each of the same past three months as you did for step G-1, and then total each category. I have tried to allow plenty of room for these. Use extra sheets if necessary.

---

[a] Life insurance premiums are usually hefty and may come due only once or twice a year. You will need to allocate an average monthly cost for these premiums into your budget.

[b] Car insurance premiums are usually hefty and may come due only once or twice a year. You will need to allocate an average monthly cost for these premiums into your budget.

Category	Month 1	Month 2	Month 3	Total 3 Months
_____	_____	_____	_____	_____
_____	_____	_____	_____	_____
_____	_____	_____	_____	_____
_____	_____	_____	_____	_____
_____	_____	_____	_____	_____
_____	_____	_____	_____	_____
_____	_____	_____	_____	_____
_____	_____	_____	_____	_____
_____	_____	_____	_____	_____
_____	_____	_____	_____	_____
_____	_____	_____	_____	_____
_____	_____	_____	_____	_____
_____	_____	_____	_____	_____
TOTAL	_____	_____	_____	_____

The number on the bottom right of this chart is your total discretionary spending incurred during your chosen three months. Use the space below to find your *monthly* spending allowance for discretionary disbursement.

Take the total of all discretionary categories for all three months (the bottom right number) and divide by three.

$_____ 3-month total of discretionary spending

÷ 3 = $ _____ Monthly discretionary spending

My current monthly discretionary spending is:

_____

H. Calculate your current total actual spending.

Do the calculations to figure your current total actual spending for the year. Add the total monthly nondiscretionary spending (from step G-1) to the total monthly discretionary spending (from step G-2) to arrive at your grand total for current monthly spending. Then multiply the grand monthly total by twelve (12) to find out your grand total for all spending for the year!

my/our current monthly nondiscretionary spending $_____
(from step G-1)

my/our current monthly discretionary spending+ $_____
(from step G-2)

my/our TOTAL current monthly spending   = $_____

my/our total current monthly spending: $_____ (from above)

my/our actual spending for the year   × 12 = $_____

Wow. That's quite a bit, isn't it? But you may not be done. . . .

Add any annual expenditures not accounted for in the three-month logging process. Examples of such items might be holiday or birthday or anniversary gifts, tuition, annual charity giving, etc. If you have already included these, that's great. Also add to it if your sales tax rate is going up soon.

$_____ annual actual spending calculated so far

+ $_____ annual spending not yet included

+ $_____ annual spending not yet included

= $_____ TOTAL actual spending for the year

So what's your final figure for what you are currently spending for the year?

My projected total actual spending for the year is: _____.

There it is!

I. Compare net cash flow to actual spending.

Look again at your final figure from step F, where you came up with your net cash flow—that is, your spending budget—for the year you're working with (your gross income, minus taxes, minus 10 percent for giving, minus 20 percent for forced saving).

Net cash flow for the year: $_____ (from step F)

My total spending for the year: – $_____ (from step H)

Surplus/deficit for the year: = $_____

This is where the rubber meets the road! If your spending exceeds your net cash flow (your spending budget), cuts are needed. Get serious!

Rewrite your budget as needed so that your spending is equal to or less than your net cash flow. Write it out in detail, by expense category. If you cannot solve one category or another, bring the problem to your discussion of the budget with your partner or mentor.

J. Agree on your budget.

Discuss and agree on your budget for the next three months with those close to you. Project budgets regularly.

Now that you have at least a sample budget, discuss what you see with your partner or mentor. Don't forget to pray together for guidance in your discussion. Agree on a budget that is achievable and that will take you toward your dreams and their goals. Decide who will do which tasks that tracking your new budget demands. Note your agreements here.

Decide when you will meet again to review your progress on this budget and when you will meet to revise the budget. Note that first meeting date here.

Post your budget wherever it needs to be, so that you will remember to use it! If it helps, post your dreams and goals there too, so you don't forget why you are forward budgeting. Use your reminder system to follow up on your decisions about who will do what and when and where you will meet next.

K. Don't be afraid to keep dreaming.

Set aside time to write alternative budgets based on dream scenarios that would require different income and giving/savings and expense. Dreaming feeds discipline and resolve!

8

FORCED SAVING

The person who achieves much, sacrifices much.

—James Allen

It is vital that you establish the habit of forward budgeting in order to achieve your goal of spiritual, emotional, and financial prosperity—what I call highest prosperity. The focus of forward budgeting on giving first, then forcing yourself to save before you spend moderately and efficiently is in accordance with the 7 Laws of Highest Prosperity that are printed opposite the first page of chapter 1 in this book. Sam the wood gatherer in the fable *7 Laws* was certainly not the only one ever to have trouble implementing forced saving and wise spending! These aspects of a sound financial plan are so difficult for so many of us that I have given each of them a separate chapter in *Wisdom and Money*. I hope the detail in chapters 8 and 9 especially will help you stick to your forward budget.

WEARING THAT CAPE WITH THE BIG *S*

In Proverbs, wise King Solomon gives us an example of forced saving. He tells us that ants have no overseer making them do so, yet they wisely save in summer the food they'll need for winter. (Proverbs 6: 6–8) Like Solomon's ants, wise people also save. The wise farmer does not sell all he reaps. During harvest, he saves in his storehouse the crops he will need for the winter; he also saves enough seed to plant at least one year's crop (he may save enough for two plantings, in case one crop fails). If we do not save part of our income for later, we are being extremely unwise. I urge everyone to be wise and save.

Saving is what will fund our short- and long-term objectives. Like the ant's or the farmer's storehouse, our savings are where we will find sustenance when unexpected costs announce themselves. Our savings are where we will find money to invest for our retirement. If we do not save, then talking about investments and investment strategies is mere fantasy, isn't it?

I state unequivocally that, stock market advertising to the contrary, saving money is far more important than investing it. It is also very difficult to accomplish if you spend first, then say you'll save with what you have left over. That is why I advocate the method of forced saving.

Besides giving us something to draw on when emergencies arise and giving us money to invest, forced saving is the spiritually, emotionally, and financially healthy thing to do. When you force yourself to save first, as you do when living by a forward budget, you are strengthening the wise habit of delayed gratification. This is a healthy discipline. If you want to be financially secure, please force yourself to pay *you* before you spend your money on other things. Not only will you help yourself, you will set a good example for your children.

Using forced saving, in my eye, makes you a kind of Superman. Let's see what we can do to help you put on that cape with the big *S*—but a cape where the *S* stands for saving, not superspending.

A SLICE OF SOMEONE ELSE'S STORY . . .

• A Savings Model

Joseph, raised as an Egyptian in the time of the pharaohs, was a descendant of Abraham, the ancient forefather of the Jewish people. In Genesis 39 through 41 we read that he fell into disfavor because of lies told about him and how he was put into prison and, in fact, forgotten—until he interpreted the pharaoh's dream. Joseph said the dream foretold of seven years of plenty to be followed by seven years of famine. He suggested that pharaoh find someone to oversee the storing of food while harvests were plentiful. Pharaoh placed Joseph in charge of Egypt's storehouses to prepare for the famine. This is the savings model he followed: During the first seven years of plenty, Joseph stored a percentage of the nation's crops in storehouses, one in each town. He did this to such an extent that the storehouses were overflowing by the time the seven years of famine began. By sacrificing, conserving, and saving their food stores, the proud nation of Egypt was fed for seven years on the harvests of the previous seven years. They not only fed themselves but those of "the whole world" (Genesis 41:57) who came asking for help, including Joseph's Hebrew family. These people, of course, increased pharaoh's wealth when they paid, one way or another, for the grain they were given.

Joseph's model, divinely inspired, is my recommended system for saving. Summarized, this simple but powerful model:

- saves a percentage of your income each week or month, depending on how often you are paid;
- keeps the savings in storehouses where it will be preserved for a rainy day;
- uses this savings to amass more wealth.

We are human and extremely prone to overindulge when times are good, spending too much and saving too little. All too often many of us save nothing at all during years of plenty. When we do save, we save far less than we could and should. Some of us even go so far as to borrow in the good times so that we can spend more than we actually make! Then, when the famine years come, we find that lack of advance preparation has made us financially vulnerable. We even have the audacity to stand around scratching our heads, saying, "Whoa, what happened? What am I gonna do?"

Before we find ourselves in this kind of situation, we should ask ourselves, *"How do I keep from getting run over by the Mack truck of famine when it comes?"* Then listen to the simple answer: *Always follow the 7 Laws of Highest Prosperity and their detailed applications shared in* Wisdom and Money.

If you do, you'll always be safe, come feast or famine.

HOW BEST TO IMPLEMENT FORCED SAVING

Throughout history, millions have discovered the huge advantages of the wise habit of forced saving. The laws of Wisdom, Priority, Motive, Preparation, and Preservation teach us to prepare for "skinny" times, those days when life's little emergencies have left our wallets lean.

What is the best way to be financially prepared? Force yourself to save the recommended 20 percent faithfully. You will benefit the most if you make these payments to yourself each time you receive income: Put your 20 percent into your savings storehouse (not necessarily a bank account!) that earns compound interest first, before spending from your checking account.

• How to Stick to Your Savings Budget Faithfully

I encourage you, as you employ the habit of forced savings, to ensure that you (a) fund your budgeted savings before you spend, using an automatic draft system, and (b) you keep your savings somewhat difficult to access.

Even if you do not like auto drafts for other purposes, like insurance payments, I highly recommend that you force yourself to save through automatic drafts. I have found that many people succeed in putting their savings ahead of spending *only when* they have an automatic system in place. This way, you do not rely on your memory and you do not fall prey to month-by-month circumstances that might affect your willingness to save.

The forced saving system that works best is the use of an automatic draft system in which predesignated amounts are automatically moved from checking accounts each month (on a specified date) to your storehouse savings accounts. Another method might allow your employer to automatically put a percentage of each paycheck into a credit union or some comparable account.

After you set up such a forced saving system, you need to protect it by ensuring that it is not easily accessible. Savings do not last long when you can get to your money just by writing a check or making a withdrawal from a bank savings account. Right? That's because cash is that stuff that never seems to stay around long—whether in our wallets or in our bank accounts. That is why I recommend a savings storehouse.

• Where to Put Your Savings: A Good Savings Storehouse

When I use the term *savings storehouse,* I am not necessarily referring to a bank account! Bank accounts do not tend to earn enough on your principal, and they are too easy to withdraw from.

When I use the term *savings storehouse* I mean "cash equivalents." Cash equivalents are short-term, interest-earning savings storehouses that offer the owner high liquidity and a high degree of safety on principal. (Translated: Savings storehouses are quite safe even though they are not usually insured, and you can get to the cash in them easily and without penalty.) Cash equivalents are as good as cash—only better. Typically, cash equivalents earn several percentage points more than a bank checking or passbook savings account, but with little or no additional risk.

Normally, cash equivalents are not earmarked for immediate rollover into longer-term investments. Instead, they are intended for short-term purposes, such as the following:

1. Your emergency fund. As mentioned in chapter 7, this fund will help you meet future living expenses in the event of a sudden drop in income due to unemployment or short-term disability, or a sudden growth of expense due to something like unexpected large medical bills or the need to pay the deductible on one of your insurance policies. Your emergency fund may also be budgeted to help with expected large expenses that come only once or twice a year, like college tuition or home insurance premiums. (You will calculate the amount you think you will need in this fund in worksheet at the end of this chapter.)

2. A place to park money until you are ready to use it for longer-term investments in more attractive assets—such as stocks, mutual funds, and long-term bonds. When short-term interest rates are high, cash equivalents themselves might be good investments. Historically, however, the rate of return on most short-term investments barely beats the rate of annual inflation.

My Favorite Forced Saving Storehouse

As you determine where best to place parts of your 20 percent savings budget, be sure you understand the compounding effect, as it applies to investments and loans. Then use this understanding to make your decisions. The compounding effect is discussed in detail later in this chapter.

My favorite forced saving storehouse is a money market mutual fund that invests in safe, short-term bonds.

Money market mutual funds are not federally guaranteed against loss of principal, but because of their diversification, strict regulations, and investment in high-quality short-term debt, the risk has historically been very low. They are generally classified in two broad categories:

1. Funds invested primarily in U.S. government-backed securities (my personal favorites);
2. Funds invested primarily in tax-exempt municipal bonds, money market savings accounts, individual treasury bills, CDs, etc.

How to Find the Right Storehouse for You

Cultivating a good relationship with your bank—and your banker—is a wise and valuable practice. Be sure you know the services your bank offers, the fees charged, and the bank's leadership and personnel. Let these suggestions help you choose a bank and a banker:

- Shop around. Examine the variety and quality of services at several banks, their convenience, and their financial stability. Ask for annual statements and learn to read them. Choose a bank that will give you the time and attention you deserve.
- Ask for a list of any and all fees charged for accounts or transactions.
- Pay attention to and read all materials carefully.
- Accept only those services and products that you really need.
- Be aware of minimum-balance requirements for all your accounts and ask how balances are figured—daily, monthly, or some other way.
- Consolidate accounts and services. The more types of banking services you do at one institution, the greater the likelihood of receiving discounts or special deals.
- Ask questions when you need help. Banks don't like losing valued customers, so it is worth asking your banker to waive a bounced check fee or other banking fees that may otherwise apply to your profile.

THE PRINCIPLE OF COMPOUNDING

Compounding means that interest is figured cyclically on the sum of the original principal and any adjustments made to account balance. These adjustments might be additions because of prior interest paid or subtractions because of bank fees or loan payments due or interest charged to a loan account. Whether for savings or for loans, account balances can be compounded daily, weekly, monthly, or annually. Compounding works for you when you are saving money and against you when you are borrowing. Compounding also works against you in other ways, such as when our economy experiences inflation.

When institutions use the terms *APY* (annual percentage yield) and *APR* (annual percentage rate), they are talking about the impact of compounding on your investments or borrowed money. (APY is explained on the next page; APR is explained under "Financing a Home" in chapter 9.) It is important to understand what compounding means, how to make it work for you, and how to keep it from working against you. So, let's look at some examples.

• Compounding as Your Friend

Compounding when applied to savings and investments works for you. In this situation compounding—earning interest on the original investment *and* on any reinvested interest—is another benefit of forced saving.

Here's an awesome example of this money-making tool. In 1626, Native Americans accepted the equivalent of $24 in exchange for the island of Manhattan. If that $24 had been saved in an interest-bearing account that earned only 5 percent annually, and all interest earned had been reinvested, that account today would be worth more than $1.3 billion!

Consider the positive financial power of compounding on a smaller scale. Assume you have $1,000 invested at a compounding, fixed annual rate of 12 percent (1 percent per month for 12 months). Here's the principle of compounding at work, on a monthly basis, to enhance your return and grow your money faster.

MONTH	INITIAL BALANCE	INTEREST DEPOSIT	BALANCE
1.	$1,000.00	$10.00	$1,010.00
2.	$1,010.00	$10.10	$1,020.10
3.	$1,020.10	$10.20	$1,030.30
4.	$1,030.30	$10.30	$1,040.60
5.	$1,040.60	$10.41	$1,051.01
6.	$1,051.01	$10.51	$1,061.52
7.	$1,061.52	$10.62	$1,072.14
8.	$1,072.14	$10.72	$1,082.86
9.	$1,082.86	$10.83	$1,093.69
10.	$1,093.69	$10.94	$1,104.63
11.	$1,104.63	$11.05	$1,115.68
12.	$1,115.68	$11.16	$1,126.84

Total (compounded) interest: **$126.84** for the year

Note that *simple* interest at 12 percent fixed, annual interest would have paid you only $120.00. So acquiring an account that features compounded interest added $6.84 to your nest egg. Letting your money compound means you earn over 5 percent more than the simple interest you would have earned over the same twelve-month period. Now, that's being a wiser investor, right?

As you can see, the compounding effect has actually raised your rate of return from 12 percent to 12.68 percent, which is the APY, or the annual percentage yield. The APY is used in connection with savings and investment instruments. It is normally higher than the simple yield since it takes into account the effect of compounding. It is a very useful financial indicator.

The longer you allow your money to compound, the more stunning the result! Applying the principle of compounding can work wonders. Since compounding makes an investment grow faster over time, it helps you achieve your financial dreams much sooner than otherwise possible. Compounding is well-known in terms of interest we pay on loans, but it is one of the best-kept secrets of accumulating wealth and becoming financially prosperous when it comes to buying rates of return on your savings. Albert Einstein once said that the principle of compounding is a very powerful mathematical concept! Now you know why!!!

Investments that offer the compounding feature include certain savings and money market accounts, individual stocks and bonds, and mutual funds. These are available from many financial and investment institutions, including banks, mutual fund companies, and stock brokerage houses. The key to finding them is knowing enough to ask for them!

• Follow the Rule of 72

The rule of 72 is a simple and valuable shorthand formula for calculating how fast your savings and investments can grow. It is a rough measure of the number of years it will take a dollar, saved and invested, to double in value—assuming a compounding, fixed annual rate of return. The rule of 72 is a wonderful preparation, planning, and preservation tool because it is easy to understand and use. It allows you to make estimates in a matter of minutes, which might take hours to calculate otherwise.

The formula is simple:

Divide 72 by the annual interest rate (as a whole number, not a decimal) to get the time in which an amount will double (after tax).

Here is an example: Let's say you invest in a corporate bond on which interest compounds. After you pay your income taxes on the earnings, assume it yields you a 10 percent increase per year. How soon will your money double?

72/10 (percent) =7.2 years

So if you invest $1,000 at 10 percent, you will have $2,000 in 7.2 years.

A corollary to the formula is this:

Divide 72 by the number of years you have to invest to get the annual interest rate (as a whole number, not a decimal) after you pay the taxes on the investment's return to double your investment.

Here is another example: Let's say the bond, after you pay income taxes on its earnings, yields you a 7.2 percent increase per year instead of 10 percent. How long will it take to double?

$$72/7.2 = 10 \text{ years}$$

So if you invest $1,000 at 7.2 percent it will take 10 years to double the initial investment.

Consider another simple, quick, and very useful application of the rule of 72 as a planning tool: Assume you want to invest $5,000 and double this money in ten years as a way to fund most of your eight-year-old daughter's freshman year of college. What rate of return will you have to earn after taxes to double your $5,000 in ten years?

This time, you divide 72 by the number of years, and you get the answer in a percentage:

$$72/10 = 7.2 \text{ percent}$$

So, to double your money in ten years, you will have to earn an annual return of 7.2 percent after tax on your investment.

Now let's say you discover that your child is another Einstein and will be off to college in five years instead of ten!

$$72/5 = 14.4 \text{ percent}$$

So, to double your money in five years, your investment will have to earn 14.4 percent per year after you have paid your income taxes on the investment's return.

• Archenemies of Your Prosperity

Let's quickly zero in on a couple of the worst archenemies of your goal of financial prosperity: The first one is inflation. The other is taxes. You will find a discussion on the tax enemy in chapter 12.

Compounding as Your Enemy

Money cannot escape the effects of inflation. And as in savings and investments, the principle of compounding applies. Only in this case, compounding works against you, not for you.

In case you are tempted to underestimate the effects of inflation on all your careful planning, use the rule of 72 to quickly show you inflation's negative power.

Corollary:
Since you are talking about a decrease in value with inflation, you would use the rule of 72 to figure the number of years it takes to half the value of an amount of money.

Example: Suppose inflation is running at 10 percent per year. How many years will it take to half the value of the dollar?

72/10 (percent) = 7.2 years

So in just 7.2 years your dollar will be worth only 50 cents.

Obviously, inflation can have an effect on your projections for your future expense budget.

A more realistic example: At 5 percent annual inflation (the inflation rate has averaged that or more over the past twenty-five years), how long will it take for your expenses to approximately double?

72/5 = 14.4 years

And this computation does not take into account that, as your wages increase with inflation, so might your taxes!

The principle of compounding that can be such a wonderful friend when it applies to earnings on your savings and investments can be a very destructive enemy when it applies to the effects of compounded inflation.

Compounding is going on all the time. If we do not make it work for us, it will surely work against us. Enemies to prosperity should motivate us to save, invest, and spend wisely. This is the only way compounding can become our friend.

What I have shared about forced saving, the principle of compounding, and the rule of 72 could seem to be just some cute mathematical parlor tricks to show off to your friends, but I hope you understand that they are much more than that. They illustrate and should bring home with a powerful punch some awesome saving, investment, and spending principles. They demonstrate the almost magical effect of compounding and the importance of reinvesting earnings on your investments.

• Using Compounding to Make Wise Choices

Let's again apply the habit of forced saving, the principle of compounding, and the rule of 72 to illustrate what a difference just a small increase in the rate of return can make over a long period of time.

For example, if your money is earning 3 percent after taxes (recognize what this might be invested in?), how long will it take to double your investment?

72/3 = 24

So it will take 24 years to double your investment (in—right!—a typical savings account offered by banks and other financial institutions).

Now let's assume instead that the rate of return is 5 percent after taxes. (Historically, money earning 3 percent after tax could have just as easily and safely been invested to earn 5 percent after taxes.) How long will it take to double your investment?

$$72/5 = 14.4 \text{ years}$$

Note that this is a whole decade sooner!

Awesome, you say? Not really. It's simple. Note that I didn't say "easy," I said "simple." Like many concepts in *Wisdom and Money,* it is easy to understand, much harder to do. But it *can* be done, using discipline, sacrifice, and the tools provided in this book.

I hope these examples give you incentive to stick to forward budgeting and forced saving. It is my experience that using these tools, together with wise, efficient spending and wise investing (discussed in the next chapters, especially chapters 12 and 13) is the only way to achieve financial success—unless of course you somehow receive a financial windfall! You already know the odds of that happening. So . . . please read on.

THE POINT OF FORCED SAVING

In my eagerness to persuade you to save at the level of 20 percent of your net income, I want to make sure I haven't taken you too far the other way. It is my firm conviction that the objective in accumulating money—for a rainy day fund, to fund education, retirement, or anything else, should be adequate provision. When anyone moves beyond that objective and begins to hoard—to focus on accumulating just for the sake of accumulating—or to focus on taking higher risk just to see if he or she can get an extra yield, then that person has exited the path of godly wisdom that leads to highest prosperity. He or she is, instead, heading for the trap of self-serving attitudes that lead to unhappiness.

If you see yourself beginning to focus on any of these self-serving attitudes, please remember that getting off the path to true prosperity is not an unusual cycle in the search for true success. Do any or all of the following before it's too late: Review the first four chapters of *Wisdom and Money.* Reread the 7 Laws of Highest Prosperity that are printed on the page facing the opening of chapter 1 of this book. Reread *7 Laws of Highest Prosperity,* and see where these attitudes left Sam the wood gatherer. Pray for guidance and talk with your partner or a trusted mentor. Do what it takes to turn back to the path of true prosperity immediately!

INSIGHTS

- Practice the wise, healthy financial habit of forced saving. Turn a trickle of dollars into a river of abundance.
- Make the principle of compounding your friend to increase your investment return and offset the ravages of the enemies of your money and prosperity.

Some people don't think money is important. I rank it right up there with oxygen.

—Phyllis Diller

Before proceeding to the next chapter, please consider and record your thoughts and work through the exercises on the following worksheet, Setting a Target Amount for My Emergency Fund.

WORKSHEET 8

Setting a Target Amount for My Emergency Fund

NOTES FROM READING THIS CHAPTER

SETTING A TARGET AMOUNT FOR MY EMERGENCY FUND

To begin to determine how much of a rainy day, emergency fund you need, use your total current monthly spending. For that number, refer to the calculation you did in step H of worksheet 7—before you multiplied by 12 to get your total annual spending. Multiply that total actual monthly spending number by 6. That six months' spending need is what I recommend you establish as your emergency fund.

my/our total current monthly spending: $_____

                                                 (from the end of step H, worksheet 7)

                                       × 6 _____

my/our emergency fund target amount: = $ _____

Now, if you haven't already, begin to build your fund by carving out part of your 20 percent savings budget and setting it aside in a separate savings storehouse earmarked for emergencies.

Congratulations! You've taken another step toward financial security and true prosperity.

9

SPENDING WISDOM

Spending efficiently and moderately are as important to achieving highest prosperity as saving and investing wisely.

—Cecil O. Kemp Jr.

If what you want is abundance, don't dwell on what you don't have. Instead, put your energy into creating that abundance by wisely managing your giving, saving, spending, and investing. Then choose wisely when you look to add material goods and services to your life.

Decide on your forward budget and set up formal times to review it often —alone and with your partner or mentor. This will ensure that your budget is up-to-date and still working for you. It will also help you stick to it, not let it fall by the wayside.

Financial success will come, not from the hottest or best investments, but from heart-based thinking and wise habits that lead you to give generously, save before you spend, and live in fairness below your means (spending moderately and efficiently). When you spend wisely you see the benefits almost immediately. You do not feet deprived, you feel energized.

Because this chapter and the previous one on saving are so important to your budget life, you may want to work on them as you work on the budget information in chapter 7. Or you may find that working through chapters 8 and 9 before or after you set your first budget works best for you. Whichever you choose, I wish you true success!

MODERATE CONSUMPTION AND EFFICIENT SPENDING

Moderate consumption means buying what you need and avoiding unnecessary purchases, especially too many consumable goods and services.

There is only so much money to be spent, right? So where will it do the most good—on peanuts, popcorn, and balloons or on saving so you have the money to pay for what you really need?

Spending efficiently means planning your purchases so that you get the most for your money when you buy. If you have planned well, you can almost always avoid taking out loans for such purchases and the consequent fees and interest that only cause you to pay too much for something you need.

Practicing moderate consumption and spending efficiency provides excellent rewards. The money you save will help you fund financial objectives that ultimately lead to financial success—no matter how you define that term.

• Finding the Incentive

The ability to practice discretion and prudence in spending will come naturally if we listen to the Wisdom that lives in our hearts. How can you tell if you have strengthened this Spirit-based thinking in yourself? Look at how you feel as you begin to see the effects of economizing. Sure, whatever your spending weakness, you will feel some resistance to change when you begin. If you've been overspending, you'll be dissatisfied at not having everything you want when you want it. If you've been underspending and defining need too narrowly, you'll probably feel some resentment at some of the new expenses. Whichever weakness is your bent, you will discover deeper satisfaction in yourself and those close to you as you gain control over your spending. Being in (appropriate) control and seeing yourself (and your family) moving toward goals you wish to achieve will pay off in all aspects of your life. And those close to you will respond to your new, happier self.

• The Basics of Moderate, Efficient Spending

I offer the following basic suggestions in the hope they will help you keep within the 70 percent guideline of the spending part of your forward budget. (By the way, I know you know it's okay to spend *less* than the 70 percent and to proportionately increase your percentages for giving and saving!)

1. Avoid buying consumable goods and services on credit.

Pay cash instead! Or pay the full balance of your credit card statement and installment account statements every month. It is not hard to see that borrowing is unwise if it is used to purchase consumable goods—things you will soon use up (groceries, fuel, etc.) or things that typically depreciate rapidly after purchase (automobiles, the latest fad)—or other consumable goods and services mentioned at various places in earlier chapters.

Borrowing money for real assets, such as the purchase of a residence or quality rental real estate, or for financing the startup of your own business, is a different matter. Real assets like these typically either maintain their value or increase in value, and it is therefore reasonable to use borrowed money to buy them. (But even then you should pay that debt off as soon as possible. The less that goes out in finance charges, the more that goes into your future wealth.)

2. Never buy on impulse.

You've probably heard this before. To keep impulse to a minimum, I suggest you follow the advice to never go to the grocery store hungry! Also, diligently plan your gift buying assiduously; it is a prime area where impulse buying tends to eat up a savings budget. Some people establish an annual budget amount for gifts—birthdays and holidays—and stick to it. Others draw names of extended family members for the Christmas season, so that everyone is included and, at the same time, everyone's holiday spending is kept within bounds!

3. Timing matters! Choose the right time to buy.

If you time your shopping wisely, you will spend less. If you need to purchase a new car, buy at the end of the model year. Take vacations in the off season—not only will you save money, you will avoid the crowds! These are just a few examples of how to carefully time your purchases.

4. Buy only what you need to fill the purpose.

Examine your motives for buying and make sure your purchases fill the need. If you are buying something simply because that's the best way a child will grow past a perceived need, buy only what is needed for that lesson, not necessarily the most expensive version of whatever the item is.

Shop for clothes in classic styles that you'll still want to wear next year and the next and the next. And if your goal is to wear a piece of clothing for several years, be sure the quality of the item matches that goal.

Question whether a new car is what you really need. Often, a used car will work just as well and cost significantly less. I often think of a used car as one that has been pretested!

Where it suits the purpose of the purchase and doesn't sacrifice quality unnecessarily, buy generic brands.

Buy in larger quantities when doing so will save you money and not overly inconvenience you in terms of storage space at home or initial outlay of cash. Be sure you'll use all you buy, of course, and compare the price per unit to be sure the larger quantity is, in fact, the less expensive one. (It isn't always so!)

5. Balance planning with benefit.

Of course, you need to be sure that the benefit of practicing any financial discipline is worth the time spent on it. Let's think, for example, about comparison shopping: If the time you spend reading labels and comparing prices is worth more than what you'll save, it is time ill spent. How do you value your time? One way to look at this is: Would you be working if you weren't reading the labels, and if so, how much would you be getting paid? Another way is: Am I already within my budget and would this time be better spent with those close to me? Watch for this potential pitfall as you look for ways to make your spending more efficient. Remember, your vision is about true prosperity, not saving every penny it is possible to save.

If you can save 15 percent overall by being efficient in your purchases, or 18 percent to 25 percent interest by not using credit (to consume what you probably don't even need), then you have "found" money you can use to fund saving and investment objectives. Remember: The number and quality of discretionary purchases is what most people get wrong when they "bust" their budgets. Kept in their proper place through a disciplined attitude and a willingness to sacrifice some today, they will bring both satisfaction today and important dreams tomorrow.

• Avoiding the Sinkhole: Credit Cards and Installment Debt

When we discussed moderate, efficient spending earlier (in chapters 5, 6, and 7) we noted how important it is to refuse to live on borrowed money, especially on debt incurred for consumable goods and services. Don't let this common, most unwise habit sap your financial energy. This kind of debt is banqueting on borrowed money! Even when not overused, it drains money out of your pocket that could be helping you meet future needs. Why let that happen?

Credit card or installment debt is also buying into a lie that says we can have what we want today without immediate cost or sacrifice. It blurs the distinction between wants and needs. Once blurred, the distinction becomes more and more difficult to see. If you are not bound by your budget you may find yourself saying "Charge it!" often and with ease. This habit of buying on credit appeals to excessive appetites and, like any appetite, will grow if not monitored. Like telling a white lie, using that charge card "just this once" without intending to pay it off at the end of the month seems like a small thing. We think it can bring no harm. But for all too many people it leads all too easily to using it that way again . . . and then again. . . . Sooner or later you will discover that there is too much month at the end of your bank account. Those eeeeeasy payments have just gotten tough! Don't let yourself get caught in a cycle where easy credit becomes a slave master.

That, of course, is just what the creditors are hoping for. Just take a moment and look at how much money they make from extending credit. Look at how many different kinds of companies—even nonprofits—now pad their profits with income from finance charges like yours. That's *your* money they're seeking. And according to *Money* magazine and other reputable sources, the average person now spends more than 22 percent of his or her income on debt interest.

Take Leo Buscaglia's advice when he said, "If we wish to free ourselves from enslavement, we must choose freedom and the responsibility this entails." We can choose not to spend our money just to be cool, to keep up with our neighbors, or to have that wonderful thing we've seen advertised. We must choose freedom from debt.

This is my wish for each reader of *Wisdom and Money.* That is why I recommend that, if you use credit cards or installment accounts, pay the balance in full at the end of each month. The first month you find yourself allowing a balance to carry over into the next month, take this as a warning sign. The second time, cut up your credit cards and close those installment accounts!

If you need more motivation to move toward being debt free, consider these three statements as incentive for not using credit:

- People who refrain from buying on credit, or who use credit as a convenience but pay for all purchases at the end of the month, spend 25 percent less than people who pay for their purchases over time. (Apparently, they not only spend less on finance charges, they buy less overall.)

- The after-tax cost of a dollar used to pay off a dollar owed on a time payment credit card can be as high as $1.18 to $1.25 (18 to 25 percent higher)!

- Filling our lives with material possessions purchased on credit and repayable over time will never satisfy our yearning. As mentioned throughout *Wisdom and Money,* especially in part I, that yearning is really about a desire for deeper spiritual connection and meaning!

Credit Card Compounding

Over two-thirds of those who use credit cards and interest-bearing debt for consumable items of any kind leave unpaid balances from month to month. Those unpaid balances average over $2,000—with interest that compounds monthly.

An unpaid balance of $2,000 on a credit card, at a rate of 18 percent per annum, compounds to an effective interest rate of almost 20 percent. That's $400 per year in interest charges alone—for one credit card!

If you had paid off the $2,000 balance on time, you would effectively have "earned" a 20 percent return on your money. Furthermore, that "return" would be tax-free. Imagine if you had invested that money in yourself instead of giving it to your credit card company! If you are in the 28 percent tax bracket (although the percentages of tax brackets change slightly from time to time, this is good figure to use for explanation), you would have to earn well over 25 percent on an investment to beat that kind of return!

If you are among the two-thirds who carry balances from month to month, stop using your credit cards and get started today paying off existing credit card and installment debt. Liquidate these debts as quickly as possible, using the 20-percent-of-net-income portion of your forward budget. Perhaps, too, you can use a tax refund, a bonus (or some of the extra monthly cash flow you have generated by cutting expenses!) to pay off these success-busters.

Once paid off, never use credit cards and other forms of interest-bearing debt again to buy consumable goods or services unless you know you can become one of the one-third of people who pay off their debt every month.

BUYING A HOUSE

A house is usually the single largest purchase a person ever makes, so be very judicious when financing either a residence that you are building or one already built that you are purchasing. In order to keep your emotions from unwisely influencing your house-buying decision, set wise, firm goals for yourself up front. As with any intended investment, you should choose goals aimed to help maximize the value of your house when it comes time to sell it and minimize the cost you put into it.

Why have I included house purchase as a spending item, rather than with the other investment assets discussed in chapter 13, "Investment Wisdom"? Suffice it to say that, as an expense, it is a given. You will need to carefully budget what you pay out for the house, both in mortgage payments and in upkeep. It is not a given that you will recoup the total cost, or more, in any major way, as you probably will with your investments. Most people who buy houses do not sell them in a way that creates significant income in retirement! Part of conservative financial planning is counting only the givens as assets or income.

• Choosing a House

You've got to like the house you buy, of course, but sound financial considerations must also be a priority since a house will involve such a large sum of money. Generally speaking, a single-family, stand-alone house holds greater promise for increase in future value and ease of resale.

Look at location as well as at the house itself: Is it in a neighborhood with good schools? Is it surrounded by well-kept houses and yards? Is it convenient to highways and community shopping areas?

Consider the reputation of the houses and how frequently they have sold in the neighborhood or area in the past. These can be clues to how secure the neighborhood is and the present and future value and marketability of houses therein.

Avoid being the owner of the biggest house on the block. Not only might it cost you too much, it may be harder to resell than a moderate-sized house.

• Financing a House

Today's homeowner is faced with a bewildering array of choices in arranging a mortgage. For example, if you take out a $75,000 loan to buy a house, that is only the principal of your mortgage. On top of that are interest, taxes, insurance, maintenance, and all the outflow that goes with owning a house. It is important to understand all the costs you will be taking on, and to compare options so that you can make the best decision for your particular situation. Ask about all the costs you can think of.

For interest, you should understand the financial buzz term *APR*. Where *APY* is used with savings (explained in chapter 8), *APR* is used in connection with loans. This so-called annual percentage rate is normally higher than the simple stated interest rate or advertised loan rate because it takes into account points and other credit costs beyond the interest factor only. It does *not* take into consideration the compounding factor, however, and thus can be misleading in terms of the true cost of your loan. Despite that financial flaw, knowing what the APR does take into account will at least allow you to compare different types of loans from different lenders based on an annual cost closer to the actual cost than rates that are advertised or stated on the face of a loan instrument.

When you work through the numbers to see what options are best for you, be sure to ask about all the costs in buying the house—insurance, points, fees such as legal, appraisal, and closing costs, and so forth.

Here are few pointers on financing a house. These may or may not apply, depending on your personal financial profile and the market situation at any given point:

Pay Cash or Pay More Than the Minimum Down Payment If You Can

Many times, people forget this is an option. If you think you have the money to do so, do a projection of the costs, taking into account that you will need money to repair and improve the property over the term of your ownership, as well as money to pay taxes. Take inflation into account when you do your projections. If it still seems like a good idea, talk to a mentor and others who have owned their houses for some time.

Assume an Existing Mortgage

Explore whether assumption rights is an option by asking your Realtor, or if no Realtor is involved, the owner of the house you are considering. This option often exists when you buy from an owner who wants to or is financially able to finance your purchase. It is also often an option for purchases of residences that have been financed by lenders such as state or federal governmental agencies. Depending on the state of present mortgage options, taking on an existing mortgage may save you a significant amount.

Study the Different Types of Mortgage Available to You

Note that some choices are better for the first time you mortgage the house you're purchasing, and others are more appropriate if you are *re*financing that house.

- *Fixed-rate, Standard-payment Mortgage: 30-year, 20-year, 15-year*

For a first mortgage on the purchase of a house, the certainty of a fixed monthly payment is still attractive to many homeowners. Because it doesn't change, it can make it easier to fit your payments into your budget.

If your budget is tight and you do not expect your income to rise significantly in the future, the 30-year term may be the best option. But before you decide, compare the monthly payments with the 20-year term and the 15-year term. Sometimes the payments on a 15-year fixed mortgage are not that much more than those on a fixed-rate 30-year mortgage. This is mostly because the interest rate on a shorter term mortgage is often lower than the rate on a longer term mortgage. Going with the 15-year option, then, has the added benefit of bringing significant savings to you!

If you are refinancing, however, and have already paid seven or more years on your first thirty-year mortgage, I recommend against setting up a new mortgage over a term of as long as thirty years. Doing so will put off your timely arrival at the financial cycle in which you can put that monthly amount to better use. I am a strong advocate of keeping house payments as low as possible while still keeping the mortgage term as short as possible.

- *Fixed-rate, Graduated-payment Mortgage*

With a fixed-rate, graduated-payment mortgage, the rate of your mortgage doesn't change over time but the amount you pay per month does. Your initial payments are lower than similarly structured mortgages at the time you buy your house, and your payments will increase on a fixed schedule, over time, to amounts higher than conventional payments. This type of mortgage is helpful to first-time buyers short on cash. It fits an initially tight budget and, since what the payments will be is predictable, it is easy to adjust that budget to prepare for the changes in expense. If you are quite confident your income will rise in the future, or if you plan to live in the house only a few years, then this kind of mortgage may appeal to you.

Over the long term, however, a graduated-payment mortgage is more expensive than other types of mortgages because the average principal outstanding may be higher.

- *Adjustable-rate Mortgage*

With an adjustable-rate mortgage (ARM), the interest rate can rise or fall during the life of the loan. Typically, the interest rate is tied to an index—such as the interest rate on a one-year treasury security. An ARM's interest rate is normally adjusted on a defined schedule—typically, once every one to three years. These loans often have a cap on them. This means the rate cannot increase more than a certain number of percentage points in a specific period of time. The initial interest rate of an ARM may run several percentage points below that of a fixed-rate mortgage.

Use caution and prudence, however, before you jump into the short-term rate trap that these loans can sometimes be. Their low initial rates make ARMs attractive to first-time buyers or to those who plan to sell a house in two or three years. If you plan to own the house for a short time, be aware that if your plans to sell change and inflation continues to grow, you may be left with a house payment you can't afford. If you are a longer-term buyer, this type of mortgage is probably not for you: Because of the potential of increasing interest and inflation, ARMs can be a time bomb waiting to destroy your budget.

In researching this option, you may be told that your offered ARM is convertible to a fixed-rate mortgage. This option usually kicks in between the second and fifth years of the mortgage. Of course, you will be paying for the privilege of this option! Look at such an offer carefully.

Another kind of ARM keeps the monthly payments the same, but lengthens or shortens the life of the loan—depending on whether interest rates rise or fall. If you consider this choice, be sure it fits what's likely to occur with your income and other expenses over the time of the mortgage.

There are many other variations of ARMs, as well. Whatever ARM option you are considering, be *very* sure you understand both the up- and down sides for your present and expected future situation. Understand, too, your choices for changing the arrangement if you need to do so. Taking the time to project the budget consequences of each mortgage option is time well spent. Listening to your partner's or mentor's views on the options is, of course, also part of the process for anyone seeking true prosperity.

• Pay It Off—Early!

If you use self-discipline and stick to your forward budget, you may find that you have more money to spend than your budget demands. If this happens, I recommend that the best thing you can do with that money is to pay down your mortgage more quickly than required and, if possible, pay it off early. To do this, as soon as it fits into your budget, contact your creditor and ask how to make a principal payment. It will not help to simply add to your mortgage payment and assume they'll know what it's for: You will need to follow their guidelines carefully.

The Benefits of Paying Off Early

If your mortgage loan carries 8 percent interest, you are in essence making an 8 percent investment with each extra payment in the normal monthly amount. It's hard to make that much in a savings account!

It not only makes wise financial sense to pay off your mortgage, it makes great emotional sense—no more stress from having to earn enough money every month just to pay the mortgage on a place the lender really owns. The rewards are worth some extra effort, wouldn't you agree?

How to Pay Off Early

One way to pay off early is to pay, along with your monthly amount, an additional amount equal to the principal (just the principal amount, not the full cyclical payment amount that includes principal, interest, and escrow). This option gives you the flexibility in tight times to cut back to your regular payment. A thirty-year mortgage can be paid off in fifteen years this way. If you use this method, be sure to ask your lender how to make certain that the extra amount goes to principal, and follow those instructions.

Another method is to save yourself interest by paying your mortgage bi-weekly instead of monthly. On a thirty-year fixed-rate mortgage, making half the monthly payment every two weeks will add up to one extra monthly payment per year. Continue this payment schedule and you'll shave off about ten years from your payback time—and thousands and thousands off the total interest you will end up paying!

One caution. Be sure you know any penalties that may apply to making extra payments and/or paying your mortgage off early. Ask your lender what those are and compare their response to your loan agreement. Weigh any such costs against the interest savings and other benefits of early payoff.

• A Tax Myth

Don't be lulled into thinking that the tax deduction you get each year for the interest on your home mortgage warrants a high mortgage balance. That deduction may not be as valuable as you think!

To take it, you need to itemize your deductions. Therefore, it's only worth the amount by which it exceeds the basic federal standard deduction (which you could automatically claim anyway if you had no house payment!). You need to figure your taxes each way—what your taxes would be if you itemize deductions and take the deduction for your mortgage, and what they would be if you took "only" the standard deduction—in order to find out if you can benefit from deducting your mortgage interest.

Even then, you should weigh that savings against what you would save by paying down the principal faster. You'll probably find that you come out ahead paying down the principal!

The peace of mind associated with a paid-up mortgage is wonderful—I know this from experience. Patty and I were disciplined and paid off our home mortgage early—and I don't miss the tax deduction at all! We were able to save over a hundred thousand dollars in interest by paying that mortgage off early. Invested and compounded for the remaining time we were to have paid on the mortgage, that sum is now a nice chunk of change!

• Equity Lines of Credit

If it looks like a spending duck, and walks like a spending duck, and quacks like a spending duck . . . it *is* a spending duck.

An equity line of credit—that is, a loan against the equity you have in your house—is just like an installment account or a credit card. It's simply another way to help you spend your money on consumable goods and services.

Unlike investment assets (what I call real assets), consumable goods and services radically decline in value as soon as you buy them. So, my very, very strong suggestion is this:

Do not empower yourself to spend the equity in your home for consumable goods and services, using an equity line of credit or loan.

"What about the tax advantage?" you may ask.

Forget it. When the purchase you are thinking about is consumable, the tax advantage has nothing to do with keeping your motives on the path of heart-based thinking!

Furthermore, this so-called advantage vanishes once you consider the cost of an equity line of credit—or any credit instrument used for the purchase of consumable items and assets like vehicles and pleasure items like boats that rapidly decline in value. The advertisers and promoters of equity lines tout the tax advantage—that is their sales ploy—but it is a grand deception in most cases. Tax advantage is a factor to evaluate only if you are considering credit to buy an investment asset that either retains its value or increases in value—something like remodeling a kitchen or adding a second or third bathroom, starting up a wisely defined business venture, or, for the very wise, making a "sure" investment.

When it serves as a liquidity tool (access to cash) for an investment, an equity line mechanism can make sense. But even then, this tool should be used only by people who have the discipline and ability to pay it back ASAP.

As with credit cards and installment debt, I strongly plead with you to never use equity lines or other forms of debt as a quick fix for either purchasing some consumable item or for trying to consolidate existing consumable debt. Why, you might ask. Doesn't an equity line have a lower interest rate than credit cards?

The problem is one of process, one of habits of thinking. Not only are you not focusing on what you could be doing for yourself and those close to you. You are opening yourself to the temptation to use such credit again. The old voices of "I'm worth it" or "I owe it to myself" are hard for many to resist!

You would be better off rewarding yourself with the feeling of accomplishment that comes from profiting from a well-kept forward budget.

• Refinancing a Mortgage

There are times, however, when you may want to consider refinancing your mortgage. The money you save can be put to good investment use—to fund college educations or retirement.

If interest rates have dropped significantly, and if you have several more years of mortgage to pay off and you intend to stay in the home you're currently in, refinancing your mortgage can be a great way to save real money—in your monthly payments and in the overall cost for your house. That is, of course, if you haven't done so recently. You need to consider how long you'll be in your house before jumping at low rates. Also look at the refinancing costs, which can often exceed one- to several thousand dollars.

Shop for the best terms for a refinanced mortgage, as you would for an initial mortgage. Make a list of the interest rate and the terms of the proposed new mortgage. Ask for the specifics on all extra charges to refinance (points, fees such as legal, appraisal, and closing costs, and so forth). These raise your effective interest rate. Then do a comparison of interest and all extra charges from each loan provider you are considering.

Since you want both lower monthly payments—(Translation: increased cash flow!)—and less overall cost for your house, you need to do the math to be sure of which choice will benefit you the most. You need to understand the "true" interest rate and cost—the one after all refinancing costs are paid.

To figure how long it will take you to recover all your fees, simply divide the total fees involved in refinancing by the amount your monthly payment will be lowered. If math gives you the willies and you have a computer, you can go online and use the formulas of any number of companies, to analyze the extra charges for an initial mortgage or a break-even analysis for refinancing. See Appendix for more sources of information on the feasibility of refinancing.

As with an initial mortgage, you will want to both shop around and negotiate for a refinance of your mortgage. You can afford to be picky these days. Competition among mortgage lenders is growing, with some offering good customers lower rates for points and other extra costs. Ask until you understand the differences between the lenders near you. Then remember that it certainly cannot hurt to ask them to waive or lower their fees!

VEHICLES

Vehicles are another common source of unwise spending for many. It is wise to examine why you are buying what you want, to be sure it is in line with the dream you are seeking to realize through your financial plan. Focus on dollars, cents, and good sense when you choose a vehicle and when you decide how to pay for it.

• Why This Car?

I believe the sole reason for buying a vehicle should be to secure safe, reliable transportation. Although style is tempting, the extra cost to get the current version of "what's cool" is often not money well spent. Compare the value of money in the bank to the value of the status that impressive vehicle might bring you. Which is more valuable to you? Which will bring you closer to that set of dreams you built your financial plan around?

In addition to which model car to buy, consider a used car as well as a new one. Since the resale value drops dramatically as soon as you drive your new vehicle off the lot, you can come out ahead by shopping carefully for a good late-model used car or truck. In addition to saving on initial price, you will save on taxes and insurance.

If you need a loan to buy the car, however, you may be offered an extremely low interest rate on a new car. To buy wisely you should take the time to do the research. What is the total cost of taxes, finance charges, insurance, parts, and service for each scenario? If you are buying new, don't forget that you'll have to pay dealer shop charges to maintain your warranty. If you're buying used, check the repair history of the car you're buying and the repair reputation for that model and year. Time spent without a car while your used car is being repaired can be more expensive to you than money spent up front that buys trouble-free maintenance. (Don't forget that most auto insurance carriers offer towing insurance for under $10 per year.)

• How to Buy

Remember, as I said earlier, that the timing of when to buy can save you money. If you are in a rush to buy, you will almost always pay more. Take your time. Look around. Read the ads. Enjoy the process. (If you don't, you're spending more time buying wisely than the money you save is worth.) For new cars, you should always purchase a vehicle at the end of the model year, at the end of the calendar year, or at the time of year when that car manufacturer runs its sales (if different from these other two times). If your state has an annual tax for owning a car, find out what date the tax agency looks at for ownership. Then do what you can to legally get the sale to occur after that date.

Price and Interest Structures

As with the purchase of a home, it is best to pay cash for a car if you can. You might make it a goal to add enough to your rainy day fund so that you have the cash to buy your next car.

If you take out a loan, compare options on how to finance the car: What is the interest rate when you pay the standard down payment? What if you pay more? What is the cutoff point where the interest rate goes up when you add to your down payment? What is the term of the loan, and therefore what is the total amount of finance charges you will be paying if you cannot pay the loan off early? How do you make extra principal payments, and is there any penalty to do so? Usually your dealer will have the best rate, but not always.

Be careful about the "promise" that leasing is cheaper than buying.

• Leasing a Car

Vehicle leasing is a notoriously murky process. Certainly there are deals out there, but leasing is an area of spending with more than its fair share of nasty secrets. Dishonest dealers use the complexity of lease contracts to take advantage of consumers. And even when everything is aboveboard, there are plenty of ways to make costly mistakes.

Listen to your dealer's proposal and ask questions until you understand it. Then take the time to determine whether you are being shown a fair comparison between leasing and buying. The biggest reason people overpay to lease is because they unwisely focus solely on the monthly payment.

Lease payments may be lower than loan payments, but that doesn't mean you're getting a better deal. You could be paying far more in interest and fees, maybe even based on a higher base price. Ask the dealer to break the costs down so that you can accurately compare the buying option against the leasing option.

Dishonest dealers might compare a lease's low monthly payment with the monthly loan payments on purchase at a different price or with the lowest down payment and over a shorter-than-average loan term, to skew you toward leasing. Be sure you're comparing "apples to apples"—the same base price and the same lease period against the same loan period.

Some dealers will say the sticker price on a car for lease is nonnegotiable. Don't believe that! Instead, go in ready to haggle with the dealer.

One key to effective haggling is finding out the factory invoice price before you go into the dealership. This is the price the dealer paid for the car. You can find it from several sources, a few of which are listed in the Appendix. The difference between factory invoice and MSRP (manufacturer's suggested retail price) is their potential profit margin, so this figure tells you how much room you have in which to bargain.

Another key to bargaining is knowing whether or not the dealer is offering you the best possible interest rates on your lease. That applies to the buying option too. Whether you buy or lease, it is helpful to know that the interest you pay comes from the rate set by the lender plus any percentage points the dealer adds. Dealers can raise the buy rate (the rate they quote you) above the lender's quote and pocket some or all of the difference! You might want to research this, either by asking the dealer how the interest breaks down or by calling the lenders in your area or by talking with your mentor or someone knowledgeable in this area; then you'll be better able to haggle over the dealer's markup.

Keep in mind that there is currently no law requiring disclosure of the annual percentage rate on a lease. There are laws for such disclosure on loans for buying a car. So if you are looking at a lease, be sure to use your calculator to determine the annual interest rate the dealer is quoting. Otherwise, you're a fish in a barrel that a dishonest or unfair dealer will hook with a good-looking deal while charging you the maximum.

There are several places you can turn to acquire or access the tools needed to figure the annual percentage rate the dealer is proposing you pay and any other aspect of the financial terms of a lease. If you own a computer, you can buy inexpensive software products that quickly do all the math for you. A few are listed in the Appendix. If you prefer to save the cost of software and learn a quick ballpark formula to estimate the calculations for different aspects of the lease, there are internet sites where you can study and learn for free. (See Appendix.) Of course, there is also the option to turn to a mentor or well-versed friend or associate to help with these calculations and analysis.

Two other important things to look for when considering a lease are: (1) Be sure the warranty period lasts as long as the term of the lease. Otherwise, if anything goes awry in the uncovered period, you're responsible for coughing up the entire cost of repairs on a vehicle you don't own and will eventually return to the dealer! (2) If you have great credit or are a repeat customer at a dealership, ask the dealer and applicable institution financing the lease to waive any security deposit and bank acquisition fees.

Other guidelines to take into account when considering the lease option:

- If the lease-holding period is going to be more than five years, you are normally better off not leasing.

- What is the vehicle's residual value (the resale price at the end of the lease period)? I strongly suggest that you negotiate a guaranteed price that you will pay the dealer to buy the vehicle at the end of the lease, so that if you use that option at the end of the lease you know where you stand.

- Remember that it can be very expensive to exit a lease early!

- Lease mileage limitations: You'll be required to pay for any mileage above the contractual limit, but this charge will go away if you exercise your right to buy the car at the end of the lease. This demonstrates the importance, when negotiating the lease, of agreeing upon a guaranteed purchase price for the car in the event that you decide to buy it at the end of the lease.

- Tax considerations: If you will use the vehicle for business purposes, the lease option may be attractive because of the normally smaller payment and more favorable tax treatment.

Always analyze the costs associated with paying cash, debt financing, or leasing a vehicle; weigh your options; and choose wisely.

• Maintenance and Repairs

Today's vehicles are more dependable and trouble free than ever, thanks to technological advances and improved engineering. But to keep your vehicle trouble free, routine maintenance is an absolute necessity. This will keep your repair bills lower in the future, help your vehicle perform at its peak, and hold the vehicle's value as the years pass.

Your vehicle's manufacturer has given you complete maintenance guidelines in your owner's manual. I suggest you browse through it and develop a list of routine maintenance items to follow.

Include on that list columns that allow you to record the dates each time each item is performed. Then develop the wise habit of either doing the maintenance yourself, or having it routinely done by trusted professionals. Keep the completed maintenance record in the glove compartment of your vehicle.

With regard to major repairs, be cautious and be sure you comparison shop. Ask a mentor or friends and associates for provider references. Also check the provider's file at your local Better Business Bureau. Then get quotes from several. In general, consider doing business only with repair providers who give written quotes, complete with price and work details. (In small towns this may not be possible, or necessary.) Ask them for customer references and check those out!

Study your vehicle's insurance policy and/or talk to your agent, to be sure you know if the repair (and any other costs like renting another vehicle while the repair is done) are covered and how the deductible applies. Before the work begins have a clear understanding with the provider about the time frame the repair project will need in order to be completed, and about the details of payment of the repair bill (including how any applicable insurance coverage will be handled).

INSURANCE

As they say, stuff happens. For the big stuff, if you don't have the financial wherewithal to absorb the loss, then you need insurance. Without it the big stuff will wipe out years of hard work and sacrifice. Insuring is like saving, investing, planning, and preparing; it's part of what responsible adults do to take care of themselves and those who depend on them.

A substantial percentage of the spending budget of most households goes for insurance in three major categories: property, life, and health. Frequently, employee benefit programs can provide coverage in some insurance areas. It is always a good idea to compare the pros and cons of buying your employer's offered insurance coverage against what you can buy on your own.

Property insurance covers your residence and its contents (furniture, mechanical and electrical equipment, clothing, and so forth), personal property (like vehicles and luxury possessions such as boats, jewelry, etc.), and other property that you own personally (such as property used in a business, rental property, etc.). The word *life* sufficiently defines its category, for purposes of this discussion. The health category includes medical, disability, and loss of income insurance.

Regardless of category, here are five suggestions for wisely managing your insurance and its related benefits and costs:

1. Work with a financial adviser who is competent in all areas of personal finance, including insurance. Guidelines on how to find one are given in chapter 13, "Investment Wisdom." Or if your financial adviser is not insurance competent, develop a relationship with an independent insurance agent (one not tied to a single insurance carrier but who represents many carriers). In that scenario, do however, include your financial adviser in the evaluation and decision-making circle.

2. Don't wear rose-colored glasses because what you see through them is not reality. When they are removed, and ego is parked, most people realize the folly of strategies such as self-insuring (which often is equivalent to having no insurance) or underinsuring, to save a few dollars in premiums (stepping over dollars to chase pennies).

   If you doubt the wisdom of this suggestion, talk to people who have been emotionally and financially wiped out by loss of a significant asset because of fire, or because of losing a lawsuit associated with an uninsured asset like a car involved in an accident that results in someone else being severely injured or even killed, or because of a sudden major health problem for which there was no medical, disability, or loss-of-income insurance. The bottom line of what I'm saying here is most people need some level of insurance in all three categories; the risks are so great that insurance needs to be a budget priority.

3. Know the basics and use that knowledge to guide you in setting the two key insurance factors in terms of risk and coverage: the insured amounts and deductibles.

   Don't over- or undervalue in setting insured amounts. And be sure your deductibles are right for your financial and psychological profile. Ask your adviser and/or agent to help you set realistic values for the deductibles and the amounts of coverage for all three categories of insurance.

   Many basics of the three types of insurance are given in subsections below this list.

4. Remember and apply my sixth financial rule of thumb given in chapter 7, "Forward Budgeting." Let your heart guide you.

   Buy insurance in an amount that, together with the net assets shown in the balance sheet (net worth) you prepared in the exercises for worksheet 6, "Finding My Net Worth," should provide as you wish for those you love in the event of loss or damage to property, your death or disability, and other events that create loss of income (for instance, a fire causing loss of income in a business you own).

5. After you, your agent, and your adviser decide what types of coverage and policy features you need, shop, shop, shop. Insurance companies will compete for your business if you take actions that require them to do so.

Ask your agent and/or adviser to shop, and do some shopping on your own. There are many internet websites that offer free quotes on coverage and rates from multiple carriers. Some suggestions for finding them are listed in the Appendix. Explore these opportunities so that you will develop ideas on how to save.

• Choosing an Insurance Carrier

After you shop and have narrowed down your choice of carriers, be sure the carrier is financially sound and handles claims in a prompt, thorough, and responsible way. There are lots of ways to verify these criteria.

There are companies that do nothing except rate insurance carriers in ways that include their financial and claims performance ratings. Ask your agent and adviser to help you gather information on the financial soundness and claims performance of insurers you and they are considering as a provider of your insurance needs. A few companies that rate insurers are listed in the Appendix.

Those are my five most important suggestions to help you understand the basics of insurance and ensure that you get value for your dollars spent on this key area of personal finance.

• Buying Through an Employer—or Not

Another important question to answer is whether you should buy some or all of your insurance coverage through your employee benefits programs at work.

There are multiple answers.

Not many employee benefit packages include property insurance as an option. There are exceptions, however. For example, your employer might provide a vehicle and pay for its property coverage or, if you own a vehicle you use for business purposes, your employer might pay for or reimburse you for the coverage on that vehicle.

Health and Life Insurance

Where health and life insurance are concerned, it may or may not be a good idea to go with your employer's offered coverage. If your employer is paying the toll, say yes! Then personally obtain the needed coverage to make up any gaps between your needs and what is being provided through your employer.

In cases where you are required to pay for the benefit, sometimes the coverage you need can be obtained at less cost through your participation in employer-sponsored plans. For example, the cost of life and health insurance can sometimes be less when it's purchased as part of an employer group.

My best suggestion is to carefully analyze the options available through your employer and weigh the costs and benefits against what can be obtained personally. Seek the assistance of your agent and/or financial adviser. This suggestion brings me to an important question that confronts many employees.

Cafeteria Plans

What about cafeteria plans? Cafeteria plans are defined under Section 125 of the Internal Revenue Code. In practice, a cafeteria plan (sometimes called a flexible benefit plan) is a benefit plan that allows an employee to have some choice in designing his or her own benefit package by selecting different types and/or levels of benefits that are funded with employer dollars on which you do not pay taxes.

Normally, the employer will adjust your compensation downward to provide the dollars to pay for the benefits selected. But that method means you are effectively buying those benefits with pretax rather than after-tax dollars, giving you both the benefits you choose and some tax savings.

Benefits which can be offered in a cafeteria plan include most benefits ordinarily resulting in nontaxable income to employees if provided outside of a cafeteria plan. Some examples are health, dental, and life insurance; accidental death and dismemberment coverage; disability coverage; and vacation leave. One exception is group life insurance with coverage in excess of $50,000. Although this is normally taxable, it can be included in a cafeteria plan as long as the amounts (of the group life insurance) in excess of $50,000 are taxed.

Although scholarships, fellowships, transportation benefits, educational assistance, and employee discounts are not taxable benefits, they cannot be included in a cafeteria plan. A cafeteria plan also cannot include retirement benefits except under a 401(k) plan. Many employers, however, will not allow 401(k) plans to be included in their cafeteria plans because the regulations governing 401(k)s are so complex, especially when combined with IRS Section 125 regulations.

The most common type of cafeteria plan provides a basic core of benefits including minimal levels of medical and life insurance, sick leave or disability benefits, plus a second layer of optional benefits. At a minimum, you want to be sure the basic benefits provide a reasonable level of protection against the major sources of personal risks—just as you would if you were buying these personally rather than through a cafeteria plan.

The employee can select the core benefit, or alternatively, purchase a

higher level of benefits with cafeteria dollars. The plan might also add benefits that were not previously offered as options.

Each employee is allotted a predetermined number of dollars, credits, or
points with which he or she may purchase benefits from options made available by the employer. If the dollar amount allotted by the employer is inadequate to purchase the desired benefits, some plans allow employees to make
additional purchases with before tax contributions through payroll deduction. If the benefits selected cost less than the allotted amount, the employee
receives the difference in cash, if the plan provides that. The cash amount is
taxable as ordinary income.

After years of exposure to these plans, I feel the reality is that many employers introduce cafeteria plans to reduce employer benefit costs. For example, I've seen many employers with newly implemented cafeteria plans
change their medical plan design by raising deductibles and/or increasing
employee contributions. My point here is that satisfying diverse employee
needs is, at best, a secondary objective in why the employer wants such a
plan. And while there is nothing wrong with an employer seeking to reduce
its costs, you want to be sure that goal is not accomplished at your expense!

The appeal of cafeteria plans is twofold: Possible tax savings and the flexibility that allows employees to select benefits that meet what they believe
their needs will be.

While the concept of cafeteria plans may seem appealing, serious potential problems do exist, including

- unwise employee benefit selection;
- reduction in previously negotiated employee benefits; and
- benefit cost fluctuation.

So, my strong suggestion is, Be careful. Before diving in, investigate the
plan well. Don't become enamored by either the potential of buying benefits
with pretax money or the flexibility angle. Seek your financial adviser's
assistance.

• The Basics of Insurance

Considerable savings can be realized if you agree to bear small losses. The
higher the deductible (the part of any covered loss you are agreeing to bear),
the lower the premium. For example, raising a deductible to $500 from $250
might save you several hundred dollars or more in premium. The old adage
"A bird in hand is worth more than one in the bushes" applies. Keeping the
savings and taking away the risk that you might have to pay additional is a
lot more financial savvy than just forking out the extra premium with no
chance of getting any of it back.

Here are the basics you should know about each of the three major
categories of insurance.

Property Insurance Basics

• *Houses*

First-time homeowners are often shocked by the lender's requirement that the property must be protected by "hazard" insurance, usually in an amount that would pay off the mortgage if the place burned down. Otherwise, the lending institution could be left with no security for its loan.

Whether you are a first-time homeowner or not, the best benefit of property insurance on your residence or other real and personal property is this: In case of damage or loss, you have switched the risk (the cost) *of replacement and payoff of any debt owed* from yourself to the insurance company for a premium that is a mere fraction of the cost of having to do either of those two things out of your own pocket! (This reasoning is equally applicable to the need for owning life and health insurance.)

The "basic" coverage form of homeowners' insurance, known as HO-1, provides coverage against damage by fire or lightning, glass breakage, windstorm or hail, explosion, riot or civil commotion, damage by aircraft, vehicles, or smoke, vandalism, malicious mischief and theft, as well as liability for injuries to others on the property.

The "broad" coverage form, HO-2, adds protection for hazards like falling objects; weight of ice, snow, and sleet; freezing and other single occurrences in heating, plumbing, electrical, and air-conditioning systems.

Further coverage is provided by "comprehensive" form HO-3, the most widely used type, and HO-5, the most expensive. In general, these two cover all hazards except flood, earthquake, war, and nuclear attack. Your agent and/or financial adviser can and should give you wise guidance on what level of coverage is best, given your financial and psychological profile.

Other property insurance policies include HO-4, the coverage designed for apartment renters, and HO-6, a broad form policy for condominium owners.

If you are a renter, don't be fooled into thinking you don't need property insurance related to your home. Don't overlook the need to have renter's property insurance to cover damage or loss of assets like computers, televisions, stereo equipment, clothing, and other items that would be expensive to replace in case of fire. Renter's insurance is relatively inexpensive, so check it out if applicable.

• *Vehicles*

The typical vehicle insurance policy includes several different types of coverage. As with homeowners or other property insurance, your premium will depend on the types and amounts of coverage and deductibles that you choose.

General liability insurance covers injuries/deaths and property damage resulting from an accident. This is the most important coverage and is required by law in many states. Each state has its own minimum liability requirement.

Some insurance companies offer "split limit" coverage (each part of the coverage is split into its own limit, for example, $15,000 maximum per person injured, $5,000 for property, and so forth) while others offer "combined single limit" (the entire combined coverage for bodily and physical damages under one limit, for example, $100,000 total). Typically, liability is presented in three numbers (each representing dollars in thousands):

- the maximum bodily injury for one person in an accident;
- the maximum for all injuries in a single accident; and
- the maximum for all property damage in an accident.

For example, 15/30/5 represents (for one accident) $15,000 per person injured, $30,000 maximum for all people injured, and $5,000 total for property damage.

I recommend your general liability coverage be equal to at least your net worth. And I recommend you carry medical coverage, collision, comprehensive, and uninsured and underinsured motorist. These options are discussed below, with a few others.

The level of coverage needed depends on your profile and the value of the applicable item. Consult with your adviser on these areas of coverage, as well as all your needed areas of property insurance coverage.

Medical coverage within your vehicle policy guarantees immediate medical payments for you, your passengers, and other parties, regardless of who is at fault. It also covers you and members of your household in any accident involving a vehicle, whether you are on foot, on a bicycle, in a friend's car, etc.

Collision insurance covers damage to your own vehicle in an accident. Collision is generally optional unless your car is financed or leased. In those cases, your lender will require collision coverage as a condition of the loan in order to protect their interest.

Comprehensive insurance covers damage to your vehicle other than collision, such as fire, flood, break-ins, vandalism or theft, and collisions with animals. It also covers natural disasters like earthquakes, hail, hurricanes, and floods (unless the vehicle is overturned, in which case it's considered a collision). Like collision, comprehensive insurance is usually required if your vehicle is leased or financed.

Uninsured or underinsured motorist insurance covers you if you are injured in an accident with others who themselves carry insufficient or no liability insurance. With the surprising number of such drivers out there, it's a good idea to have this coverage. Some states require it.

There are also other optional features that I recommend you carefully consider, weighing the premium cost against the potential need.

Rental reimbursement covers vehicle rentals required because your vehicle is damaged or stolen. Towing and labor covers charges in case of a road breakdown. Replacement coverage is available that covers the complete cost to repair or replace your vehicle under certain conditions, even if those costs exceed the vehicle's depreciated value. This option is not available from all carriers.

Life Insurance Basics

• *Use of Life Insurance*

Life insurance can be used for any number of reasons. The most common is compensating for the loss of earnings. Some would say it is creating an estate where time or other circumstances have kept the estate provider from accumulating sufficient assets to care for his or her loved ones. However you say it, I almost unconditionally recommend this use of life insurance. The exception is where sufficient assets to care for your loved ones are already in place.

Other uses of life insurance should be carefully considered, in consultation with your financial adviser. They include

• Paying estate taxes and other estate settlement costs.

• Funding college for children or grandchildren. (I do not recommend this strategy.)

• Paying off a mortgage. (I do recommend you have enough life insurance to pay off any indebtedness you have and to provide enough additional funds to cover any difference between the assets you've accumulated and what you feel in your heart is sufficient to take care of your loved ones in case of your death.)

(That does not mean I recommend buying what is called credit life. I don't recommend that because it normally is much more expensive than simply adding the indebtedness into your overall insurance need and covering the risk through your overall life insurance plan.)

• Protecting a business from the loss of a key employee. (I routinely recommend this, where applicable.)

• Creating a retirement fund. (I don't recommend this.)

• Replacing a charitable gift or equalizing inheritances.

Where appropriate I do recommend the above-listed uses not otherwise recommended against.

• *Cost of Life Insurance*

The cost for life insurance varies widely depending on the health and age of the person to be insured and the coverage amount of the policy. Individuals are rated by their age, health history, and in some cases, by their careers. All other things being equal, younger people will generally have lower premiums than older people.

The best way to find out how much life insurance will cost is to get quotes from multiple carriers. This can be done by calling insurers or by searching the internet.

• *Term or Whole Life?*

If life insurance terms leave you confused, here's a quick summary of the four major types of life insurance policies. Keep in mind that definitions may vary slightly from carrier to carrier and from state to state:

- *Term insurance.* The simplest form of life insurance, you purchase coverage for a specific price for a specified period. If you die during that time, your beneficiary receives the value of the policy. There is no investment component.

- *Whole life.* Similar to term, whole life is a policy you purchase to cover not just a set period, but you your "whole life." Premiums remain level throughout the life of the policy, and the company invests at least a portion of your premiums. Some firms share investment proceeds with policyholders in the form of a dividend. Many companies will offer "a relatively low guaranteed rate of return," but in reality often pay at a rate in excess of the guarantee. The remaining two policy types discussed below are variations of whole life that have evolved over the years.

- *Universal life.* You decide how much you want to put in over and above a minimum premium. The company chooses the investment vehicle, which is generally restricted to bonds and mortgages. The investment and the returns go into a cash value account, which you can use against premiums or allow to build. With some policies, sometimes called Type I or Type A, the cash account goes toward the face value of the policy on the death of the policyholder. With a second variety, sometimes called Type II or Type B, the beneficiary receives the face value of the policy plus all or most of the cash account.

  While Type II is meant to provide a partial hedge against inflation, it demands higher premiums than Type I as you get older.

  A variation of a universal policy, often called universal variable life, allows policyholders to choose investment vehicles.

- *Variable life.* With a variable life policy, there is usually a wider selection of investment products, including stock funds. As with a universal policy, returns on investments can offset the cost of premiums or build in the account. And depending on the type of policy, the beneficiaries will either receive the face value of the policy or the face value plus all or part of the cash account.

  Having read the material under this topic and other material on insurance throughout *Wisdom and Money*, some will still have at least two questions, one of which is: Should I own term or, instead, some form of whole life insurance?

I've personally owned term and a form of whole life, plus I have helped thousands answer this question for themselves. My bottom line answer is, I feel that term is best in most cases. That's because it is almost always better to buy term and invest the difference between its cost and that of a whole life policy, or some variation thereon. Please note the latter part of that suggestion: Invest the difference!

Many undisciplined people wholeheartedly agree with the first half of my suggestion—to buy term—but when faced with the choice would spend rather than invest the difference. I'm certainly not by these comments intimating that an undisciplined reader should buy whole life. I am strongly recommending they buy term *and* invest the difference in accordance with the broad investment guidelines given in chapter 13, "Investment Wisdom."

• *Insurance for Spouse/Children?*

Another question readers may have is: What about insurance on my spouse and children?

In rare circumstances, it may be advisable to purchase life insurance on children. Generally, however, such purchases should not be made and they should never be made in lieu of purchasing appropriate amounts of life insurance on the family breadwinner(s).

It is of utmost importance that the income earning capacity of the primary breadwinner be fully protected. In a dual-earning household, it is important to protect the income earning capacity of both only if the loss of both incomes would create a genuine need (financial hardship).

I do recommend consideration of purchase of some life insurance on a spouse who doesn't work outside the home. But coverage is necessary only if the loss of that spouse would create financial hardship on the remaining spouse. The purpose of that coverage would be to pay for household and child care services lost at this individual's death.

Health Insurance Basics

This category includes primary and supplemental medical coverage, like disability and cancer or major health issue policies. There are numerous plans with many kinds of coverage and options you can tailor to your needs. The sections below outline only the common types of policies, what they cover, and options available.

• *Secondary Medical Coverage*

If you are considering supplemental coverage or Medicare, Medicaid, etc., I suggest you consult with an agent especially competent in these types of insurance. He or she can provide many helpful brochures and information packages on these specialized types of insurance. You can also call applicable local and federal agencies to gather information to discuss with your agent and financial adviser. Or you can obtain information on your own by going online and searching, using the terms "supplemental insurance," "Medicare," or "Medicaid." Some such sources are listed in the Appendix in the section for chapter 11, "Funding Retirement."

In all instances, I strongly suggest that you work with your financial adviser to help you create a health benefits package that's right for you.

Below are a few basics on three of the most important types of secondary medical coverage.

Medicare. Medicare is a two-part health insurance program for three categories of people. It is funded from payroll taxes and managed by the U.S. government. The three categories of covered individuals are Americans who are: (1) sixty-five years of age and older, or (2) less than sixty-five but with specific disabilities, or (3) in the end stage of renal disease (permanent kidney failure requiring dialysis or a transplant).

Part A of Medicare is the hospital insurance coverage component. Most people eligible for Medicare do not have to pay for Part A coverage. Part B of Medicare is the medical insurance coverage for which most eligible individuals do pay a monthly premium.

Part A helps pay for care in hospitals as an inpatient, critical access hospitals (small facilities that give limited outpatient and inpatient services to people in rural areas), skilled nursing facilities, hospice care, and some home health care. Most eligible people get Part A automatically when they turn sixty-five. They do not have to pay a monthly payment called a premium for Part A because they or a spouse paid Medicare taxes while they were working. If you (or your spouse) did not pay Medicare taxes while you worked and you are sixty-five or older, you still may be able to buy Part A. If you are not sure you have Part A, look on your red, white, and blue Medicare card that comes to you automatically from the government when you turn sixty-five. It will say HOSPITAL PART A on the lower left corner of the card. Where to get more information on Medicare is in the Appendix in the section for chapter 11, "Funding Retirement."

Part B (medical insurance) of Medicare helps eligible participants pay for doctors' services, outpatient hospital care, and some other medical services that Part A does not cover, such as the services of physical and occupational therapists, and some home health care. Part B helps pay for these covered services and supplies when they are medically necessary. More specific information about coverage under Medicare Part B can be found on the Medicare internet website given in the Appendix.

Medicaid. Medicaid is a jointly funded, federal-state health insurance program for certain low-income and needy people. It covers millions of individuals including children, the aged, blind, and/or disabled, and people who are eligible to receive federally assisted income maintenance payments.

Eligibility requirements for Medicaid benefits vary for each state. For information beyond that shared above and the coverage and eligibility requirements, contact your state Medicaid office. There is also a website listed in the Appendix.

Long-Term Care Insurance. Medicare, HMO's and Medigap insurance do not pay for nursing-home care for long-term stays or for assisted living. Insurance can be purchased to help pay for these costs. Without such insurance, a one-year stay in a nursing home, estimated at $25,000 to $42,000 per year, can wipe out a family nest egg. It can leave the well spouse without financial resources for living expenses. When shopping for long-term care insurance look at

- premium costs;
- how long the company has been writing this type of insurance;
- what the company's history on payouts is;
- whether or not the company has a history of premium increases;
- whether or not a "partnership" policy is available;
- whether or not the policy is tax qualified;
- how the policy treats preexisting conditions;
- what the insurance policy will cover:
  - nursing home?
  - home care?
  - caregiver training for home care?
  - which medical benefits are covered besides basic nursing home costs
- how the policy fits with your managed-care coverage or Medigap insurance coverage;
- for how many years the policy will pay out;
- how much it will pay per day;
- what the daily benefit maximum is;
- whether or not it is indexed for inflation, and if so, how is the indexing is calculated;
- how many days (referred to as the "deductible") must you wait before coverage starts:
  - 1, 30, or 90 days?
- for how many years, months, the coverage lasts (is there a maximum pool of money?)

- under what conditions premiums are waived; and
- what optional benefits are available, and at what cost.

It would be good to compare all this with what the daily rate for nursing homes is in your area now.

- *Primary Medical Coverage*

     Let's review the four most common policy types for primary medical coverage:

- Indemnity policies allow you to go to any hospital or doctor. You submit a claim and pay the invoice (to be reimbursed later) or authorize the hospital or doctor to collect their fees directly from your insurance company. Although this plan is flexible as to who provides your care, the premiums are typically higher than other types of primary medical health insurance. Also, indemnity plans usually do not provide any coverage until the deductible has been satisfied.

- PPO (Preferred Provider Organization)-based policies exist where an insurance company has a working agreement with a network of "preferred providers" (hospitals, doctors, clinics, etc.). These providers discount their service fees to the insurance company in exchange for being part of the network. If you use a provider from outside the network, you'll have to submit a claim and likely pay a higher deductible. A PPO-based policy is usually less expensive but not as flexible as the indemnity plan.

- HMO (Health Maintenance Organization)-based policies exist where all your medical services are provided by the organization of doctors, hospitals, etc., who have working agreements with the HMO itself. This is different from a PPO, where the agreement is between an insurance carrier and the health care providers. The HMO is, however, like a PPO in that you must use the providers they authorize (except for emergencies as defined by your plan). One of the most unique—and sometimes irritating, inconvenient, and frustrating—procedures that HMOs require is that your doctor must refer you to other doctors within the HMO as need for care within their specialty arises.

HMOs and people who sell their policies tout the fact that there are no deductibles, usually only a small co-payment for each service and often a (comparatively small) maximum you pay annually "out-of-pocket," but the premium you pay each month may be high.

Insurance companies have wised up and now offer PPO plans that not only compete with HMOs but also often offer better benefits for lower premiums. Another advantage of a PPO over an HMO is that your policy is with the insurance company, and if you pick the right carrier, it is many times far more financially sound than an HMO organization.

• POS (Point-of-Service)-based policies are, in reality, an HMO with greater flexibility. Your primary doctor may refer you to someone outside the HMO with minimal or no additional cost. You may also refer yourself to a non-HMO provider, but you'll normally have to pay coinsurance.

In selecting a primary medical insurance plan, you should evaluate not only the type of provider organization but also the deductibles and coinsurance requirements. Those items represent risk the policy provider is asking you to take, in addition to the premium and the following costs, if applicable:

Co-pay. This is the fee paid each visit to the doctor. This usually isn't subject to the deductible and coinsurance provisions of most primary medical plans. Co-pays usually range from $10 to $40. When you shop, ask for prices for different levels of co-pay, deductible, and coinsurance features.

Prescription card. This shifts some of the prescription costs from you to your insurance carrier. Usually this card is presented at a pharmacy, where you pay only a fraction of what it normally costs depending on your policy and type of prescription (brand name or generic). The pharmacy collects the rest from your insurance carrier.

Accident supplement. In case of an accident, this option would pay for any medical treatment up to the predetermined amount without a deductible. Any costs in excess would normally be subject to the deductibles and coinsurance features of your policy.

Preventive care. Some policies may offer this as either an option or an inclusion. Routine physicals, immunizations, and tests may be covered, with or without a deductible, co-pay, or coinsurance. Your carrier may also include visual benefits ranging from co-payment eye exams and discounted glasses. They may also offer dental services that cover general cleaning and other basic dental care. If so, co-payment or coinsurance is often required for extractions, crowns, and other advanced procedures.

Keep in mind that your premium will increase if you carry such features as prescription, supplemental accident, or preventive care coverage. These options can be added, if needed, or limited or not used, to tailor a package that fits your financial and health needs.

My personal experience, and experience from helping thousands of individuals and businesses make their health insurance decisions, is that a PPO is the best from among the four options, whether you are looking at the question from an employer or employee perspective. There are, however, exceptions.

From the employer perspective, it might seem wise to pick the type of plan based on premium considerations alone. Certainly that is important, whether you are paying all or some of the employee premium or whether the employee is paying it. In other words, a good price is important to both employer and employee, regardless of how the employer is offering primary medical care—through an employer group plan or through some form of reimbursement to the employee for the cost of an individual policy. But . . . there's more to cost than premium.

There are quantitative factors that add to cost, such as co-pays and deductibles. And there are qualitative factors that may not add to premium cost but that affect you as an employer. For example, if claims service is poor in terms of both which claims are allowed and how promptly and professionally claims are handled, you can bet this is costing you in terms of employee morale and productivity—and perhaps eventually in good employees!

A wise employer knows the importance of developing and maintaining what I call "family culture" in their business. In a nutshell, the employer and its leaders develop and maintain an environment where employees are seen as part of the family and family is very important. These employers profit the most and last the longest, because they look at value and not just surface cost when making decisions involving employees.

• *Disability Insurance*

I'll close the discussion of health insurance by giving you a quick overview of disability insurance.

Disability income insurance coverage provides monthly payments, up to a specified amount and for a specific time period after a covered illness or injury occurs. Of course, such insurance must be purchased prior to your illness or injury. Disability insurance provides a way to protect you and, if applicable, your family by effectively guaranteeing your income and your standard of living for a specific time frame. You might say it protects one of your most valuable assets—you and your ability to earn income. If you become disabled, you may not have enough assets or be able to earn enough income to cover your continued living expenses. Within the defined parameters of the policy, disability income insurance will provide monthly payments to help meet your daily living expenses.

I suggest you consider carrying coverage that would pay at least 70 percent of your gross income. That is consistent with my spending budget recommendations shared earlier in the book.

I strongly suggest that you work with your financial adviser to help you create a disability insurance plan that fits your financial and psychological profile.

GROCERIES AND HOUSEHOLD PRODUCTS

It is likely that much more of your income than you realize goes toward the purchase of groceries and household products. In order to get this expense under control, before you leave home each week and especially on "emergency" stops at the store:

1. Establish what your grocery and hygiene product budget is and determine to stick with it. Find a way to make this work. If you are over budget in the first time period or two, choose sticking to the budget and not having what you need. In terms of process this will take you a long way toward your goal of learning what you can afford within your forward budget and what you cannot afford. You might find that putting the allotted funds—either by week or month—in a specified envelope or "cookie jar" and not spending over that tangible limit works for you! Or you might find that keeping receipts and totaling them weekly and bringing that total to your next scheduled session with yourself, your partner, or mentor helps. Or you might decide that keeping your accounts in a computer program gives you the framework you need. Many of these programs have a budget feature that will even pop up and remind you that you're over budget for that particular expense category when you enter too much within the time period you specify. (These programs can take a lot of time to learn and set up properly, so use this option only if you enjoy it and have the time or if that time will pay off in the long run.)

2. Clip coupons, shop for advertised specials, and comparison shop.

3. Eat more fruits and vegetables and less red meat. Most would agree this strategy is healthier and potentially less expensive, if you shop wisely.

4. If you do not yet have a system that is keeping you to your budget, or if you do but still have trouble keeping to it, establish a dollar amount that will not be exceeded on each shopping trip. Take that exact amount with you to the store. Or carry a calculator and stick to your budget. (These methods will also make you all too aware of the high cost of sales tax.)

5. Have a written list prepared before you go shopping. Make your written list as specific as you need it to be: Include the number of containers, the size of containers, and even the brand name if this will help you.

6. Avoid shopping for groceries when you are hungry. Avoid eating "just one" on the way home—this will add to what you have to buy the next time!

7. If it has proven to add pressure to spend more when you do so, avoid shopping with children or spouse present. (But balance this against

teaching your children or encouraging your spouse to shop moderately and efficiently.)

8. Buy in large quantities when they are less expensive and you have the need for that much of the item and you have adequate storage and can cope with the larger size containers. Make fewer, longer shopping trips. This saves on grocery costs and transportation costs. (Several quick trips a week tends to feed impulse buying—and this can kill your budget! But sometimes buying a few items at a time enables you to check prices as they are being rung up in the store. And the savings on errors can be quite large!)

9. Buy generic brands when they are less expensive and just as good. (Sometimes the brand names, on sale, are less expensive; sometimes the generics won't satisfy you as much and are therefore not as good a buy.)

10. Before you leave the store, compare the price of items to your copy of the cash register tape. Why? Because you may have been overcharged —for items you did purchase or for items you didn't put in your basket or, as mentioned below, for errors in the store's cash register pricing. (This can be done later at home, but it's easier to do at the time, even holding up the checkout line if necessary. Since the price is not usually on the item, the only way you can check a price is by comparing with the store's shelf labels.)

11. Firmly but respectfully (consistent with the way you want to be treated) request that incorrect pricing labels on the shelf be corrected and that missing labels be put in place. This responsible consumership will make shopping easier in the future.

RECREATION

We all need recreation, alone and with those close to us. There are many ways to get this inexpensively, and even free, without transportation cost. Look for these. Cultivate new ways to spend time at home, and away from home, with those you love. This will add to your family life and keep you within your forward budget.

• Dining Out

As with groceries and household products, establish an allotted amount to spend each week or month on dining out. Stick to that budget—without exception. When you have spent the budget, don't eat out anymore.

Be moderate about where you eat. Splurge infrequently, be moderate in your selection of appetizers and entrees, avoid desserts, and don't spend so much on your meal that you have to be unfair in your tipping in order to stick to your budget. You will feel better about yourself and attaining your goals if you tip generously.

• Vacations

Vacations are very important, a critical part of personal and professional development. Getting away from work and personal schedules and demands is key to rest and renewal. Just as balance calls for vacations, vacations should be balanced with your financial reality and some semblance of reason overall. Vacations should:

- be budgeted and pre-funded from the 70 percent spending budget, not financed with debt;

- be planned in agreement with the axiom: Timing matters! Choosing the right time to take a vacation can save you a bundle. Taking them in the off season is the best option—not only will you save money, you will avoid the crowds!

- be planned to take advantage of bargains on hotels and air and ground transportation, where bargains still suit the purpose and don't unnecessarily sacrifice quality. With the advent of internet and other travel related companies, a little time spent on your computer can pay big dividends (see Appendix.)

There are many other ways to reduce vacation costs without compromising the benefits. For example, buy groceries and eat in while on vacation, rather than always dining out. Pack food for travel rather than buy at roadside, train/bus station, or airport eateries, saving buying out for when the need is for more than food (rest, change of milieu, etc.). Have a want-to attitude and take the time to look for and consider alternative vacation ideas and destinations. Cultivate new ways to spend time at home and away from home with those you love, ways that will add to your family life and keep you within your forward budget. Those can be very restful and inexpensive vacations, as well as opportunities for personal, relationship, and family growth.

Kept a proper, balanced perspective through a disciplined attitude and a willingness to sacrifice some, vacations will bring both satisfaction today and savings that can help fund important dreams tomorrow.

• Music, Movies, and Other Entertainment

Concerts, recorded music, movies, video/DVD, and other "canned" entertainment can eat your money. As trite and repetitive as the following strategies may sound, the keys to managing these recreational and educational items wisely are:

- Setting a weekly or monthly budget and sticking to it;

- Never using debt to purchase these discretionary expenditures. Instead, fund them from the 70 percent spending budget;
- Shopping for bargains, including purchase of used items.

As with any category of outflow, especially discretionary items, money expended on these items should be balanced with your financial reality and some semblance of reason overall. That means perspective and a disciplined attitude take precedence over always being hip!

BACK TO THAT CAPE WITH THE S

Learning to spend wisely, moderately, and efficiently can give you the feeling of being the master of your money rather than letting your money rule you. Living spiritually and generously is a powerful antidote for excessive ambition and material greed. Using our money wisely can enable us to discover true significance, satisfaction, security, and sanity. Living within boundaries and practicing deferred gratification is the only way to attain the highest and lasting prosperity. Let the wisdom of God lead you toward this wise, pressure-free life.

INSIGHTS

- Efficient spenders live below their means with generosity, approach consumption reasonably, and are rewarded financially, emotionally, and spiritually.
- Getting out of debt—and staying out—should be priorities.
- The greatest dangers of using debt are its assumptions about tomorrow and the habits it creates in us, making compromise too familiar a companion.
- There is no sanctuary of peace like a debt-free home with love as its foundation.
- We only get to spend the currency of our life once. Spend yours wisely!

Before proceeding to the next chapter, please consider and record your thoughts and work through the exercises on the following worksheet, Cutting Loose.

Cutting Loose

NOTES FROM READING THIS CHAPTER

CUTTING LOOSE

You may decide to do this worksheet before you write your first forward budget or after you've tried living with your first budget and see or sense the problem areas. You may want to redo this worksheet about once a year, as your insight and needs change, and as you move from cycle to cycle in your financial life. As always, seek guidance from the Spirit within before you begin and as you work, and go over your worksheet with your partner or mentor after you have worked through it.

Now . . .

Write down ten ways to cut spending.

Focus on whatever you think will enable you to fund savings—and start down the road to financial freedom if you choose to use that method. Include both new ways you've heard about and ways that have already worked for you.

1.

2.

3.

4.

5.

6.

7.

8.

9.

10.

Keep this list in a prominent place.

Look at it frequently. Use it when you do your budget checkups with your partner or mentor. Add to it as you gain new insight. Subtract from it when insights don't pay off, financially or in terms of where that method is taking you spiritually, emotionally, and in terms of your goals and dreams. Use the list as incentive to ask friends and acquaintances how they keep spending in line. You will not only gain wisdom this way, you may begin to lead them on the path to true prosperity.

Remember, you can do all things through the power of Divine Wisdom. I promise you, it is worth your very best effort to get Superspender under control and become a model Supersaver!

10

Planning for Major Expenses Part I:

FUNDING A COLLEGE EDUCATION

Children are messengers we send to a time we will not see.

—Neil Postman

Now that you have saving and spending in line, it is important to start planning for the two major expenses most of us will incur: educating our children and retiring in a way that will keep us from being a burden on them or anyone else. Even though you need to invest money to fund a college education, I have chosen to treat the expenses first, then how to handle taxes in a way that will legally maximize the amount you have to invest, and then the wisdom and tactics of investing. You may choose to read these chapters in a different order.

Educating your child well is an investment in his or her future and it is therefore a wise, honorable, and hopeful thing to do. It is also a legacy you leave for the betterment of society: The more equipped your child is, the better he or she will be able to add to the balance of wisdom, honor, and hope in this world.

As stated earlier in *Wisdom and Money,* I do not believe a college education is necessary to attain everyone's vision of what life should be. And I do not believe the reason for going to college should be simply the better paying job it often brings with it. But if your children show interest and ability for college, opening their minds to a deeper knowledge of our world and to more critical ways of thinking, as well as to skills that apply to specific jobs, is hardly ever a bad choice.

In case your children end up going to college, I suggest you plan early to fund for their college years. If they choose another path in life, the money can be used to their benefit in other ways. For example, you may choose to use the funds to help them buy a house, pay for health or child care expenses, or begin funding their retirement. Be sure, though, to take into consideration the tax ramifications of alternate use of these monies. And if you feel you need assistance, consider the suggestions in *Wisdom and Money*'s chapters on taxes and investing, and talk with your mentors about how best to proceed.

(Throughout this chapter and its worksheet, please substitute the term *post–high school* for the word *college*, where applicable.)

To fund a college education you will want to initiate a savings and investment program and you want to be aware of how tax planning can help you do so. Here are some tips for beginning this plan.

DON'T GET BLINDSIDED BY TUITION TICKET SHOCK

Tuition ticket shock strikes when parents learn just how high the cost of college is. The fact is that four years (or more) of higher education are not cheap! And merit scholarships—those not based on financial need—are few and far between, particularly at choice schools.

This ticket shock sets in either because parents underestimate all the expenses that come with a college education or because they overestimate the amount of financial aid—need-based or otherwise—their children are likely to receive. As a result, many have inadequate pre-funding in place when their children are ready to start college.

Those with little or no pre-funding find themselves having to borrow in order to fund college needs. They may have to take hard-earned equity out of their house or money from their retirement investments, often at high tax disadvantage. Their other choice is to ask their children to shoulder the entire cost burden. College students who do this may work while attending school, which is not a huge problem if the hours are kept in line. In fact, some kinds of work will help them build their résumés. But in addition, they may need to take out loans. It is not uncommon for these young adults to graduate with significant debt that will then be a handicap as they begin their new careers and (probably) marry and want to start a family.

Parents should therefore begin to plan for their children's education as soon as possible. In doing so, college expenses should be realistically anticipated, as should the amount of financial aid that will be extended.

There are three important parts to planning the funding of college education. First, include your children in the process to assure they become aware of the cost of their education and ask them to make appropriate financial contribution to it—because we value what we pay for! Parents and children working together this way also helps avoid the extremes and hardships previously mentioned.

The second part of the process should be projecting what the real costs will be when the student is ready to go to school. Parents should look at the projected changes in their income and expenses between the time the plan is begun and the time the student will begin college. Usually this means they should assume their income will go up as their children get older. Thus, if at the time planning begins you are eligible for a high percentage of need-based aid, the financial plan should only include the amount of such aid the student will receive based on the income the family is likely to have at the time the student is ready to go to school. (If you manage to increase your income above a certain amount, there will be no need-based aid.) The plan should also, of course, assume that costs of schooling will increase over the years at least as much as inflation.

Part three, of course, will be to put a savings and investment program into action.

THE TRUTH ABOUT COLLEGE COSTS

The true cost of college may be higher than you think: Once your child is ready to attend, cost includes tuition, required fees (there are many—be sure you understand them!), books, room and board, snacks, clothing (does your child have a reasonable amount of the right kind of clothes?), furnishings for the dorm or apartment (just leaving home means many things you take for granted—towels, toiletries, desk lamps, etc.—will need to be duplicated; in addition, dorm beds are often longer than standard beds and require specially sized sheets), a computer, yearbooks, entertainment (cost to attend cultural events as well as the cost of just socializing), transportation for the student (both while at school and to get the student to and from school at various times of the year), transportation for the parents (cost to visit for parents' weekend and other functions, or just to make sure they are all right), and so on. Some kinds of classes also involve additional expenses, as do sports and extracurricular activities.

Don't forget the costs of getting there, either! These costs include fees for taking college-entrance tests, application fees for each school applied to, travel costs to take your child to see the schools he or she is potentially interested in, and the cost of any course your child takes outside high school to help his or her application or to test interest in a given field of study.

Oh yes, and finally there will be high school and college graduation costs for your child and your cost to attend them!

To avoid being overwhelmed by the college cost crunch, start planning and saving well in advance. This will not only make the college experience of your children more enjoyable, it will give a good example to them for their own future parenting years.

Begin by determining the current annual estimated costs of each item of college-associated expense. Collect figures from sample private and public colleges. List them and refine them as your child grows older. As it becomes clearer what kinds of activities and courses he or she is likely to take and which schools he or she is likely to attend, you can fine-tune your projections.

• Look Realistically at Financial Aid

Research your eligibility for need-based or other financial aid. These formulas are available from the schools of your choice or from publications your library probably has. Be aware that there are two basic formulas for how a school awards aid based on your income reporting. Most publicly funded schools use the government formula. Most private schools use their own institutional formula. Talk to parents who have put children through the schools you are looking at. This is always a good reality check! And don't forget that financial aid, when awarded, comes in many forms: scholarship, grants, work-study (of which there is more than one type), and loans (of which, again, there is more than one type).

Armed with truth about cost, you'll be more motivated and inspired to apply the following tips to your planning.

7 COLLEGE PLANNING TIPS

1. *Start saving now.* The sooner you start, the less money you will have to beg, borrow, or work an extra job for, to meet college expenses when the time arrives.

2. *Save regularly,* even if it's only $50 or $100 a month. That may not be enough to pay all the bills, but it's a start. Increase the amount periodically. Savings should be carved out of the 20 percent savings budget discussed in chapter 7, "Forward Budgeting."

3. *Invest wisely.* Invest the education savings for growth. (Growth means increase in the value of savings set aside and invested to fund college education, *after taking into consideration any applicable taxes and inflation.* Please revisit the discussion of those two archenemies of your money back in chapter 8, "Forced Savings.")

   If your child is more than five years away from entering college, increase in value of these monies will likely require that you invest in assets that offer higher returns than savings accounts. For example, you may want to consider investing in growth stock mutual funds.

   As your child enters the senior year of high school, begin to gradually shift assets into income investments like stock and bond mutual funds that offer the option of monthly payout of investment earnings rather than reinvestment.

As part of a wise investment plan for monies saved toward college education, you should also look into putting some of your savings for college education in the name of your child. But be sure to consider the tax ramifications before doing that. And look into the advantages of tax-deferred savings instruments like an education IRA. (More is given on this and on for-growth investments in chapters 12, "Saving Taxes" and 13, "Investment Wisdom.")

4. *Strongly consider sending your child to school in your home state.* Tuition costs are considerably lower for in-state than out-of-state public or private institutions. If your child wants to go to a particular out-of-state school, find out if they have tuition reciprocity with your state. And remind your independently minded child that going to school in-state does not mean he or she has to go to school right down the road, or come home every weekend.

5. *Consider alternatives to doing four years away from home.* Remember that four years of college is not the only post–high school path to their living up to potential. For college, for example, your child can attend two years at a community college and transfer to finish the last two years in a four-year school. It worked for me! Or it might pay to look at a technical school or a working apprenticeship in a business or other organization in the area of interest. Some states even have apprenticeship programs.

6. *Get the most bang for your buck.* Do some homework. Go to the library or go online and look through the publications available for bargain colleges. There are many excellent but overlooked schools, public and private, that cost less yet offer education comparable to some of the higher-priced ones. Remember, it's the strength of the department of interest at a given school that matters most. (Balance this bargain hunting with any justified desires of your would-be student, of course!)

7. *Encourage finishing college in fewer than four years* if it doesn't put too much pressure on your child. Generally speaking, the sooner your son or daughter finishes college, the less it will cost. Cutting the time spent in a four-year school can be done in many different ways. Advance placement courses or dual-enrollment courses (either locally or via distance learning, which can be taken via video or other means) while in high school can knock off as much as a semester or two. Taking CLEP (College-Level Examination Program) tests can give your child credit for courses that cover knowledge they already have. School-specific tests or SAT IIs can sometimes either exempt you from courses or put you in a higher-level course in that area. Extra courses while in college can help. If you feel that an extra-heavy class load is not best for your

child, it is possible to take courses at the local community college or elsewhere during summer. (If you are interested in this option, check with your school and with your major department to be sure the credits will transfer!) Any and all of these will help save the cost of the degree sought. (See Appendix for some specifics on funding a college education.)

However you proceed, if college is likely to be on the horizon for any of your children, it is wise to look ahead and plan. And as with any other area of expense, the more informed you are, the more likely you are to spend an appropriate amount and receive satisfaction from your expenditure.

To become more informed, there are many free or low cost tools available on the internet and from high schools and colleges, state and federal government agencies, and retail stores that offer computer aids and books on topics related to college education. Some internet sites are given in the Appendix.

PAYING FOR EDUCATION FROM THE MONEY YOU HAVE SAVED

If you plan, save, and invest those savings wisely, you will have the money you need to pay your share of your children's education expense. And you will be able to guide them to make wise choices on how to handle the part you ask them to pay. They will want to choose how much, if any, to work during those four years, and whether to go only for income or to choose jobs that give them experience they can put on their résumés.

As you draw on those funds earmarked for college education, be sure you understand the tax repercussions. If you feel uncomfortable with your knowledge and skill in this area, talk with a mentor.

And don't forget about tax credits for educating those young adults! There is more on this in chapter 12, "Saving Taxes." For now, suffice it to say these credits can mean substantial tax savings that increase your cash flow and thus afford you a painless way to save more toward college education.

INSIGHT

- Focusing on goals and taking habitual positive action greatly enhance the probability of success.

Before proceeding to the next chapter, please consider and record your thoughts and work through the exercises on the following worksheet, Estimating My Children's College Expenses.

WORKSHEET 10

Estimating College Expenses

Throughout this worksheet, substitute the term *post–high school* for *college*, where applicable. Don't hesitate to ask for help from a mentor if you feel uncomfortable or overwhelmed with doing the calculations in this worksheet.

NOTES FROM READING THIS CHAPTER

PART I
ESTIMATING PRECOLLEGE EXPENSES

For precollege expenses, list as many as you can think of. Use as a model the oldest child who is likely to attend college. You can find basic costs at your library, through the guidance office of your local high school, and on the internet at the websites of the schools you are considering or of the college testing agencies. Some of these websites are listed in the Appendix of *Wisdom and Money*.

Begin this calculation by putting the cost as of today in the "cost now" column.

After you list the current expense, use inflation (4 to 5 percent per year) or some other method to estimate the cost of these expenditures in the year you will begin to spend them for this child.

A. Cost of prep courses or summer courses.

These may be taken either to enhance the child's application or to help the child gain experience in the field he or she is interested in or to test his or her interest in that field.

(cost now)   (cost in 20____)

$_____ $_____

B. Cost of college testing.

The main tests many colleges require are the general SAT or ACT exams. Many students buy prep books and practice the test at home, to prepare. Also, some students opt to take these tests several times, to improve their scores.

Information on cost and procedure may be obtained from your high school's guidance counselor or online at the websites of these testing agencies. Be sure to ask if you qualify for a fee waiver for any of the tests you are contemplating.

Information on which tests are accepted at the schools of interest can be found by contacting the school or your high school guidance counselor. Don't forget that some colleges also require subject-specific exams for admission, while others want you to take them for placement. Find out which, if any, your schools require, then add in those extra test costs as applicable.

	(cost now)	**(cost in 20____)**
test prep books	$_____	$_____
SAT or ACT test, per test	$_____	$_____
number of times test is taken	_____ ×	_____ ×
Total cost of general tests	$_____	$_____
Cost of subject test	$_____	$_____
Cost of subject test	$_____	$_____
Cost of subject test	$_____	$_____
Cost of subject test	$_____	$_____
Total cost of college testing	$_____	$_____

C. Cost of application fees.

If you are in a need-based category, you may be eligible to get a waiver for some or all of the application fees for the schools you're applying to. Ask your high school guidance counselor or the schools of your choice for guidelines.

(name of school)	**(cost now)**	**(cost in 20____)**
school 1 _____	$_____	$_____

	(cost now)	(cost in 20___)
school 2 _____	$_____	$_____
school 3 _____	$_____	$_____
school 4 _____	$_____	$_____
Total application fees	$_____	$_____

D. Travel expense to visit schools:

Unless your child has already visited the schools you're contemplating, he or she should visit. Make an appointment with Admissions. Be sure to wander around campus as well, to get "the other side of the story" and to give your child the chance to get a feel for the school. This gut feel is often the deciding factor! Many children also stay overnight and attend classes at least once. This kind of stay can be arranged through Admissions if you don't already know someone attending who will help you.

(name of school)	(cost now)	(cost in 20___)
school 1 _____	$_____	$_____
school 2 _____	$_____	$_____
school 3 _____	$_____	$_____
school 4 _____	$_____	$_____
Total travel expense	$_____	$_____

E. Total all categories of precollege expense.

Total each of the above categories, and add in any expense you're aware of that I left out! Note the total precollege cost for your first child to be attending college below.

	(cost now)	(cost in 20___)
Total precollege cost:	$_____	$_____

F. Adjust for the number of children likely to attend college.

Extrapolate the cost for the number of children you have who are likely to attend college. Multiply the total "now" precollege cost by the number of younger children you have who are likely to attend college. Adjust the inflation column to take into account the additional years it will take for these younger ones to be ready to begin preparing for college! Note that number below.

	(cost now)	(cost in 20___)
One child's precollege cost:	$_____	$_____
number of children	× $____	× $____
Precollege cost/all children:	$_____	$_____

The number in the "20__" column is your goal amount for savings for precollege costs. The inflation-adjusted precollege total just calculated should be added to the totals at step F in part II of this worksheet.

You can refine both the precollege and college expense numbers as the years pass.

PART II
ESTIMATING COLLEGE EXPENSES

Choose two sample schools, one public, one private, that you think your oldest child might choose to attend. Research the current costs of attending. (You can get them from your library reference desk or from your high school guidance counselor or by writing or calling the colleges/universities you have in mind or by browsing the websites of those schools on the internet.)

A. Current costs of one year.
List those costs here.

School 1 _____   School 2 _____

Per year:

	School 1	School 2
Tuition	$_____	$_____
Required fees	$_____	$_____
Extra course fees	$_____	$_____
Dorm room/rent	$_____	$_____

Dining plan/
Food budget $_____ $_____

Computer cost $_____ $_____

Clothing $_____ $_____

Child's transportation
  to and from school $_____ $_____

× number of trips/year   × _____   × _____

Total transportation $_____ $_____

Furnishings $_____ $_____

Books $_____ $_____

Entertainment $_____ $_____

Your travel expense
    to visit $_____ $_____

× number of trips/year   × _____   × _____

Total travel to visit $_____ $_____

**Total annual expense
for one child** $_____ $_____

B. Adjust for inflation.

Using an annual inflation factor of 4 to 5 percent, calculate what the above total annual cost per school would be at the time of the projected entrance date for your child. Note those figures below.

Notes here:

Inflation-adjusted annual cost:
                        $_____ $_____

C. Adjust for number of years at school.

Multiply by the number of years you anticipate your child being in college. *Don't forget to add in the one-time cost for graduation!* Note that cost below.

Notes here:

Inflation-adjusted total cost:

$_____ $_____

D. Adjust to the "net" amount you will pay.

If you are in an income bracket that is eligible to receive financial aid, study the guidelines for aid at the schools of your choice. These can be found through the school and also from basic financial aid advice books. Familiarize yourself with the FAFSA (Free Application for Federal Student Aid, a form everyone must fill out if they apply for aid) and the CSS/Financial Aid PROFILE (another form that some schools also require; this form costs money to file at the time of this writing) and find out if your schools use only one or both. Then study how the schools of your choice use these to grant aid and which forms of aid they are likely to give you. Write those numbers below and total them.

If you are not in an income bracket where need-based aid is an option, consult resources in your library reference collection on independent scholarships that might apply to your child. There are also online references for scholarship search. The free ones are just as good as the ones that charge you to search! Some are listed in the Appendix of this book; others can be found by asking the financial aid office of your school.

estimated aid in grants $_____ $_____

estimated aid in work/study $_____ $_____

estimated aid in loans $_____ $_____

Total estimated aid $_____ $_____

Subtract this amount from the inflation-adjusted total costs above and write the inflation-adjusted net cost for one student below.

Inflation-adjusted total cost $_____ $_____

Total estimated aid $_____ $_____

Inflation-adjusted net cost/child $_____ $_____

Note here the terms of loans likely to be taken out by your child and, if you can ascertain it, the total debt upon graduation.

E. Adjust for the number of children.

Now multiply by the number of other children you have who will likely attend college. Adjust the financial aid as needed (for increased income, more than one child at school, schools of choice). This is your goal savings amount for the college education of your children.

Inflation-adjusted net cost/child $_____ $_____

adjustments $_____ $_____

                                      ×_____   ×_____

Inflation-adjusted total college
cost for all children $_____ $_____

F. Total of precollege and college expenses.

Two more adjustments and the calculation will be complete. The inflation-adjusted total cost for all children above will need to be increased to reflect the precollege expenses from step F in part I of this worksheet.

Inflation-adjusted:
Precollege cost/all children:

                             $_____ $_____
(from part I, step F, "20__" column)

College cost for all children
                          + $_____   + $_____
from part II, step E, above)

Grand Total college cost
for all children $_____ $_____

G. Tax-adjusted total of precollege and college costs.

Then I strongly recommend you add a tax factor, to ensure the most conservative estimate. Of course, the tax factor amount added can be reduced over the years as you apply the tax reduction strategies discussed in later chapters.

The easiest way to determine the tax factor is to guesstimate what tax bracket you realistically expect to be in during the time you are accumulating funds to pay for your children's college education. Then add that percentage to 100 percent and multiply that percentage by the inflation-adjusted grand total cost for all children.

For example, if you expect to be in an average tax bracket of 15 percent, add 15 percent to 100 percent, to get 115 percent. Then multiply 115 percent by the grand total college years' cost for all children.

Grand Total college cost
for all children $_____ $_____

Tax factor
(100 % + tax bracket)   × _____%   × _____%

Inflation- and tax-adjusted
college cost/all children
Grand Total $_____ $_____

This is your current goal amount for saving now for future costs of college education (precollege and college costs included) for your children. You can refine these numbers as the years pass.

The inflation- and tax-adjusted grand total cost above should be accumulated by carving a monthly amount out of your 20 percent savings forward budget and earmarking that as college education funding. As your college education fund savings accumulate, you will want to invest them. Investment guidelines are given in chapter 13, "Investment Wisdom." And ways to save taxes, so that you lower the total inflation- and tax-adjusted amount above, are given in chapter 12, "Saving Taxes."

11

Planning for Major Expenses Part II:

FUNDING RETIREMENT

Bridge the gap which exists between where you are and the goal you intend to reach.

—Earl Nightingale

Retirement ticket shock is similar to college ticket shock, *except most of the time the ticket price is much higher for funding retirement!* It is a sad truth that most people are not prepared for retirement. A recent study found that half of all retirees enter retirement with less than $10,000 in savings! Scary, isn't it? Lack of appreciation for the cost of retirement, reliance on the myth of Social Security, and a failure to save even minimally from income in the years before retirement all help account for that phenomenon. A few avoid looking at the cost of retirement, hoping on the one hand they'll be able to, but on the other hand never have to cope with the financial and planning realities of what must be done in preretirement years to make that dream come true. If this is part of your money personality, I suggest you overcome your repugnance by thinking of the example you are setting for your children or of the justice issue in funding your retirement: If you don't plan for it, someone else will have to take care of you. And while they may not mind doing that (especially if you have planned and something unexpected has been the cause of your inability to support yourself), doing so will keep them from doing something they might deserve to do. Not planning is not unlike refusing to work during your working years, and expecting others to take care of you. It is not an honorable way to live. (Here, I am speaking of deliberately not planning, which is very different from trying and not succeeding!)

In order to accumulate enough money to retire on, we must first look at how much money it is likely to take, then at where that money might come from. Since there is so much misunderstanding about this, let's start by looking at common misconceptions about retirement.

7 MYTHS ABOUT RETIREMENT

Let's begin by identifying seven common myths that can lead to disaster after it is too late to remedy the situation. Then we will look at my counter-proposal to each myth. As you read them, identify which ones are part of your current belief system or money personality, then begin to think more effectively. As always, recognizing flaws in our thinking is the first step to becoming more truly successful.

1. *Social Security will take care of me.* If you are a married couple making between $50,000 and $100,000 a year in the last few years before retirement, Social Security (if it is still around when you get to your retirement years?!) will probably pay you less than a quarter of your preretirement income. Could you live happily—and stay retired—on 25 percent of your current income?

   You can request a benefits statement from the Social Security Administration in Washington. (See Appendix.) The statement lists your payments to the system and expected benefit payments. It is a good idea to request such a statement regularly during your working years, in order to get a good idea of what to expect.

   After you study how Social Security applies to your situation, it would be wise to plan at a minimum to personally provide the other three-quarters of income you will need for retirement.

2. *Retirement expenses will be lower than my current expenses.* This may be true, but only if you intend to stay home for the rest of your life, are lucky, and live very frugally to compensate for inflation. This assumes, too, that your mortgage is paid off, your health remains good, and your children and their families and/or your parents don't develop need (or you don't intend to help them if they do). Be aware that study after study has shown that retirement expenses do not really go down—in addition to inflation, there are still the utilities to pay, cars to maintain, and home maintenance costs. As you age, prescriptions and medical bills tend to increase, and the need (and joy of) financially assisting your loved ones often arises. In addition, most people look forward to retirement as a time when they can "finally" do what they really want to do. If that's the case, you are going to need the same—if not more—

income to enjoy those dreams: traveling, doing service or mission work, buying hobby supplies, fixing up the ol' homestead, visiting grandchildren, contributing to charities, taking some courses, etc. Remember my fifth financial rule of thumb from chapter 7? Fund retirement based on 100 percent of preretirement income! Be safe, not sorry.

3. *My employer will take care of me.* If you subscribe to this myth, I have to ask, Which company? Statistics suggest that the average person changes jobs, sometimes even careers, seven to eight times in their lifetime. That makes it very difficult to receive the kind of pension you might have received by working for one company that has an honest, successful retirement benefit for thirty years. If you are, or are likely to be, one of these "average" people, take heart: Traditional pension plans—ones where an employer pays you a monthly amount based on your preretirement salary—are rapidly going the way of the dinosaur. Those plans are being replaced with plans where the retirement benefit you receive will depend primarily on how much you contribute, not how much your employer contributes, and on the rate of return you have earned on the investment choices you made for your contributions. Given this situation and the scandals involving foul play by employers' funding and management of retirement plan assets, it might be better to do the investing on your own.

4. *Personal investments will take care of me.* This will be true for you if you follow the suggestions in *Wisdom and Money.* I have listed this statement as a myth, though, to remind you that the average family saves less than 5 percent of its income. And many who do save make the big mistake of investing their savings in so-called guaranteed investments, investments that I call sticker-shock investments and that, as explained in chapter 13, "Investment Wisdom," guarantee only one thing—you lose!

5. *Retirement is years away. I can always start saving later.* Here is some incentive to start now: For every ten years you wait to start saving for retirement, you will need to save about three times more per year to have the same size retirement nest egg. Do you remember the old Fram oil filter commercials? Their spokesman said, "Pay me now or pay me later." What's true for oil filters is true for retirement funding. Later is more expensive and a lot more painful.

6. *I don't ever plan to retire. Or if I do, it'll be a short retirement.* According to current U.S. statistics, approximately 50 percent of people reaching age sixty-five can expect to live almost another two decades. That's at least twenty years you need to fund for. In addition to having this kind of life expectancy, forced or voluntary early retirement means that some people will be retired nearly as long as they have worked. If you subscribe to this myth, I suggest you reread my encouragement earlier in

this chapter to lay avoidance aside and begin to plan now. If you don't, this myth may indeed come true for you because you'll be forced to work due to lack of preretirement financial preparation.

7. *My ship is going to come in when my parents pass their estate to me.* This sounds nice, but statistics suggest that those who believe this might also want to buy stock in the company that owns oceanfront property in Arizona! It is more realistic, and sobering as well, to realize this: Until they die, your parents face the same challenges with money as you do, and often more. Statistics indicate that a substantial percent of one's lifetime health care expenditures, for example, is spent after age fifty. So money your parents have now may not exist when they die. Please look at this realistically, given expenses they may incur, the cost to bury them when they die, and the net of what you will inherit after taxes and lawyers' fees are paid (not to mention that your parents may leave some or all their money to someone else or to some other cause). In addition, remember that counting on others to take care of your responsibilities is a self-serving attitude that will hinder your spiritual, emotional, and financial growth. Consequently, in terms of character development, it might be better to plan to take care of yourself (and your spouse), and if you do inherit something substantial someday, use it as a bonus.

PLANNING THE AMOUNT NEEDED

The first step to planning realistically for retirement is, of course, figuring how much income you will need to live the way you want to live in what should be your "Golden Years."

Here are some questions to consider, regardless of current age, that will give you some idea of the cost.

- Where do you want to live?

- How do you want to live?

- What do you want to do in retirement?

- How much cushion (emergency fund) do you need in case you change your mind about what's adequate? Or inflation and tax rates are more than you projected? Or the stock market goes south? Or you or your spouse become very ill or, God forbid, divorce?

Consider the answers to these questions. Then plan, save, and invest accordingly. This will help ensure that you are being safe not sorry in terms of the amount of income you deem adequate.

• Narrowing the Options

Take a long, hard look at your dreams about retirement and then look at your current house and how it fits with those dreams. Ask yourself questions like:

- As you age, will you feel more comfortable in it or in a smaller home?
  - In a condo or an apartment?
  - In an individually run residence or in a retirement complex that allows progressive supervision in case you become ill?

Be sure to think it through completely, taking into account the different subcycles you are likely to encounter as you (and your spouse) age. Then go through questions like:

- Is your current residence in a safe location?
- Do you like your current neighborhood, or is it time for a change?
- Is your current address really convenient for those things you envision doing during your retirement years?
- If you plan to stay where you are, will there be significant expenditures for upkeep?
- Do you really want to (and can you) handle the upkeep of your yard and current residence?

Be sure not to make rash decisions. For example, if your spouse dies, standard advice is to wait two years before making any major change in your life (unless there is a need to make the change sooner). This two years can be spent reevaluating who you are as a newly single person.

If you decide you would like to move, ask yourself questions about what the move will do to help you live your retirement dream, questions like:

- Do you want to maintain independent ownership of some sort, or do you want to live in a retirement community?
- Where do you want to live and what do you want there?
  - Do you want to live near your children or special friends?
  - Even if you are not particularly close to your children, if you or they became gravely ill, would you want to be closer?
  - If climate is a factor, do you want to live year-round somewhere warm (or cold)?
  - Or do you want to maintain both a winter home and a summer home?
- Do you want to live in a big city or small town?
  - Do you want some land to be a hobby farmer?
  - Or do you want to be in a city, close to a particular set of activities or institutions or people?

Retirement is a new phase of your life. What level of income and expense will make your dreams come true? How do you want to spend time during this new phase? Traveling? If so, where to and what will it cost? Maybe you want to spend your time on crafts and other hobbies, return to the classroom, or volunteer your time. You may even want to start your own business or work part-time for an employer.

Consider pacing the timing of these changes. Moving a thousand miles away from your present residence and starting a business at the same time might be a little too much for you and your financial resources. Remember: It takes most people longer to adjust to change as they get older. You may want to stay in your current home for several years after retirement, for example, before you move.

Note your answers in part I of the worksheet for this chapter, and share your findings with your partner or mentor as appropriate.

• A Ballpark Formula for the Annual Income Needed to Live Retired

Let's make the chapter's opening quote from Mr. Nightingale come alive. After you have considered and answered the retirement-related questions posed above, you'll want to determine how much money it will take to achieve your retirement dreams.

I offer a simple formula ballpark method—not intended to be precise—that should allow you to get an overall grip on where you stand with retirement funding. This formula ignores all rules of thumb you may have heard and used before reading *Wisdom and Money.* It uses the fifth financial rule of thumb I noted in chapter 7, "Forward Budgeting."

The formula to adequately fund your retirement is simply this:

1. Take 100 percent of your current annual gross income.

2. Figure the number of years you expect to be retired. (That is, of course, how long you and your spouse expect to live after retirement.) Some financial pros recommend that you determine your postretirement life expectancy and double it! Count me in with that group.

3. Multiply your estimated annual gross income by the number of years you anticipate living in retirement.

4. Add inflation's impact to that, from now through your anticipated retirement life span. Use 5 percent annual inflation (unless inflation radically changes as you approach retirement). Remember: Using the rule of 72, at 5 percent inflation, you can see that your expenses will approximately double in 14.4 years ($72/5 = 14.4$)!

So, for example, if you are fifty, you might need to double the income figure you arrived at in steps 3 and 4 above and then double it again, if you believe you'll live to be eighty.

You might need to get up off the floor! (Please?) You are almost ready to figure out where all that money is going to come from. But first, you have to remember one more thing: Just as is true in your preretirement years, retirement income is not (usually) tax free. That is why in step 3 I recommended you begin with annual gross income—income *before* taxes, giving, saving, and spending. To determine the annual gross income figure for step 1 that you then use in step 3, you should use your current annual gross income unless that is not your desired income in retirement. In that case, I suggest you substitute an annual income figure that, while representative of your desired income, also reflects the realities of your earning capabilities and opportunities in your remaining preretirement years.

This easy formula to get at the income you'll need to cover the cost of living when retired will serve you well, once you get used to it. There is space in part II of the worksheet at the end of this chapter to note your figuring for the above four steps.

Once you've completed that entire worksheet exercise and thus calculated the amount of money you'll need, you are ready to look at how to come up with that money! That is discussed later in this chapter, and in chapters 12, "Saving Taxes," and 13, "Investment Wisdom."

• A More Specific Formula?

If you wish to do a more detailed projection than this ballpark formula, either consult a financial adviser especially competent in the areas of retirement and tax planning or go online and search for free assistance sites and those that offer inexpensive software that includes a tutorial and walks you through a detailed projection. A few ideas on sites are listed in the Appendix.

If you opt for a more detailed calculation, you should understand that most of these formulas will be expense-based rather than income-based like my ballpark formula. Thus you'll need to be sure to anticipate both the usual costs you assume you'll have and the unusual costs you may encounter as you age: big-ticket vacations, medical expenses, taking care of an aging parent or an adult child, providing gifts to your grandchildren, the different costs involved in retiring in a different state or a foreign country (should this be part of your dream), and so forth.

You may also want to break down these expenses into subcycles: One for the years left to retirement, one for the early years of retirement, and one for the remaining retirement years you expect.

When you have projected expenses, be sure to adjust for inflation and taxes.

Whether you use my ballpark formula or a more specific one, once you've calculated how much you will need to fund retirement, you are then ready to learn *how* to fund it!

WHERE RETIREMENT FUNDING WILL COME FROM

Now that you have a pretty good idea of what it will cost to live in retirement, and therefore what income you'll need, let's look at where that income will come from. Generally, speaking, it will come partly from Social Security (if it's still viable when you retire), from your savings and investments, and possibly from distributions from any self-funded and/or employer-based retirement plans that exist. But the specifics on these are important to understand.

• Social Security

Count on Social Security benefits for only as much as 25 percent of the inflation-adjusted total estimated income, if you count on it at all.

The Social Security Administration in Washington, DC, will tell you, given your past employment history, how much they estimate you will receive if you retire at 62, 66, or 70. Write to them (see Appendix) for your latest records. (You should do this at least every three to five years, anyway.)

If you count it, remember that other income will affect the taxation of Social Security benefits. This could mean that, after tax, the benefits will be worth less than you or the government may project.

Be sure you understand the factors that may cause you to receive no Social Security benefits or less than your benefits statement suggests. For example, such factors as the rates for inflation and return on investment the government applies in making their projections.

Note this in the appropriate step of part III of the worksheet for this chapter.

• Other Sources

The other 75 percent of the inflation-adjusted figure you established as your desired gross retirement income will come from the other sources you have put in place and carefully managed. Here, as in other areas of your finances (funding college education, for example), is where the laws of Preparation and Preservation come alive.

First, determine how much the accumulation programs you already have in place (and plan to keep funding until retirement) can provide of that total need. That should include the following.

- What you think your total distributions will be from employer-related pension and profit-sharing plans if you have them.

- The amount you think you will have at retirement from your private retirement programs that are sanctioned by the IRS, such as IRAs (individual retirement arrangements), Keogh plans, and 401(k), 403(b), SEP retirement plans, and others. (See basic information on these below, and more detailed information in chapters 12 and 13.)

- The amount you expect to have at retirement from currently owned personal investments, which you are funding each month. (See chapter 13 for suggestions on personal investments beyond those within formal retirement plans like those mentioned above.)

As you figure what you expect to have from programs you already have in place to fund your retirement, note what I did *not* include, and why:

- Please do not include that expected inheritance from Uncle Joe or Mom and Dad. I strongly suggest planning as though this will not happen, then take such an inheritance as an extra gift, if it materializes.

- Do not include the highly unlikely scenario that you will sell your house at a profit and invest part or all of that money to generate retirement income. Don't do it! Believe me, selling a house for this purpose rarely occurs. A wise planner will prepare for retirement without making this assumption and instead treat such income as an extra gift, should it happen. Please understand that years of history say a house is a wonderful investment. *But* a house should not, in my view, be an investment that you count as part of the assets you will need to generate the income to cover your living expenses in retirement.

- Do not count earnings you anticipate from working full- or part-time after you retire. Leave this as a bonus, should you decide to do it.

Conservative planning takes into account only what you believe will happen in all likelihood. It treats any other income as a bonus. I argue strongly on the side of such conservative planning!

After you add up the amounts that you can reasonably count on to fund retirement and subtract this from the 75 percent income figure you arrived at earlier, don't be surprised if your projections show that you don't have enough. Most people don't.

If that calculation actually projects that you will have enough or more than needed, congratulations! You're in the vast minority of overprepared future retirees. Keep going down that path!

If you have a fairly large deficit left after the subtraction, take heart: You're with the majority. And because you're reading and working through *Wisdom and Money,* this computation will change as you initiate financial change in your life. You'll begin to walk the path to genuine prosperity.

The bad news, in this common situation, is that this is the capital you will have to make up in extra savings between now and retirement.

The good news is that you know it now and can get to work making up the difference—unless, of course, you are already retired or near it. In that case, you'll have to face the reality of either continuing to work full- or part-time in your current job or a new one.

If you still have some years left before you retire, plan and prepare in your preretirement years so that your retirement years can really be golden! Note your deficit or overfunding amount in the appropriate step of part III of the worksheet for this chapter. And begin immediately to take savings and investment actions to fund any deficit. Begin now to close the gap between where you are and where you want to be in funding your personal retirement. You'll be glad you did!

A FEW RETIREMENT INVESTMENT SPECIFICS

As mentioned in chapter 8, "Forced Saving," you will pay for your major expenses like your share of shouldering the cost of your children's college education and funding your retirement through an informed, disciplined savings plan that I recommend be based on 20 percent of your preretirement, after-tax income. If you're in your late forties or in your fifties, or if the recent downturn in the stock market has set you back, then the reality is you may have to increase that 20 percent to be able to accumulate the assets needed to retire in your sixties.

Because of inflation, the only way to come out ahead over the long term for big-ticket expenditures like these is to find a way to invest your savings wisely. Over time, any deficit revealed by your ballpark formula calculation should be replaced with assets earmarked for retirement. Again, this should be done by carving an appropriate amount from your 20 percent savings budget. You may want to use some of that to increase funding of retirement-related assets already in place, provided that doesn't create too much concentration in one place and thus violate the principle of diversification discussed in chapter 13, "Investment Wisdom."

Some of that increased savings should be used to invest in asset categories you've not yet begun to fund. For example, if you don't already contribute to a 401(k) plan through your employer, this is a good time to start! Some investment guidelines are given in chapter 13. Other investment ideas may be obtained by going over the specifics of your situation with a wise, objective financial planner. This is not a copout! You may really need to find one. Suggestions on how to select one are found in chapter 13, "Investment Wisdom."

• Become a Wise Investment Manager

With the decline of traditional employer-managed pension plans, more and more employees are managing their own retirement accounts by choosing what types of assets to invest in and how much to allocate to each category.

A 401(k) or a SEP retirement plan are good ways to do this. So is the use of IRAs. More information is given about them in chapters 12, "Saving Taxes," and 13, "Investment Wisdom."

Judging from the thousands we helped in our planning practice over a fifteen-year period, I can say that far too many 401(k) participants are constructing unwise investment paradigms.

They are either underestimating the capital they need to fund their retirement living years or they are being too conservative in their 401(k) investment selection. (Using the ballpark formula I've provided can help keep you from underestimating the capital you'll need. The guidelines in *Wisdom and Money* and a professional adviser can help you invest your 401(k) wisely.)

Another major mistake employees are making in managing their own retirement plans is avoiding diversification. You need to invest in many different companies and make many different kinds of investments. So, if your salary, benefits, and retirement funding are all tied to the same employer, be careful! You may be overconcentrating your assets, and this can be devastating. If your employer goes out of business: no salary, no benefits, and too much worthless stock. Please: Diversify, diversify, diversify. (There is more on the need for diversification in chapter 13.)

Please read on, so that you will not be one of these unwise investment managers!

HOW TO MANAGE YOUR RETIREMENT DISTRIBUTIONS

The point of planning well is having the money when you need it. It is good to understand how and when to best take your money out of your retirement plan(s).

• Switching Jobs?

If you are switching jobs, you may be required to leave your pension money with the company for later distribution as an annuity, or you may have the choice to take a lump sum now. If you have a choice, I suggest you look at how taking it in a lump sum might help you.

Take into account your money personality, and if you will do what you plan to do with it. If you are one who fears that taking it in a lump sum runs the risk of spending the money before retirement even begins, look at what you could do to prevent that.

Talk to a wise, honest financial adviser. Get a candid opinion on whether the company you're leaving would continue to invest it well, and how that compares with the return you're likely to get if you decide how it is invested. Talk to him or her, too, about how to move the money without tax penalty. There are specific methods and time frames to follow, some of which are covered in chapter 12, "Saving Taxes."

I normally recommend that you commit to financial self-discipline and take it with you in one lump sum. If you properly roll it over into an IRA, you will avoid any federal taxes and penalties. And you have more control over your investment options. There is more wisdom about this in chapters 12 and 13, "Saving Taxes" and "Investment Wisdom."

• Ready to Retire?

A similar choice comes up when you are ready to use your retirement savings and investments. Should you take it in a lump sum or bit by bit?

This is a difficult financial question and one better to consider early, when you can put into place the strategies that minimize unpleasant consequences.

I want to pause here to repeat my earlier caution that I am giving only general information and suggestions. You should consult a qualified professional who is familiar with your individual circumstances. There is no way that a basic book, or any book, can speak to your specific, ever changing needs.

Lump Sum or Annuity?

After you retire, should you take your qualified retirement plan distributions in a lump sum? Or in an annuity that pays a fixed amount each month until death (and if you made the proper election, pays your spouse under a joint-and-survivor payout option)?

The answer depends upon your individual financial circumstances. But it is good to look at how the answer should be arrived at.

Some make their choice, not on good advice, but simply because they do not like to think about having to invest and manage a large sum of money, so they go for the monthly annuity payments. This may, in fact, be the right choice for these people, but the process of their reasoning is far from commendable. Being lazy or fearful is not a reason to avoid a lump sum payment when a qualified financial adviser can help you keep the money invested wisely.

It might be that you could earn better returns with some investment help than if you leave your money under the control and investment direction of your former employer. Whether you and your adviser or your employer's advisers have better chances of increasing the money depends upon your particular situation.

Others take the monthly amount because they are afraid a lump sum will be frittered away long before their retirement ends. Again, it is better to get good advice based on who you are. There may be a way around this temptation.

If you are tending toward taking annuity payments, remember that they are based on average life expectancy. Your adviser will probably ask you what your family's history is in terms of actual life expectancy. If your parents and aunts and uncles are still alive when you retire, you might beat the actuarial odds and come out well ahead. But then again, you might not want to play the odds game, remembering that you may lose big-time if you live less than the life expectancy used in these calculations!

Finally, because annuity payments are fixed, they lose ground to even modest inflation. The longer your retirement, therefore, the less likely the monthly payouts from an annuity election will cover your actual retirement expenses.

By taking a lump sum, you can roll the money over into an IRA or if for some reason, that option is not available to you, invest the money (after taxes) in growth assets that preserve your purchasing power. As I stated in the section above, I normally recommend taking the lump sum distribution. Two of the most attractive features, as I see it, are the following.

- You have more control over your money and, typically, more invest-ment options.

- You have greater flexibility to choose the size and timing of payments. Perhaps you need larger amounts of cash early in your retirement. An annuity will not provide this. What if you do not need payments at all for a few years? In this case, you can roll the money over into an IRA—you will not have to pay taxes on it until you use it.

Tax Considerations

The decision of whether to take your pension in a lump sum or as an annuity is certainly complicated by the very large question of taxes. An advantage of choosing annuity payments is that they are paid out over a number of years, making it easier to avoid the higher tax brackets. Please read the additional information about the tax side of this decision in chapter 12, "Saving Taxes." Then do please get advice.

GET ADVICE

Preparing for retirement is one of your most important financial objec-tives. It involves emotion as well as large sums of hard-earned money, and the tax laws for retirement plan distributions are especially complicated. These are all very good reasons for me to repeat my earlier suggestion: It is prudent to seek the help of a trusted, competent financial adviser—someone who spe-cializes in these critical areas—to help you allocate and perhaps manage and modify your plans over time. Suggestions on how to select an adviser are found in chapter 13, "Investment Wisdom."

INSIGHTS

- Putting thought, time, and energy into securing funds for the future is not being materialistic—it is being realistic.

- For those who claim that they can be content to live meagerly during their retirement years, I offer the following honest comment:

  I'd like to live like a poor man—only with lots of money.
  —Pablo Picasso

- I've been rich and I've been poor, and although money can't buy happiness, rich is definitely better.

- Enjoy the journey to retirement. And be sure to put enough money in the tank so that you not only get to the destination but also have fun when you get there.

Before proceeding to the next chapter, if you haven't already done so as part of working through this chapter, please consider and record your thoughts, then work through the exercises on the following worksheet, My Retirement Plans.

WORKSHEET 11

My Retirement Plans

NOTES FROM READING THIS CHAPTER

PART I
MY RETIREMENT DREAMS

Look at the dreams you have for your retirement. If you haven't already, make notes on these crucial elements of your dreams and discuss them with your partner, using all your discussion and listening skills. If the suggested topics don't cover your dreams, use the space to write what your dreams *are*!

My dream is:

I/we want to retire in _____ years.
    because:

I/we will live in _____ (kind of dwelling).
    because:

I/we will live in _____ (place or kind of place).
    because:

I/we want our quality of life to be _____
    because:

I/we want to be near _____ (people/activities, etc.)
because:

We definitely want to be able to _____ (activities)
because:

Other dream notes:

PART II
MY/OUR RETIREMENT WILL COST

To determine how much money you will need to save now to achieve your retirement dreams later, use this worksheet to do the calculations called for by the ballpark formula I gave in chapter 11. Refine your calculations as time passes and you get closer to your retirement goals.

A. Note what gross income you need per year.

From the ballpark formula, I think I'll need $_____ a year when I retire in 20___.

B. Note the number of years you expect to live after retirement.

I/We'll probably live _____ more years after I retire.

C. Figure the total amount of retirement income needed.

$_____ a year × _____ years in retirement = $_____

D. Add in inflation's impact.

At 5 percent annual inflation (a pretty good gauge), your expenses will approximately double in 14.4 years (72/5=14.4). So if you are retiring at sixty-five and plan on living fifteen years as a retiree, double the number in step C.

If you're figuring to live about thirty years beyond retirement, double it again!

$_____ amount of total gross income needed in your retirement years, after adjusting for inflation.

Please note that the above amount reflects the projected total gross income you'll "consume" in retirement. Said another way, this is what you project you'll spend in retirement.

If you don't want to do the remaining steps called for below by the ballpark formula, then at least do this. Calculate the amount of preretirement assets you'd need to accumulate to have a base of capital that would generate the inflation-adjusted income you've estimated you'll need in retirement. That can be done, within reason, by using the information in steps B and D above. Here's how:

1. Divide the amount needed after adjusting for inflation (step D) by the number of years you projected you'll live after retiring (step B). The result is the average annual inflation adjusted income needed during your retirement years. Let's assume that number is $50,000 for purposes of the projections immediately below.

2. Now project an average pretax rate of return you feel you could realistically earn on assets during your retirement years. Let's assume you say 10 percent per year.

3. To determine the amount of assets you will have to accumulate by the date you retire, divide the annual income calculated in step 1 by the rate of return assumed in step 2. If $50,000 (per step 1 above): $50,000 divided by 0.1 (10 percent) =$500,000. If your rate of return projection is only 8 percent, then the assets you'd have to accumulate before retiring would change to $625,000 ($50,000 divided by 0.08, which is 8 percent). If it were projected at 12 percent, then the amount of total assets you will need to accumulate before retiring will drop to $416,667 ($50,000 divided by 0.12, which is 12 percent).

The above calculations are more conservative than the calculation results you'll get by completing the ballpark formula worksheet below. That's because they assume you never actually consume the accumulated assets and, instead, have them available to pass to your heirs as part of your financial estate.

I strongly urge you to complete the ballpark formula calculations below. Why? You will then have a good idea if there's a gap between where you are and where you desire to be when you retire, and how much the gap is.

Knowledge of the gap can be powerful motivation that leads to positive action to assure the gap is closed by retirement.

And who knows, after you finish the ballpark formula calculations below, you may decide not just to close the gap but also to begin to save and invest so you have assets to pass to your children and other heirs of your choice!

PART III
HOW I/WE WILL PAY FOR RETIREMENT

A. Figure the amount you can expect to cover from Social Security.

To calculate your Social Security benefits for up to 25 percent of the total amount needed after adjusting for inflation, multiply the amount in step D of part II of this worksheet as noted below:

$\$\underline{\hspace{2.5in}} \times 0.25 = \$\underline{\hspace{2.5in}}$

Order a benefits statement from the Social Security Administration (SSA), if you haven't already, and compare this figure with what the SSA says you are likely to be eligible for. In addition, ask them for the rules that may further limit your Social Security checks. And ask your financial adviser or tax preparer how income in other categories may affect the taxation of your Social Security benefits.

B. Figure the amount you'll cover from your savings/investments/ retirement plans.

Multiply the inflation adjusted figure from step D of part II of this worksheet as noted below:

$\$\underline{\hspace{2in}} \times 0.75 = \$\underline{\hspace{2.5in}}$

This is the amount of total gross income you project you'll spend in your retirement years beyond your Social Security income.

C. Note your assets and their value below.

(These should already be on your net worth statement from worksheet 6. Please only include assets below, in accordance with the guidelines shared earlier in chapter 11.)

Asset   **Value**

_____ $\$\underline{\hspace{0.8in}}$

_____	$_____
_____	$_____
_____	$_____
_____	$_____
_____	$_____
_____	$_____
_____	$_____
_____	$_____
_____	$_____
TOTAL	$_____

In case you ignored my suggestion above, I urge you to cross out any assets you cannot reasonably count on and put the adjusted total below.

D. Figure the amount still needed to fund retirement.

Subtract the amount in step C of this part of the worksheet from the amount in step B. This is the amount you are short (or over) in funding goals.

$ _____ minus $_____ = $_____ Total

Add in any part of the first 25 percent that Social Security won't fund, as far as you can tell from your statement, and write the total below.

Take heart! Reread suggestions on how to make up the difference, if you're short.

PART IV

HOW I/WE WILL STRUCTURE OUR DISTRIBUTIONS

After you read through all the pertinent chapters, begin to note your thoughts on how best to take your distributions during retirement. You may not be close enough to retirement to make any final decisions, but it's good to begin to gather information for the sources recommended in chapter 11, and take notes as you see considerations important to your situation. You can then bring them up when you get closer to that time.

A. Specifics I want to bring up with my partner or mentor.

B. Specifics my partner or mentor has suggested I/we take into consideration.

C. Decisions we have made on how to take distributions.

Once you get close enough to retirement, you will want to make up a whole new budget. of course!

12

SAVING TAXES

Nobody owes any public duty to pay more than the law demands.
—Learned Hand (renowned New York judge)

Tax planning is an effective, painless way to save significant amounts of money. It effectively increases your net income and thus the amount of cash you can dedicate to saving for goals like educating your children or retiring well. If you're having trouble saving the recommended 20 percent, then tax savings will help. Or if you want to increase your savings rate above the 20 percent level, tax savings is one way to do that.

Paying taxes is an inevitable part of life, but you do have some control over the amount you pay. The secret to this control lies in knowing the tax laws, then making a conscious choice to apply the tax code to your financial situation for legitimate gain. Keeping your hard-earned dollars from taking a one-way trip to the government's coffers is indeed a constant challenge, especially as your net worth and income grow, but it is one worthy of your careful attention.

These suggestions are based on the U.S. federal tax laws in effect at this writing. Be alert for tax law changes and remember that *Wisdom and Money*'s suggestions are not meant to refer to state or local taxes. Residents of a different country should remember that, although many of the principles in *Wisdom and Money* are universally applicable, its suggestions are not meant to apply to the tax laws of their country.

TO PLAN FOR TAX ADVANTAGE OR NOT: SOME COSTLY MISPERCEPTIONS

Not everyone knows that many of us—perhaps you among them—work the first half of every day to satisfy their tax liabilities. That's a situation crying out for an alternative, don't you think?

If you don't want to pay the government a single, solitary penny more than you are legitimately required to in your situation, you need to move past your false perceptions about what must be paid in taxes.

Perhaps you have shied away from tax planning over the years because you have considered it somehow immoral. If this is the case, you are the victim of inaccurate thinking: You are probably confusing tax avoidance with tax evasion.

It is true, some are willing to do *anything* to lower their taxes. Tax evasion is illegal and severely punishable and you are right to avoid it like the plague! And besides violating tax law, tax evasion definitely does not align with the 7 Laws of Highest Prosperity.

Legitimate tax avoidance, on the other hand, can come from using spiritual and financial wisdom to make the tax laws work to your advantage. Wise tax avoidance is not only legal, it is also quite proper. It uses accurate thinking to ensure that you legitimately save as much as possible of the income you earn, so that you can use it to help fund your dreams and goals. It is in agreement with *part* of the above-mentioned inaccurate thinking: Legitimate tax avoidance states that we *are* morally obligated to pay all the taxes that are due. The point where thinking becomes inaccurate is where the word *due* is misunderstood.

Calculations of what is due that are arrived at by using sound tax planning can be (and often are) very different from calculations arrived at without wise tax planning. Why not let your spirit-person allow you to see that taking care of yourself and your family by saving on taxes, where allowed by tax law, is a way of responding to the responsibilities you have been blessed with?

Another group who duck tax planning are those who just don't want to take the time to learn what is needed to save in this way. Why *not* take some time to see what you can save? It will be at least as advantageous as other methods of saving money you have probably already put into place. For example, it will pay off at least as much as the time you spend shopping for bargains on consumable items! I suggest you take a hard look at this ineffective train of thought, and see if it is, in your case, a cloak for laziness. If so, change your ways and read on!

The third major misperception is the same one that keeps many from investing wisely. It says that planning for the best tax advantage is too risky. They are afraid of an audit and of being slapped with fines, so they choose to pay a higher tax than they are required to pay just to feel safe. If this is a temptation for you, it is important to understand where this part of your money personality comes from. Ask yourself, *What is the risk of losing a dollar paid in taxes that did not have to be paid?* Then answer yourself, *100 percent!* As with any aspect of a money personality that instinctively keeps you from managing your resources in a way that leads to true success, I suggest you use prayer and practice (to establish wise habits) and advice to move toward a more effective use for your natural caution. In addition, reading through the material, later in this chapter, about the realities of a federal tax audit may help allay some of your fears.

Inaccurate or lazy or fearful thinking can cost you a bundle! Some of those unwise ways of thinking come from believing and acting on the five myths below. Why not understand the myths, commit to learn to think more accurately, and get help looking at the how-to's and the rewards of wise tax planning?

5 COMMON MYTHS ON SAVING TAXES—AND HOW TO RESPOND TO THEM

The great enemy of the truth is very often not the lie—deliberate, contrived, and dishonest—but the myth.

—John Kennedy

I agree. One common attribute of truly successful people is their ability to determine the truth and make decisions based on that truth.

As you begin to save significantly and invest some of those savings in order to gain assets that will fund your dreams and goals, your tax situation will change. Don't use the excuse that, because funding your goals leads to new situations, you should not proceed. Don't proceed in ignorance, either. Be careful to make wise (informed) choices as you save and invest. Acting on assumptions can lead to significant loss.

Five common myths about taxes and the tax ramifications of certain investments—myths that can cause us to make unwise and costly financial choices—are listed below. They are accompanied by wise, honorable, hopeful truths that debunk them. Before listing them, though, I want to give a few definitions.

• Definitions

The terms *tax free* (exempt), *tax deferred*, and *tax sheltered* are not interchangeable. Indeed, they are completely different things.

Tax free (exempt) generally refers to income that by law is not taxable.

Tax deferred means payment of taxes is deferred by law until a later date.

Tax sheltered means the law permits legitimate current avoidance of taxes, either through use of specific deductions, credits, and so forth, or through specific structures permitted by law.

Examples

Deduction of depreciation against rental property is an example of a tax shelter. Using a corporation to operate a business is another example of a structure that legitimately shelters business income from personal income taxes. *But* . . . unlike tax-exempt income, eventually some level of tax is paid on income involved in tax-deferred and tax-sheltered strategies. This is why the use of various ways to reduce taxes must be carefully planned so that, when all is said and done, you don't end up paying more taxes in the long run.

These thoughts are shared, not to create more confusion or fear, but to debunk myths born out of confusion and also to once again point you to the importance of working with a competent tax-planning professional and tax preparer.

• 5 Myths About Saving Taxes

1. *An IRS audit notice is the kiss of death.* In fact, audits can be handled without a huge time loss and without ruffling your spirit if you keep careful records and if you have someone to help you through the audit session(s). I was audited three times and I handled them fairly calmly by applying this piece of wisdom: *You have rights—exercise them and pursue them wisely.* There are a lot of myths out there about what triggers an audit and what doesn't. In fact, audits occur fairly infrequently, and they are not usually difficult to respond to. There is more on how to face an audit later in this chapter.

2. Interest paid on a home-equity loan is always tax deductible. In fact, interest paid on a home equity loan, the proceeds of which are used for personal purposes other than home improvements, is not deductible unless you are itemizing your deductions. Since itemizing is not always to your advantage, you need to look at your whole tax picture before assuming that your home-equity loan will be tax deductible. Basic guidelines on when taking out a home-equity loan or when refinancing your mortgage will benefit you can be found in chapter 9, "Spending Wisdom."

3. *Tax-exempt investments are always better than taxable investments.* In fact, a tax-exempt investment such as municipal bonds often pays less interest than a taxable investment. It is therefore possible that a taxable investment like many stock mutual funds could provide a better return overall than a tax-exempt investment, even after taxes are taken into account. Be sure to look at this area of cost to see what's best in each instance. General guidelines on this can be found in chapter 13, "Investment Wisdom."

4. *A tax-exempt investment is never taxable.* In fact, when you profit by selling a tax-exempt investment, the resulting capital gain is almost always taxable. And the amount of that tax depends on your tax bracket and whether or not you have accumulated other capital gains in your life.

Be sure you take the time to look at this area of tax-exempt investing before you jump in. General guidelines on this can be found in chapter 13, "Investment Wisdom."

5. *An investment program designed to fund a child's future college costs should be registered in the name of the child to gain tax advantages.* In fact, although you may save on your income taxes now by doing this, your child could be penalized later when applying for financial aid at college time. Look into the formulas used by the colleges of your choice, as discussed in chapter 10, "Funding a College Education." Many, for example, take up to half of the student's assets the first year. Talk to your financial adviser and your tax-planning professional before you make this choice. Be sure to look at all sides of this decision before making it.

I hope you are inspired to seek the details of the truths in this list by now. I hope the list reinforces my basic suggestion that, especially in terms of taxes and investing, you need advice specific to your financial situation (as it changes through the years) and specific to the financial markets of the day (as they change through the years) to wisely move along the path to true prosperity. Here is a little more encouragement before you read on.

Any fact facing us is not as important as our attitude toward it.
—Dr. Norman Vincent Peale

WAYS TO GET ADVICE ON TAX PLANNING

To improve your skills at tax planning, you can talk to others in similar income situations as you. You can read books and subscribe to magazines and newsletters, some of which are listed in the Appendix in the section for chapter 13. You can talk to tax preparers. All of these are good ways to begin planning for the best tax advantage.

You can also study tax law yourself. To do so, I suggest you read books that are tax-topic intensive and written by qualified professionals. Some of these are listed in the Appendix in the section for chapter 12.

But the best way to prepare is to engage the services of a wise, honest tax-planning professional. A tax preparer comes in handy to get your taxes filed, but he or she is not necessarily a tax-planning professional. (In the same vein, since a tax-planning professional is not necessarily a tax preparer, you may not want to ask him or her to prepare your tax return!) The tax-planning professional helps you plan for the future; the tax preparer records your tax history. Be sure that you've hired the right person for the right job. In the next chapter, I provide guidelines on selecting a financial adviser. I strongly believe that person should, among several credentials, either be qualified as a tax planning expert or associated with others who are and can consult with you and your adviser.

KEEPING MORE OF YOUR BREAD

As you make your savings and investment decisions, you must take the tax bite into consideration. When you learn to use tax incentives to your best advantage, you will be saving and investing as much as possible.

Over the years, Congress has passed laws designed to encourage a shift of funds from some taxable sectors of our economy to areas of public need or good. These tax incentives designate the investments the government encourages, investments that will be tax free, tax sheltered, or tax deferred. (I repeat yet again that those terms do not mean the same thing. If my earlier explanation is still fuzzy in your mind, then a qualified tax-planning professional can help you understand the differences.) These tax incentives can help (legally) minimize your income and estate taxes. They include IRAs, 401(k)s, and SEPs; utility company stocks and municipal bonds; credits for education and for investing in real estate; and more! Many of these names sound like something only accountants could love. But the potential results of using them as part of your financial plan will definitely appeal to nearly everyone.

• Saving/Investing With a Full Loaf

What I call the *full-loaf* dollar is your money before taxes.

Using such a full-loaf dollar to save or invest can obviously lead to your financial prosperity much sooner than using the after-tax dollar. Instead of thoughtlessly giving away up to a half of our income to taxes, shouldn't we inform ourselves about how to pay only what the law requires of us?

Yes, it can be done legally, without sacrificing wise priority or motive. I know you probably realize this immediately, intellectually, but let me demonstrate in black and white how working with a full loaf is far superior to working with a half or even two-thirds of that loaf.

Full Loaves for Retirement: the 401(k) and SEP Plans

In terms of retirement, you may wish to take advantage of the black-and-white language in the tax code that allows you to contribute money to a tax-deferred retirement plan.

There are many different kinds of retirement plan structures, and each category has its own rules and regulations. If each were discussed in-depth, the pages of a good-size book could be filled. For those reasons and because this book is intended as a basic resource rather than a cover-everything-under-the-sun compendium, I'm going to provide overviews and some working examples of the three most frequently used retirement structures: (1) 401(k) retirement plans, (2) SEP retirement plans, and (3) IRAs. That will give you a taste of the benefits afforded by such plans.

Some of the other kinds of retirement plans include those authorized under various sections of the IRS tax laws. For example, there are 403(b) plans that are available to employees of institutional and governmental employers such as schools, colleges, and federal, state, and local government agencies. And there are what some refer to as Cafeteria Plans that, in my view, are in reality not retirement plans, but rather a structure through which a business can offer employee benefits like health insurance, etc. I have commented on Cafeteria Plans in my discussion of insurance back in chapter 9, "Spending Wisdom." And, to name one more of many others, there are 457 Plans.

- *The 401(k)*

A 401(k) is a type of retirement plan that allows employees (as well as those who are both owners and employees in any of the business structures mentioned in the next sentence) to save and invest for their own retirement. Employers that can offer a 401(k) plan include corporations, partnerships, and self-employed people. Through a 401(k) you can authorize your employer to deduct a certain amount of money from your paycheck before taxes are calculated, and pay it to the 401(k) plan. Your money is then invested as you choose from the investment options offered through your company's plan.

Each employer's 401(k) plan has different limits on contributions, but the overriding limit is this: The IRS limits what you can contribute each year as an employee. And different limits apply to what the employer can contribute. For 2002, the maximum pretax contribution allowed to an employee was $11,000. For 2003, it increased to $12,000. Thereafter, tax law in effect at the time of this writing increases the maximum amount you can contribute by $1,000 for each year through 2006, to a maximum of $15,000. After 2006, these pretax contribution limits will be increased in $500 increments to factor in the effects of inflation.

Some plans allow you to contribute on an after-tax basis as well. I don't recommend these for two reasons: (1) they don't get the same favorable tax treatment as pretax contributions, and (2) you have more control over that money when you invest such after-tax dollars outside formal retirement plan structures.

It is important to note that, depending on your plan, you may find yourself eligible for a "hardship withdrawal" if you encounter certain unexpected circumstances that require your money before retirement. According to IRS regulations, your hardship must represent an "immediate and heavy financial need" and there must not be "any other resources reasonably available to you to handle that financial need." The IRS recognizes four reasons for a hardship withdrawal:

1. Certain unreimbursable medical expenses;
2. Purchase of a primary residence;
3. Payments of post–secondary education tuition for the next year;
4. Prevention of eviction from, or foreclosure on, your home.

Generally, you must begin to take distributions from a 401(k) no later than April 1 of the year following the year in which you turn age 70½ or following the year in which you retire, whichever is later.

Before getting into the tax-related nitty-gritty, here's one other important fact about a 401(k). The Employee Retirement Income Security Act of 1974 established guidelines for how money in 401(k) plans is maintained. The bottom line is that your 401(k) plan account is not considered an asset of your employer—it is supposed to be held in trust in a separate account for you. This means that your plan money (which includes all your own contributions and all vested company contributions) is not supposed to be commingled with your company's money. Your company is not supposed to be able to access your plan money for any purpose related to maintaining its business.

The 401(k) and other plans cited above are invaluable if you are employed by others or self-employed and interested in sheltering part of your income from taxes while saving for your future dream of retirement. Many of these salary reduction plans are frequently overlooked by employees or are underutilized.

Since contributions to a 401(k) plan are made with *pretax* dollars, you do not pay income tax on a current basis for the money you contribute to the plan. That is because contributions within the legally allowed contribution limits are not included in your income reported currently—that is, they are excluded by your employer from income reported on your annual W-2 (for income tax, but not for Social Security taxes). Plus, that money grows, tax-deferred, as long as it is in the formal retirement plan. (You will, of course, pay taxes on what you later take out.)

- *The SEP (Simplified Employee Pension)*

A SEP (Simplified Employee Pension) is the simplest type of retirement plan available for businesses. It requires minimal reporting and disclosure, whereas a 401(k) and others require lots of both! As with a 401(k), any business—whether a C corporation, S corporation, partnership, sole proprietorship, or self-employed individual—can establish a SEP plan.

The most unique features of a SEP plan are that

1. contributions are made directly to each participating employee's SEP IRA, by the employer; and
2. if an employee leaves the employer, he or she simply rolls the account into another personal IRA.

Depending on your tax bracket, it's possible to have a tax deductible IRA, a non–tax deductible (Roth) IRA, and a tax deductible SEP IRA.

- *Advantages*

Both 401(k) and SEP plans utilize automatic deduction by employers from payroll to collect the employee contributions to the plan; those funds are then paid to the plan by the employer. These plans are thus in agreement with the procedures referred to in earlier chapters as the "forced saving" mechanism, ensuring that your money is saved and invested *before* you have an opportunity to spend it!

And just as importantly, these plans allow you to invest with a full loaf of your bread—*before* taxes are taken out of it—helping your money to grow much more quickly.

Let's say out of your 20 percent savings budget you decide to contribute $1,000 to a 401(k), SEP, or another one of the pretax-dollar tax-deferred retirement plans. Since you will pay no taxes on that $1,000 before it is invested, the whole shebang is earning more money for you. What happens if, on the other hand, you elect not to contribute the $1,000 to one of these plans but take it as compensation from your employer and then invest in a savings account or non-IRA mutual fund or CD, or in non-tax-deferred stocks or bonds? Regardless of how wise the investment, you will pay income tax on the $1,000 because it will be considered compensation. In a 28 percent tax bracket for example, you'll have $280 less to invest. Plus, the earnings on the $720 you invest will normally be taxed when received. You not only lose the $280 to taxes, but you lose what it would grow to be in a tax-deferred plan had you chosen that option.

When you combine these benefits, you can understand my reason for suggesting these plans be utilized where available and to the extent your profile will allow. It does not take a rocket scientist to realize that we are talking about a ton of money, added and compounded over the course of your working lifetime.

The value of tax deferral added to the benefits of compounding are staggering when you realize what these can mean for the growth of your retirement funds: You are effectively being allowed to invest both the contributions and earnings on the investments that otherwise would be money Uncle Sam would already have taken. When the time comes to pay taxes on it, you will have accrued a nice amount you wouldn't otherwise have.

- *Look for Employer-match Benefits Too!*

Some companies make their 401(k) or SEP plans even sweeter by kicking in money from the company kitty for every dollar you contribute to the plan. That's like receiving a bonus, only it's better than a bonus because you do not have to pay tax on it currently until you take it out of the plan. Again, the principle of compounding as well as tax deferral makes this money look very sweet a few years down the road!

- *As Always, Be Careful!*

In my years of helping employees (and stock owners, partners, proprietors, and self-employed people who are paid wages, salary, etc., by the applicable business that sponsors the retirement plan) maximize their 401(k) and SEP plan investments, I saw many underinvest, that is, place their money in safer, low-return investments. There is a balance to be found between too much risk and not enough. I am sure, however, that by the time you've read through the previous two chapters and the next one, chapter 13, "Investment Wisdom," you will be ready to talk to a wise, objective financial mentor and become a wise manager of your investments inside and outside formal retirement plan structures.

• IRAs (Individual Retirement Accounts)

Individual retirement arrangements have been around for quite a while. I believe the traditional IRA is an excellent resource for accumulating and growing assets for your personal retirement. I'm not an advocate of Roth IRAs, however, even though this Johnny-come-lately is touted by many as the best thing since sliced bread. I'll speak more specifically to Roth and education IRAs (which I do recommend) momentarily, but first a brief overview of the traditional IRA.

Traditional IRAs

With the traditional IRA, you can enjoy the benefits of compounding growth and tax savings. At the time of this writing, contributions to these IRAs are limited to $3,000 a year for those younger than fifty and $3,500 a year for those fifty and older, as long as you've earned at least the amount you're contributing in the year you contribute. (Unearned money cannot be used to help you meet that threshold.) (*Unearned income* is a tax-law term referring to passive income like rents, interest, and dividends, rather than active income like salary, bonus, etc.)

Contributions to a traditional IRA are tax deductible if you are not covered by your employer's retirement plan. Even if you do participate in a company plan, you still may be able to deduct contributions to a traditional IRA, depending upon your income and filing status. As with a 401(k) and SEP, investments within a traditional IRA grow tax-free until money is withdrawn. (Unlike the 401(k) and SEPs, though, you are putting post-tax dollars into the IRA.)

Money withdrawn from traditional IRAs before age fifty-nine will usually get hit with a 10 percent penalty. Generally, a traditional IRA owner must begin taking money out of the account by April 1 of the year after he or she turns 70. The amount is a minimum distribution determined by the account holder's age and life expectancy. The IRS has established simplified tables that a traditional IRA owner can use to figure the required distribution. Those tables can be found in the written and online resources I've cited in the Appendix.

When transferring assets from one tax-deferred retirement plan to another, many people use what is called a rollover IRA. That is done, as discussed in more detail later in this chapter, to legally avoid paying what would otherwise be significant taxes and penalties. A traditional IRA can also be used for rollovers.

You can take money out of your IRA, tax free and penalty free, as long as you repay the full amount within sixty days. It's a good way to give yourself an interest-free loan. You can only do this once every twelve months.

Roth IRAs

Now back to those Roth IRAs. The two most notable things about a Roth IRA are that

1. contributions *are not* tax deductible; and
2. withdrawals are tax free if the account has been open for at least five years and you're at least fifty-nine when you start to withdraw money.

To all those people who tout Roth IRAs as if they are a kind of financial wunderkind, I ask these questions. Why a Roth IRA, when there are other options that offer tax deductions for my contribution? (Like increasing my 401(k) contributions.) Or, why would I want to lock my money in a structure that penalizes me if I tap into that money, when there are alternatives that don't?

Education IRAs

Individuals can make annual contributions of up to $500 per child into an account that's exclusively for helping to pay higher-education costs. The money contributed to an education IRA doesn't count against the annual total individuals may contribute to their combined IRAs. The earnings and withdrawals from an education IRA are tax free, but you can't deduct the contributions from your income tax.

I do think education IRAs can make sense as a tool for helping fund the college education savings plan you created when you worked through chapter 10, "Funding a College Education."

OTHER WAYS TO MINIMIZE THE CUT IN YOUR LOAF

There are several more sound, legitimate ways to save big on taxes in terms of managing your investments and your estate. Some are listed below.

- Take advantage of exemptions and timing provisions when you sell your residence.
- When you decide on where to invest:
  - Consider tax-advantaged investments such as municipal bonds. You can generate tax-free income from investing in certain types of mutual funds, or investing through insurance structures such as annuities,

etc. To find out more about these types of investments, see chapter 13, "Investment Wisdom."

- When selling a mutual fund at a gain, select the best tax reporting method.
- Remember that tax rates on capital gains are capped at 28 percent, whereas other forms of income—like compensation, interest, dividends, and rent—may be subjected to rates as high as the mid-30s! This makes owning capital assets like mutual fund shares and individual stocks and bonds more attractive.
- Maximize tax deductions. Keep good records.
- Look for ways to legitimately qualify for tax credits. There is more on this in the next section of this chapter.
- In planning your estate, disinherit the government. Instead, leave a legacy through a planned charitable giving program and other strategies to maximize your estate by minimizing estate taxes (see chapter 14, "Preserving Your Estate").

These are just a few ways to save big on taxes. There exist many more tax reduction strategies that lawmakers are not likely to touch. These reduction strategies are meant to be tax-saving incentives for the wise. For more information, see suggestions on how to learn more given earlier in this chapter and also in the Appendix.

• Tax Credits / Tax Deductions

The tax code provides for many tax credits. These are direct reductions of what would normally be the amount of tax you pay, dollar for dollar. Because it comes off your "bill," a credit is worth much more than a deduction. A dollar of deduction is worth only a percentage of each dollar owed, based on your tax bracket.

Therefore, for example, a $1.00 *credit* (like the child care and the Hope and Lifetime Learning credits) is about seven times more valuable than $1.00 of a mortgage interest deduction if you are in a 15 percent tax bracket. The credit is $1.00 off what would have been your tax bill without that credit. Compare that whopping benefit to the much smaller benefit that comes with $1.00 of, for example, the deduction from income for mortgage interest. The mortgage deduction shelters from tax $1.00 of your income, which in a 15 percent tax bracket means you pay 15 cents less in taxes. It doesn't take a rocket scientist to understand that $1.00 of tax reduction from a tax credit is 85 cents better than the 15 cents you save by having $1.00 in mortgage interest deduction!

TAX CONSIDERATIONS ON RETIREMENT PLAN DISBURSEMENTS

Some parts of the decision on how to take your distributions from an employer-sponsored retirement plan are discussed in chapter 11, "Funding

Retirement." That decision is further complicated by the very large question of taxes. That part of the decision is discussed below.

A tax advantage of choosing annuity payments is that they are paid out over a number of years, making it easier to avoid the higher tax brackets when you receive them. But if you handle lump sums correctly, you can minimize taxes while gaining a benefit you lose if you opt for the annuity form of payout. With the lump sum option comes opportunity to personally control the future investment of the money.

There are several options you have, if you leave the employment of an employer and are faced with the question of what to do with your money in that employer's retirement plan. The annuity option is available if you are formally retiring. In all other scenarios involving employment termination you can (1) leave the money in your former employer's plan, or (2) roll it over to a 401(k) or other qualifying plan of your new employer, or (3) take what I believe is the best, most flexible option and roll it into a rollover IRA.

In the United States, at the time of this writing, if a lump sum is not rolled over into an IRA or a qualifying plan of a new employer within sixty days of distribution, it will be taxed in the year the distribution is received. But you can postpone the tax bite by rolling over the lump sum directly into one of the places just mentioned. You avoid potentially huge current income taxes and penalties. And rollover allows your money to continue to grow on a tax-deferred basis. And there's also this potential benefit: If your future income goes down, as often is true in retirement years, the final taxes may be less because you end up in a lower tax bracket.

You can also minimize the initial tax bite on a lump sum distribution by paying the tax based on a five- or ten-year averaging option. (At the time of this writing, the longer period is available if you turned fifty by 1986.) You can learn more about this option from the J. K. Lasser and other tax books mentioned in the Appendix. You can and should also learn more by talking with your tax preparer and/or financial adviser.

HOW TO HANDLE AN IRS AUDIT

Here are eleven tips to use if you receive notification of an upcoming IRS audit. In the more than thirty years I have been in the workforce, I opened that envelope announcing an audit of my return three times. Twice, the end result was no proposed changes. The third time, my representative and I still felt my return did not warrant the changes the IRS insisted on. But we ultimately accepted them in order to avoid pursuing a process that could have cost more in money and time than making their changes did!

Here are my tips for facing an IRS audit:

1. Don't panic.

2. Read the notice carefully. Is it notification of an actual audit or is it a

correspondence audit, which only asks for details about a particular deduction or calculation?

3. Has the statute of limitations expired? The audit process must start within three years of the due date of the return or of the date you actually filed the return, whichever is later, with certain exceptions. (So, for a year 2002 return filed in April 2003, you would normally have to be notified of an audit by April 2006.) More about this can be learned from the tax-topic books listed in the Appendix.

4. Don't send what the IRS asserts is an overdue payment without verifying that they are correct. Read the taxpayer rights sheet that should arrive with the mailed notification.

5. Don't respond immediately. Allow yourself ample time to prepare and become organized. Time and location for an audit are usually flexible.

6. Take only what you need to the audit.

7. Be honest.

8. Answer only the questions posed to you. If seemingly unrelated questions are asked, ask for time to gather the needed documentation.

9. Be pleasant and businesslike. Just say "No" if unrelated questions are asked. You can send a legitimate representative (i.e., accountant or enrolled agent) in your place.

10. Consider an appeal if your position justifies it.

11. If you end up agreeing with the IRS position or if, for the sake of saved time, money, and frustration, you decide to pay even though you don't agree with their position, consider making an offer to pay less than what is legally owed immediately, if your financial circumstances allow that. (This might come from your rainy day fund or from liquidating other assets like stocks, mutual funds, etc., but where the liquidation is done in a way that creates minimum new taxes. All this should be thoroughly discussed with either the person who is representing you before the IRS or your financial adviser, if those are different people.) Remember that I said my third time was not a charm? I exercised this option. It worked out well for both sides, so don't think you're doing something morally wrong if you pursue this option. On the contrary, you're doing the morally right thing to own your debt and do the best your financial circumstances will allow in order to repay it. If this option is refused, you could consider paying over time, so you won't get off the track of living by your forward budget. Simply make this payment a nondiscretionary expense and adjust your budget.

• How to Handle Correspondence Stating You Owe More

Sometimes the IRS sends letters to taxpayers stating more is owed than what has been paid. This can be the result of the IRS finding a math error in your return or the result of an internal audit (one where they've looked at your return and those of your dependents but have not asked you to come in and explain yourself). This type of letter does not request you to come in and talk with anyone. If you get one of these, and the demand for payment is not because of an error in math, try doing exactly what the IRS requests to correct the error. Call the phone number in the letter and get instructions on how to maximize the chances that this error will be corrected easily, minimizing the amount of your time needed to give them more (or the same) information. If things go well, all will be resolved cleanly.

Sometimes the internal structure of the IRS leads to the error not being corrected despite your compliance. This kind of situation is very frustrating. But instead of getting frustrated if you receive a second or third notice, take advantage of the system the IRS does have in place that will allow you to speak to a person "higher up the pecking order." Simply ask whoever you have been dealing with at the IRS who their supervisor is and ask to speak with that person. Keep going up the pecking order until the correction is made.

Or if the correction is still not made, then call the IRS office near you and set up an appointment to meet someone in management in a one-on-one setting. When you make the appointment, ask what you should bring with you. (Usually you will need copies of your returns and the backup paperwork associated with the specific matter giving rise to the difference of opinions.) Some kinds of IRS errors are more easily fixed in such a one-on-one climate. And the background frustration that comes from not knowing if the situation is resolved yet will disappear.

INSIGHTS

- Make your money work as hard for you as you worked to earn it!
- Base your financial decisions on truth and nothing but the truth!
- Giving is a powerful spiritual and financial tool. Remember, besides the personal joy of helping others, charitable contributions save you taxes!

Before proceeding to the next chapter, if you haven't already done so as part of working through this chapter, please consider and record your thoughts, then work through the exercises on the following worksheet, My Plans to Minimize My Taxes and Maximize Money for Me.

My Plans to Minimize Taxes and Maximize Money for Me

NOTES FROM READING THIS CHAPTER

MINIMIZING MY/OUR TAXES

A. Record the investments you now have.
Use the space below.

B. Categorize them.
Arrange these same investments by what they are for: education or retirement or some other specific goal.

C. Mark the ones that may be candidates for greater legitimate tax savings.
After researching if any might be changed, list the ones that might possibly be better if financed with a full-loaf dollar.

D. Note your action plan.

Look at all sides of the math: money in, tax advantages now. Tax repercussions later. Market fluctuations in between. Decide what you would like to do and note it below.

E. Get advice.

Now pray, then talk over your inclinations with your partner. Then make an appointment to talk them over with a tax-planning professional to see if you've overlooked some aspects in your plan.

F. Act.

Now you are ready to make your changes! Note them here and use your follow-up system to be sure you've done all you meant to do. Enjoy the rewards!

13

INVESTMENT WISDOM

The typical question people ask: "Is this a good investment?"
It is better to ask: "Is this a good investment for me?"

—Justin Heather

If you have followed my suggestions thus far, you have established a forward budgeting system that features forced savings (paying yourself before you spend) and you have got your spending under control. You have made plans to meet your major expenses, like educating your children and planning for your own retirement. Once any past debt is paid back and your emergency fund is full, you are ready to invest a proper percentage of your savings to meet those needs. To make wise investment choices, you have to take into account how much you will eventually need to get out of those investments as well as when you'll make them, how much risk you are willing to take, and how your choices are affected by the tax bite. These topics are treated in their own chapters. Please review them as you feel the need.

Becoming a wise investor is critical not only to accumulating material wealth but also to achieving genuine prosperity. The spiritually wise person will give priority to eternal values and make choices according to the Truth that has withstood the test of time. These choices lead to the betterment of many and must include taking reasonable risks. With investments, as in every facet of life, one must look at the potential good that can be gained, set goals for attaining it, hone the skills needed to meet those goals, and then map out a plan that will aid in achieving those goals while helping all along the way.

THE WISE INVESTOR

A wise investor lives by the values and principles of the Philosophy of Wisdom that was discussed at the beginning of the book. Living by it shapes heart-based thinking that ensures that one's investment decisions are not controlled by cleverness of mind or unwise motive. Heart-based thinking ensures that one understands his or her money personality and uses this understanding to avoid extremes. He or she takes good advice and moves past "safe" saving without taking excessive and unnecessary risks. He or she focuses on the goals set by a vision of true prosperity, not just one of material wealth. Consequently a wise investor avoids the pitfalls of a goal of maximization (the foolhardy pursuit of wealth for its own sake) or of giving in to a penchant for taking risk for the sake of risk.

A wise investor acts with the quiet confidence and certainty that come from heart-based thinking and wise habits. This wise investor avoids willful, unilateral decisions and, instead, discusses an investment plan, step by step, with his or her partner and mentors. Refusing to remain in the overly "safe" place of saving in types of accounts that are insured by either a federal agency or a credit union agency, a wise investor finds contentment with investments that prudently balance safety and growth.

• True Success

This is more easily achieved when one remembers that success—in life and with money—is not measured by knowledge or cleverness. It is not measured by the accumulation of assets or material possessions. True success is measured with the eternal yardstick.

True success comes from how we conduct our lives, how we handle the resources we have been given. Have we been afraid to use them? Have we used them for our improvement and for that of others? Or have we used them selfishly and narrowly to fill the desires of the moment?

Answering these questions regularly, in prayer, alone, and in our regular discussions with those close to us, is essential to working toward true success. And so is moving beyond being a mere saver.

MOVING BEYOND BEING A SAVER ONLY

Those who never invest come in two major categories: the ones who squander their money and have nothing to invest and the ones who grasp their money so tightly and fearfully that they never move from saving to investing. Either type of noninvestor is just as unwise as the unwise ones on the other side of the spectrum—investors who allow greed or "winning the game" to control their common sense, those who seek the highest return and foolishly risk their principal unnecessarily. Do not let any of these unwise behaviors keep you from true success. Move beyond saving to investing and learn to establish and live within wise investment boundaries.

• Stuck in the Saving Mode

Some folks have the idea that making money through investments is somehow a greedy undertaking. It is not. If you need to be reminded of this, think about whom the wealthy man admonished in Jesus' parable in Matthew 25:14–30. Was it the two servants who invested and doubled their master's money? Or the servant who buried his money (to "save" it) and had only the original amount at the time of reckoning? One guess. . . .

Many other people think of investing as a sport for the wealthy and for gamblers, and saving as the sport left for everyone else—the little guys like them. Whether from looking only at investors who unwisely go to extremes or from having a money personality that finds risk taking difficult, they think of saving as the "safe" thing to do. This is faulty thinking.

Saving does, of course, serve a valuable purpose. It is, in fact, critical to a wise, forward budget. But there is a problem with saving and never investing. As you have already seen, if all you do is save your money, inflation will eat away at your capital! And as you saw in chapter 12, taxes on savings income can do the same unless you wisely plan with tax savings in mind. To achieve highest and lasting prosperity, we must leave faulty thinking behind and move to a higher level of understanding. In terms of financial management, this certainly includes moving from saving to investing.

• Incentive for Investing

> *You must lose a fly to catch a trout.*
>
> —George Herbert

Fear of investing stands in the way of financial success in the same way that fear of losing your lure will keep you from catching a trout! Remember those examples on compounding in chapter 8? Remember the rule of 72? Examples like those will help you see the necessity of wise investing. So should the following ones.

One dollar saved at a fixed compound interest of 3 percent per year after tax will double in 24 years. At the time of this writing, you would be very lucky to find a savings account that yields as much as 3 percent before taxes, much less after tax! In an investment that pays 8 percent per year after tax (as has been true many times the past three decades, though not true at the time of this writing), this same dollar will double in only 9 years, so in that same 24 years your dollar will become over $6. And an investment earning 11 percent per year after tax (which again, though not frequently the case at the time of this writing, has been true quite often in the past three decades), that dollar will double in a little over 6.5 years, making that dollar worth about $8 in 24 years. Would you rather have $2 or $6; $2 or $8?

And consider this: If inflation ran 5 percent per year over that same 24 years, the dollar you began with would be worth only 50¢ after 14.4 years pass; and after 24 years, that initial dollar would be worth about a quarter!

Obviously, these examples, and the bear market that exists at the time of this writing, speak volumes to any fear you might have about investing. Without mixing words, the bottom line is that fears must be overcome and wise investments must be made to realize your life vision and its dreams. Now, and almost always, is a time to move beyond low-yielding savings accounts and into investments that over and over, down through history, have proven their superiority for building material wealth.

• Heart-based Investing

I recommend a three-plank plan to minimize risk and maximize potential rewards.

1. Guided by your wise, divinely led heart, be sure your investment strategy is motivated by enduring goals, principles, and values. This approach will enable you to continue to live a generous life that benefits you and others and thereby fills you with happiness.

2. Leaving your emergency fund in a savings storehouse, regularly transfer the excess of your savings into higher-yielding investments. Do not call guaranteed savings accounts "investments."

3. To invest wisely, follow the basic guidelines of wise investing given later in this chapter.

GENERAL INVESTING GUIDELINES

Wise investing begins with knowing who you are and how to plan. Chapters 1 through 5 in *Wisdom and Money* are about who you are and what you want from life. The rest of the chapters are about planning. Review those five chapters as needed. Please don't forget that when "you" is plural, investing includes taking into account those close to you and how your investment plan will affect them. You will need to discuss investment planning with your mentor or partner before putting it into action. Unilateral decisions lead to dissension, and dissension is not part of true prosperity.

• Avoid Sticker-shock Investments

As you begin to look at the general guidelines for wisely investing the savings you accumulate beyond your rainy day fund, please make the first step this one: Understand the meaning and implications of the word *guaranteed.*

Why is that important? Let me answer that with another question: Why will over 90 percent of people not be able to retire in the financial comfort and lifestyle they had hoped for?

We have already looked at the first reason so many do not have adequate retirement funds when they need them: the fact that many never save at all or woefully undersave. Since you are now living your forward budget, you are probably not in this group.

I suggest that you look closely at the second reason: Far too many consider investing to be putting their savings in what I call sticker-shock investments. These are the so-called guaranteed investments—like savings accounts, CDs, and other such "investments" backed by the guarantee of federal or credit union deposit insurance. This type of "investment" appeals to those who are not risk takers by personality, and to those who misunderstand the pitfalls of unwise investing and who are committed to not falling into one of those pits (as they misunderstand them).

Sticker-shock investments frequently give you a negative net return on your capital. (There is an example of how, below.) So, if you buy only sticker-shock investments, you will find that, by the time retirement rolls around, you have indeed fallen into a common investing pit: You will have lost huge chunks of savings and buying power because of their low yields over time when compared with inflation.

If you own only sticker-shock investments, you are not alone. Millions of people buy and hold billions of dollars' worth of sticker-shock investments because they are buying into the half-truth of guaranteed principal. It's easy to see how this happens: The fear of losing money in an investment that is not insured is a normal human instinct, and it is deliberately and constantly reinforced. The sponsors of sticker-shock investments spend billions of dollars every year marketing this message of fear!

I encourage you to look at the half-truth in the message so that you will invest more wisely. Such a message overstresses the guarantee of your principal while it intentionally sidesteps all the other relevant facts you should consider before investing, like your need to have enough money put away by the time you retire so that you will be able to live on it at the cost of living that will exist in your retirement years.

In fairness to the sponsors of sticker-shock investments, the fear may seem justified (notice I said *seem*) at first. Sponsors of the other kinds of investments—non-sticker-shock investments (investments that may actually make some money!)—sometimes confuse potential buyers. They offer investment opportunities so complex that buyers feel they need to be financial wizards to understand them. Even when the investments are not difficult to understand, some investment and financial professionals use complex language to describe investing concepts. In their minds, this helps justify the buyer's need for them (which is a real need). It often backfires and simply reinforces consumers' fears of non-sticker-shock investments, sending them back to staying with what they understand—a need for security.

In so doing, many people place too much emphasis on the guarantee of their principal and thereby take huge risks, knowingly or unwittingly, by ignoring how inflation and taxes may well eat away at the very outcome they seek: having enough money to cover cost when it is needed.

And to that I add this strong caution. The risk of investing in sticker-shock investments is probably greatest at times when market conditions are as they are at the time of this writing. Yet fear causes money to literally fly from non–sticker shock investments into those "guaranteed" loss investments. The reality is that this strategy makes sense only in the short run—that is, while an investor assesses the best non-sticker-shock investments to own in bear markets. Nearly always, it makes no financial sense to stay heavily invested in so-called guaranteed investments.

Sticker-shock Example

If you still need convincing, consider this scenario. You have $10,000 "invested" in a savings account that earns 4 percent per year. You are in a 28 percent tax bracket. Inflation is 4 percent per year.

Every year you stay with this sticker-shock investment strategy, you are in reality losing more than 1.1 percent of your capital and earning nothing! This loss of $110 per year comes from the following calculation:

The 4 percent interest on one year is $400.

The 28 percent tax on $400 is $112. This leaves you $288 in income from the savings account, which is a 2.8 percent post-tax return on your $10,000.

At 4 percent inflation, you may initially think that this $288 at the end of the year is comparable to more. But that's a false perception, based on very faulty beliefs!

It is indeed true that your account balance will go up by $288. But you need to also look at what has happened to your principal of $10,000. Because of the 4 percent inflation it now has the spending power of $9,600. This loss of $400 is partially offset by the $288 (which will begin to be affected by inflation the following year) you gained in spending power on your post-tax interest, leaving you with a net loss on your investment of $112, or over 1.1 percent! This means you're starting the second year of such an investment with an effective principal of only $9,888, or slightly over 1.1 percent less than what you started with!

And what you see in this example is, in reality, happening over and over every year you allow fear and other things to unnecessarily cause you to keep your savings invested in sticker-shock investments. If you were to continue this approach for the forty years you will probably work before retiring, this 1.1 percent annual loss would become nearly a 50 percent loss in the buying power of your money.

Believe me, this is not a cheap parlor trick. This is not nonsense. It is black-and-white, pen-to-paper truth.

Since the money with which you buy *anything* (except things like special pretax plans instituted by Congress and mentioned earlier in *Wisdom and Money*) is after-tax money, you must look at how inflation affects you on an after-tax basis. Inflation reduces the buying power of your capital.

Seem like a no-win proposition?

Take heart. Fear and intimidation about investing can be overcome if you let your investment strategies be guided by the Philosophy of Wisdom and its principles and values of eternal truth that include the 7 Laws of Highest Prosperity.

Take heart—and then take part in your own financial success story!

USE THESE STEPS TO INVEST WISELY

You invest so that your hard-earned money does not lose value. Remember the assets on that net worth statement you worked up in worksheet 6? As you look at ways to increase the buying power of your assets, you will look at different investment asset types. Some are "safer" than others. When to invest in which type can be learned.

These are the basic investing guidelines I recommend:

1. *Seek the help of a competent, trustworthy, objective financial adviser* who shares your values and has a proven history of helping people achieve success with money. Be sure he or she is compensated primarily for his or her counsel, not for selling you investments. More detail on this important topic is given in "Hiring Your Financial Adviser," below.

2. Even as you listen to the adviser you hire, I still encourage you to invest some of your time in learning about the financial markets and your investing options, in order to increase and maintain your financial intelligence. Just as being a savvy patient comes in handy when speaking with medical doctors, being a savvy investor will come in handy when you make your investing decisions. There are some basic websites and magazines listed in the Appendix that may help you gain a context for the advice you receive. Remember: Responsibility is yours, both in where you seek advice and how you structure your investing budget.

3. Develop a personal investment model using minimal-risk investments for its base. If you own a computer, there are many companies that offer investment model software. Some are listed in the Appendix. All these software and information tools can be helpful in applying the other suggestions below.

4. As you choose where to make your investments, be certain you are investing in worthy endeavors. Since investing is an awesome privilege and responsibility, the wise investor will seek information and, as appropriate, pray about the options and discuss them with those close to him or her. Some questions to consider are: If I invest in this organiza-

tion, what will they do with my/our money? Do they make a product or perform a service I/we agree with? Do they also do things I/we disagree with? Where is the balance? Are they exploiting their workers or do they provide good working conditions and share the profits with them? Do they work toward self-sustaining economies wherever they are located, or do they support an economy that is dependent on ours? Where does the company distribute their largesse?

5. Decide which portion of investments will be used for income. Invest these only in asset types like bonds, stocks, mutual funds, and money market accounts that generate regular dividends or interest.
   (I recommend you stick with these types of investments and with the growth assets described below that do not include hard assets like real estate (except your house) until your net worth exceeds several hundred thousand dollars. Then you should look at adding a layer of investments that include commercial and/or residential rental real estate. At this level of investment, I recommend that you buy these investments outright, not take out loans to own them. Be sure to maintain your integrity in how you operate these investments! Serving those who use what you own will keep you on the path to true prosperity.)

6. Decide which portion of your investments you will use for growth.

7. Balance risk and reward by diversifying these investments among several asset categories.

8. Add up to four levels of investments, only graduating to riskier, higher-return investments when all other base investments (your emergency fund, income investments, and growth investments) are covered.

9. Don't jump in and out of the market.

10. Review your investments with your partner and adviser at least yearly to ensure that your allocation mix still fits your investment budget needs and the cycle of life you are in.

• Why No More Specific Suggestions

One final comment on the above suggestions. Some will criticize me for not being more specific or for not giving a lot of detailed examples on how to apply those suggestions.

Wisdom and Money is a basic book especially targeted at helping those who are not advanced in their financial skills or who have no adequate plans in place. It also attempts to address many, many aspects of planning that even the advanced person will find very helpful.

Each reader's money personality, goals, and profile are unique. Rather than mislead someone whose needs are different from a given specific example, *Wisdom and Money* gives general suggestions and focuses on concepts and philosophy of planning. I strongly believe this will take each reader further than specific examples that may not apply.

If you are one who is set on managing your own finances despite my suggestion that you hire a financial adviser, let me say that, based on over a quarter of a century of observing and helping thousands of people and businesses of all economic strata and sizes to manage their money, I agree there *are* some who for various reasons don't need a financial adviser. But most people *do* need one and they miss opportunity when they try to go it alone. Most intelligent people would never consider taking care of their physical health without having relationships with trusted, competent health care professionals whom they gladly pay, recognizing that the benefits are worth the cost. Where their physical health is concerned, they check their egos at the door, recognize their limitations, and trust themselves to others who they feel are far more competent than they are. So it should be with financial health. The reality is that our economic and education systems are such that not to have a financial adviser, assuming you can afford one, may well be the greatest risk you take with your financial well-being.

You deserve the personalized attention a trusted, competent paid financial adviser can and should provide you. Armed with the information in *Wisdom and Money,* you can move much more rapidly from beginner to advanced student of money than someone without the guidelines and suggestions contained herein. And you will be better able to choose a trusted, competent adviser who is not intimidated by informed clients, and to maintain a relationship with that adviser!

So, you might ask, How does one find an adviser who meets the criteria shared above and who also provides benefits that clearly exceed his or her compensation?

• Hiring Your Financial Adviser

To locate potential financial advisers in your area, all you need do is call the Association of Certified Financial Planners in Denver or look them up on the web. (See Appendix for specifics.) Their website also gives some excellent tips on hiring an adviser.

I highly recommend you first consider hiring someone who holds the Certified Financial Planner designation from the association. Then ask for professional and client references and check out the advisers you're considering! Finally, interview the advisers you are most strongly considering.

As you interview potential financial adviser candidates, don't give too much weight in your decision to gut feelings or personality quirks. Instead, balance the potential adviser's apparent quantitative skills (knowledge of the field) with his or her qualitative skills (communication and other interpersonal skills). Certainly you want someone who is sensitive, who talks to you as much as possible in ordinary language, who will take the time to thoroughly explain whatever recommendations are being made regarding your finances, and who will pleasantly and thoroughly answer any questions you have.

Questions to Ask Financial Advisers When You Interview Them
- What is your background and experience?
- What are your financial planning credentials?
- How are you compensated by your clients? (By product sponsors?)
- What services do you offer?
- Could I review the written agreement you use to document the relationship with a client?
- What is your financial philosophy?
- What initial process do you carry your clients through? What are your ongoing processes to service your clients?

Their answers to these last two questions will indicate whether they do the following things that I consider the minimum such an adviser should do when working with clients:
- Go through an information-gathering process before developing a plan and recommending any strategy or product;
- Analyze and evaluate your profile;
- Develop a written plan and present it with their specific recommendations (which should include alternatives);
- Work with you to implement recommendations;
- Regularly monitor and tweak the plan, based on face-to-face meetings.

EMPLOY THE PRINCIPLE OF DIVERSIFICATION

You have heard the adage that you shouldn't put all your eggs into one basket. In the area of investing it is certainly true that too many people lose out because they have invested too much of their money in one type of investment or one category of investments. Studies continue to indicate the advantages of diversification. By employing the principal of diversification—that is, by buying among different asset types—investors can accomplish two things at once:

1. They can increase their overall portfolio return; and
2. They can reduce the chance of financial disaster should one investment turn sour.

The principle of diversification tends to be most effective when one invests in asset classes that do not correlate with each other. This is true because, historically speaking, when one class of investment is down in value, the other is usually up.

• Signs That You Have Not Adequately Diversified

Let me assure you that diversification is a linchpin of your financial train: It holds together all the parts of your investment portfolio. Because of ignorance or fear or bad advice, too many investors fail to diversify adequately.

If you do not diversify, you probably will not see your money grow even as well as it would in those infamous "guaranteed" savings accounts. Here are some signs that you may have failed to diversify adequately.

1. You are invested too heavily in one or two individual stocks and bonds, thereby betting on the financial strength of a single entity;

2. You have concentrated too much of your money in one asset category, such as stocks, mutual funds, or hard assets (like real estate);

3. You own too much stock in your current employer's organization. (Even when your employer funds a 401(k) or other formal retirement plan with company stock, you need to sell off some of that when and if the plan allows, then reinvest the proceeds in assets not tied to your employer.)

4. You are relying on your employer to fund your future retirement. (Instead of taking the company-recommended investments with your 401(k) money, look at your options outside these recommendations and bargain for what benefits you, and possibly other employees, the most. For example, you may want the option to invest in no-load stock mutual funds with a proven performance history.)

5. You have bought too much house. As you did when you looked at how your spending and saving budget would be affected by the price of the house you buy and how you decide to pay for it, you should also look at that house as an investment. If too much of your money is tied up in that asset and the housing market in your neighborhood takes a tumble or your house burns to the ground or gets hit by a natural disaster, you may find that the return you expected is in the negative amount. Look at the investment value of your house carefully.

• Some Diversification Ideas for the Beginning Investor

While it is not the scope of *Wisdom and Money* to try to give investment advice, there are general guidelines for those who have just completed filling their rainy day fund. Here are some ways to consider diversifying investments for a beginner:

1. As just stated, don't own to much house! Otherwise the mortgage pay-

ment will eat up the cash flow you could otherwise use to save and invest in other categories of assets.

2. Put your rainy day fund into a money market mutual fund;

3. Begin to fund a college education plan by transferring money from savings into investments like no-load, stock-based mutual funds that have good performance records over the long term;

4. Buy shares in one or two no-load, bond-based mutual funds that have good performance records over the long term;

5. Fund an IRA and/or begin contributing to a formal retirement plan sponsored by your employer.

Keep in mind that a single mutual fund will normally own shares of stock or bonds of quite a number of entities. This further broadens your diversification.

Don't forget to study which options seem best for you, then discuss what you are tending toward with your partner and your adviser!

• Some Diversification Ideas for the More Advanced Investor

Here are some ways to consider diversifying after your net worth has passed several thousand dollars.

1. Still don't own to much house! Otherwise the mortgage payment will eat up the cash flow you could otherwise use to save and invest in other categories of assets.

2. With the monies earmarked to pay for college education for your children, buy shares in several no-load, stock-based mutual funds that are more aggressive than those a beginner would want to pick. Of course, no matter how aggressive, you want to pick those that have good performance records over the long term;

3. Buy shares in one or two no-load, bond-based mutual funds that are more aggressive than those a beginner would want to pick. Of course, no matter how aggressive, you want to pick those that have good performance records over the long term;

4. Maximize your allowable contributions to IRAs and formal retirement plans sponsored by your employer;

5. Shift you monies in formal retirement plans into more aggressive investments, like those mentioned above. Of course, no matter how aggressive, you want to pick those that have good performance records over the long term.

As you advance, be sure to invest money outside formal retirement plans in different mutual funds than those owned with monies inside formal retirement plans.

Don't forget to study which options seem best for you, then discuss what you are tending toward with your partner and your adviser!

GUIDELINES FOR INVESTING FOR YOUR CHILD'S EDUCATION

In chapter 10, "Funding a College Education," we looked at the need for your saving and/or investing to accumulate funds for your children's education. In chapter 12, I recommended you consider funding education IRAs and traditional IRAs. If you do, I recommend you apply the above investment guidelines to those monies. Also take a look at the additional guidelines given below for employer-sponsored plans, and consider applying them as appropriate to your IRAs as well.

MORE GUIDELINES FOR INVESTING IN EMPLOYER-SPONSORED RETIREMENT PLANS

In chapter 11, "Funding Retirement," we looked at the 401(k) and other employer-sponsored retirement plans as a major consideration in how to accumulate what you need for retirement.

Studies have shown that perhaps over half of 401(k) fund assets are in fixed-income type instruments—those with low percentage point returns, or sticker-shock investments. A difference in return of a few percentage points may not seem like much, but over a long period of time it adds up to a huge difference. For example, if you save $300 a month in a 401(k) for thirty years and invest those savings in investments earning 5 percent, you will accumulate roughly $250,000. Alternatively, if you choose a mix of assets with a slightly higher risk—say, an overall portfolio that includes mutual funds invested in stocks and bonds and that collectively earns 8 percent per year, your retirement nest egg will almost double that amount! Change the mix to higher risk, bump that hypothetical rate of annual return another two percentage points to 10 percent per annum, and your account will grow to slightly less than $700,000—almost triple the first example of investing solely in low-yielding, fixed-income instruments (those dreaded sticker-shock investments).

There are some specifics to consider when you and your financial adviser decide where to allocate your funds for 401(k) or similar plans:

1. *Your investment options:* Some 401(k) plans and similar employer-sponsored plans offer only limited choices. Most employers with these type plans, however, have adopted provisions that offer the plan participants a diversified menu of investment options. Some employers did this on their own; others were forced to do it by changes in the law. You must by law receive a disclosure of your options from your employer. Those options should include frequent opportunity to switch your in-

vestments in response to your own or market and economic conditions. At the time of this writing, most of these plans don't allow you to switch on a whim, but changes in the law have made it easier to switch more frequently and thus give you greater flexibility in maintaining growth in your money. I suspect the law will continue to change more in participants' favor, in the aftermath of recent stock market performance and business scandals.

2. *Your age:* Generally, the younger you are, the higher the percentage of more aggressive investments you can and should invest in.

3. *Your overall total asset portfolio:* When investing your retirement assets in employer-sponsored plans, the investment portfolio mix you choose for that money should take into consideration the mix of your other assets (such as personal investments listed on the balance sheet you prepared for the exercise in worksheet 6, "Finding My Net Worth.").

4. *Company participation in funding:* Some companies contribute a certain amount for every dollar the employee puts in; but some require the employee to use that money to purchase *their* company's stock. This can skew the balance of your portfolio in an undesirable direction that violates the principle of diversification. You don't want too many eggs in one basket. So, as you are permitted by plan rules, sell some of that stock and diversify into assets unrelated to your employer.

MY FAVORITE INVESTMENT: MUTUAL FUNDS

My personal favorite investment, a mutual fund, is a government-regulated company that pools money from many individual investors through the sale of shares in a particular investment company. The fund's managers buy stocks, bonds, or other assets for their shareholders. The price of the shares (called net asset value or NAV) increases or decreases depending on the current value of the fund's investment holdings and its liabilities.

Mutual fund shareholders may receive income from the increase in the fund's share price or they may receive a profit from the sale of their shares in the mutual fund company if the value goes up (much as they would by investing in individual stocks and bonds). Of course, if the fund's share price goes down, then the fund shareholder will lose money if he or she sells at a lower price than the purchase price. (On the other hand, if you are open to waiting, you can reinvest in shares at that lower price and hope to profit all the more at a later date. Making such a decision is where a good, objective adviser comes in!)

Mutual funds offer many advantages that have led me to believe so strongly in them, making them the centerpiece of my recommendation for the portion of assets allocated to long-term investments. Four advantages in particular stand out:

1. *Diversification.* A single mutual fund holds many, sometimes hundreds, of stocks and/or bonds.

2. *Professionalism.* Full-time money managers make the investment decisions.

3. *Small fries welcome.* It takes as little as $25 to start (or per month) to get you into a fund.

4. *Compounding and liquidity..* You can choose to compound your earnings through automatic reinvestment or to receive income through the withdrawal of earnings. (Shareholders can also sell their mutual fund shares on demand).

• But Bear in Mind . . .
On the down side:

1. Mutual funds are not federally insured like CDs or savings accounts—even if you buy them through a bank or other financial institution. Neither the investment return nor the principal is guaranteed.

2. You can lose money if you sell your shares for less than you paid for them.

3. There are risks of loss due to market conditions, such as interest-rate fluctuations.

On the up side:

1. That risk of loss due to market conditions such as interest-rate fluctuations is not unique to mutual funds.

2. Even though they are not insured, mutual funds are closely regulated. Past closures of mutual funds that resulted in loss to investors have been nominal when compared to the number of FDIC-insured institutions that have been closed.

3. All mutual funds are not the same. Since there are thousands of different funds, with different investment objectives and different levels of risk, you can choose which you want to invest in.

• What to Look At in a Mutual Fund
As you look at the types of mutual funds, look at their objectives, level of risk, and costs that reduce your investments' return. These are stated in a brochure called the fund's prospectus and annual report. Also look within the prospectus at what the fund invests in, to be sure you are not indirectly underwriting uses you don't agree with. Is the fund trying to generate lots of current income? Or is it a fund focusing on the appreciating value of fast-growing company stocks as its principal objective?

As the mutual fund industry has evolved and matured, some funds have become highly specialized. So, for example, look at whether the mutual fund you're considering fits this category and, if so, ask questions like: Does this fund invest exclusively in U.S. government securities? Does it invest only in tax-free municipal securities? Does it invest some of its money in corporate bonds? Does it invest only in larger company stocks? Does it specialize solely in small company stocks? If the answer to any of these questions is yes, then be sure their objectives are consistent with yours, given the cycle of financial life you are in now and the ones you anticipate for the future.

Also be sure not to concentrate your money in any one category of mutual funds, including those just mentioned.

In addition, you might look at mutual funds that have been specifically set up to invest in companies with a global presence. Or you might consider funds that invest in specific sectors of the economy such as health or technology. Or you might prefer funds that invest in what you deem morally responsible companies (which are among my favorite specific funds).

• How Many Mutual Funds to Aim At

How many different mutual funds you should consider owning depends, among other factors, on your individual investment goals, the amount of money you have to invest, and the time you have to monitor your funds. Ideally, you should diversify among several funds with different objectives. This effectively reduces risk.

• How to Choose a Fund

So, how should you go about picking mutual funds? Very carefully.

I encourage you to gather as much of the above kinds of information as suits your style, then consult the qualified financial adviser you have chosen. If you have not yet chosen an adviser, please use the basic guidelines given in the subsection of this chapter called "Hiring Your Financial Adviser." Also consult the Appendix, which has further guidelines on where and how to look for such an adviser. Then hire one!

WHAT TO DO IN BEAR AND BULL TIMES

When bear markets and recessions hit, it's important not to panic.

If you see the advance signs that would indicate a need to move your investments back to the savings sidelines for a while, then do so. *But* if you miss or misread them and get caught by the bear, the best thing almost always is to ride out the storm. Never allow fear to cause you to jump out of the market and take huge losses. Take heart. Rocky times often present bargain purchase opportunities that are the sunshine of such times.

Whether in bear or bull times, keep on saving and moving your savings into growth-oriented investments.

INSIGHTS

- Guarantee lasting success by following the 7 Laws of Highest Prosperity.
- Move from saving to investing: Don't own too many sticker-shock investments.
- Avoid greedy and foolhardy investment approaches.
- Choose investments balanced for safety and growth.

Before proceeding to the next chapter, please consider and record your thoughts and work through the exercises on the following worksheet, My Investment Plans.

WORKSHEET 13

My Investment Plans

NOTES FROM READING THIS CHAPTER

PART I
NOTES ON SETTING MY INVESTMENT GOALS

PART II
NOTES ON HIRING MY INVESTMENT ADVISER

PART III
NOTES ON ALLOCATING MY INVESTMENTS BY RISK

PART IV
NOTES ON DIVERSIFYING MY INVESTMENTS

PART V
NOTES ON MY METHOD TO TRACK INVESTMENT PROGRESS

PART VI
NOTES ON INVESTMENT DECISIONS

PART VII
NOTES ON FOLLOW-UP

14

Preserving Your Estate

The baby boomer and subsequent generations will inherit the largest intergenerational transfers of wealth in U.S. history. And with wisdom applied, these transfers could make history too, by being done more beneficially than estate transfers usually are, both for heirs and for society.

—Cecil O. Kemp Jr.

To maximize the benefit of your assets to your heirs, your estate plan should be part of your overall personal financial plan, not something done at the last minute (or not done at all). If you and your spouse have been working through *Wisdom and Money* to plan and manage your finances, then life will be simpler for whichever one is left after the first one dies. The widowed one will not be left with debt or with inadequate income. If you work through this chapter together, you will also save your surviving partner a seemingly insurmountable learning curve while grieving.

Estate planning is clearly in keeping with the seventh law of highest prosperity, the law of Preservation. Two of its primary objectives are to preserve and pass along your (1) life values and priorities, (2) earthly material wealth so that the transfer is made to desired beneficiaries.

A will, letters of instruction, a living will, durable power of attorney, and the formation of trusts are all common elements to good estate planning. It is critically important to work with a competent attorney and a wise financial adviser in order to achieve the desired results.

YOUR WILL

When someone dies, it is not uncommon for the children, spouse, ex-spouse, relatives, business partners, and everyone else who knew the decedent to break into arguments, sometimes even bitter warfare, over the division of the estate. Often the battle does not involve money, but who gets some item like Uncle Henry's old pickup truck or Grandmother's china collection. Sometimes the dispute ends up in court, costing the estate heavily in attorney's fees. At other times it poisons relationships, temporarily or permanently. Always it makes grieving for the deceased more difficult.

Do not assume that only large estates become embroiled in this type of squabble. While it is true that wills involving small estates are less likely to be challenged, it is also true that many families actually have much larger estates than they realize, once retirement accounts and insurance policies are considered.

A will may be the single most important document you sign in your lifetime. It is important for the estate planning for both your personal finances and your business's. (If you own a significant part of a business, it will also affect ongoing operations.) Preparing your valid will well is your way of ensuring that your estate and its portions go to those whom you choose, at the least cost in administrative expenses and taxes. It also can state who will do what jobs in your business or how your assets in that business should be dispersed.

Making a will or updating an old one follows the sixth and seventh laws of highest prosperity, the laws of Preparation and Preservation. These are the laws that speak of wise planning and stewardship, in which spiritual values and material goods should be passed on to the next generation. If you are tempted to avoid this task because you are nonchalant or because you don't want to think about your mortality or because it seems like a big hassle to you or because you think you own too little to make a will necessary or because you think the law will distribute your estate just as well, please stop sticking your head in the sand! Any of these attitudes is naive and a recipe for financial disaster—for you *and* for those you love.

• Avoid Dying Intestate

Not having a valid, up-to-date will can lead to your money going to someone you wouldn't want to have a penny of your material resources. If you die without a written will, you will have died, according to the law, "intestate." Let me explain that fancy word *intestate* very simply. If someone dies without a written will, the state they lived in has preset rules to divide the estate. Often, that division does not come close to the decedent's desires or the needs of his or her closest heirs. For example, some states have laws that divide the estate in equal portions between the deceased's spouse and children. Those laws could be applied in a scenario where there are two adult children who have no need for the resources due to their own financial profiles, but the surviving spouse is elderly and in need of all the financial resources. In that situation, two people who have no need get two-thirds of the estate and the one who really needs it all, instead, receives only one-third.

Prepare Your Will

To avoid dying intestate, prepare your will carefully, and with an adviser. This will allow you to

- choose your heirs;

- reduce or minimize taxes on the transfer of your estate;

- decide who will be the guardian of minor, handicapped, or disabled children;

- identify a qualified person as your executor; and

- designate a state of residence for tax purposes.

To help make it more difficult for someone disgruntled to challenge your will, follow these four tips:

1. *Confirm your mental state.* Doctors can determine competency with simple mental tests. If you alter your will while confined to a hospital or nursing home, the staff—or even roommates—can be interviewed as to your state of mind. Put it in writing.

2. *Involve a competent attorney and financial adviser when making substantial changes to your will.* Your adviser can question you about your estate's assets, any changes you want made, and why you want them made. Be sure he or she takes extensive notes and keeps them in a file, giving you a copy to hold. The adviser can also testify about your state of mind at any trial contesting the will.

3. *Don't involve beneficiaries.* Do not let any of your major beneficiaries pay for the preparation of the will, or even give the appearance of unduly influencing the will's preparation. Don't have your beneficiaries present at the signing of the will.

4. *Videotape the signing.* At the time of this writing videotaped wills—in and of themselves—are not valid in the United States. The will must be written, witnessed, and properly signed. A videotape of the signing of the will, however, can be a powerful defense against challenges because it can establish the grantor's state of mind. Read the entire will before the camera. Be sure the witnesses are independent and are shown watching you sign. Have your attorney explain the will on camera after it's been read; then have the attorney question you about your understanding.

Select Your Executor

Selecting a qualified executor is just as important as making a written will and proving it valid. Your executor (your personal representative) will carry out your instructions according to the terms of your will.

If you make no valid will or if your executor is either not available or is declared legally incompetent, a court will appoint an administrator after your death. Usually a bank trust department or an attorney will then handle your estate.

Make your own choice while you are able to do so. Discussing your will and your wishes with the executor will benefit your estate and beneficiaries—and help the executor. Explain your choice of executor to other family members and review your choice periodically. You have the option to change your selection throughout your life.

Most people simply choose their spouse, an adult child, or a close relative for the task of executor. While this is often a good choice, the decision should not be made hastily. An executor must make numerous critical decisions, meet court-dictated duties and deadlines, prepare complicated tax returns, and spend considerable time wrapping up your affairs.

LETTERS OF INSTRUCTION

A letter of instruction is a good companion document to a will. A letter of instruction is not legally binding, but at a very stressful time it can help your heirs and those responsible for administering your estate. Specifically, a letter of instruction can

1. help ensure that your wishes are carried out;
2. help ensure that none of your estate is wasted or lost; and
3. be a way of forcing you to organize your financial affairs.

A letter of instruction can include such things as:

- A list of things to do, including whom to notify of the death: names, addresses, and telephone numbers of friends, relatives, employer(s), life insurance companies, and the Social Security office. It would help your surviving spouse and/or dependent children if you include specific information on which forms to file with Social Security and what will be needed to support the claim.
- An organ donation request, with applicable forms attached to the letter of instruction.
- Burial arrangements, describing what you want.
- A detailed list of your assets and liabilities. Detailed means detailed: It should include a list of assets, including where the assets are physically located (such as in safe deposit box Y at X bank). The list should especially include details of time-important assets like your insurance policies.
- Directions for the disposition of your personal effects if your will doesn't already state specifically who gets items like clothes, rings, cars, etc. This can head off conflicts such as Aunt Sue and Uncle Joe both

claiming that you promised *them* the fine china, when actually you wanted it to go to your son or daughter. When there has been bad blood between you and your spouse, children, and others, the post-death scenario can worsen these relationships, resulting in increased isolation, alienation, shame, and hostility. A letter of instruction and, where applicable, other estate planning tools mentioned in this chapter probably will not cause such bad blood to disappear, but they may help minimize or avoid new conflicts at an already difficult time in the lives of all those you love and leave behind.

- A list of your advisers—financial adviser, attorney, banker, and insurance agent—with their addresses and telephone numbers.
- Personal messages (thanks, encouragement, etc.).

LIVING WILLS

A living will is an individual's written declaration of what life-sustaining medical treatments the individual will or will not permit in the event the individual becomes incapacitated. For example, the person may request that artificial nourishment or artificial resuscitation be withheld if he or she is terminally ill or in a coma.

The debate over health care reform has sparked renewed interest in living wills because of the high cost of dying. Approximately one-third of the total U.S. health care bill each year is associated with patients in the last six months of their lives. In these situations, artificial life-sustaining treatment is frequent even when the patient and/or the patient's family and doctors believe that such efforts will be futile. This happens because almost all of us are reluctant to take on the responsibility to stop such efforts (there's always the *what if . . .*), or because doctors are reluctant to stop these efforts for compassionate reasons, and because they run the risk of being sued by a family member who disagrees with the decision made.

Having a living will drawn up and executed prior to such a situation can provide you with peace of mind while giving direction to your family members and doctors. Having a living will can minimize the medical expenses that will be paid by either your family or taxpayers. This is certainly a minor consideration, as far as I am concerned, but it is a consideration, nonetheless.

No, I am not an advocate of assisted suicides.

I *am* strongly in favor of dying with dignity and having one's affairs in order. That is why I recommend that you thoughtfully consider what *you* want done in such a situation—before the situation arises. Then write it down in a living will.

Most states have enacted laws pertaining to living wills. The details vary from state to state, but generally the document must be in writing, witnessed, notarized, and made while the individual (eighteen or older) is competent.

State statutes may describe in some detail the circumstances for implementing a living will that requests not to be resuscitated. For example, two doctors often have to certify that the patient's condition is terminal. The patient (almost always) cannot be pregnant. If the patient is in a coma, he or she almost always must be so at least several days before life-sustaining treatment can be stopped.

You can find out about the laws in your state in several ways, by talking to your financial adviser, attorney, and/or life insurance agent or by looking some of the estate planning websites listed in the Appendix.

HEALTH CARE PROXIES

Because living wills cannot anticipate every type of medical circumstance or may be restricted by state statute, a recommended companion document is the health care proxy, sometimes called a health care durable power of attorney. This legal document allows an individual, called a principal, to appoint someone (called their agent) to make health care decisions on their behalf, should they become unable to do so themselves. A health care proxy is more flexible than a living will and can deal with a wider variety of circumstances. Since a health care proxy is a limited power of attorney, the agent is not authorized to make financial or business decisions for the principal. Usually that power, if necessary, is assigned to someone else through a separate power-of-attorney document.

I urge you to discuss these issues in advance with your family and your financial adviser. Thinking "the unthinkable" now can prevent much heartache and agony later for everyone involved.

DPAs

A durable power of attorney (DPA) is a simple and normally inexpensive legal document that allows one person to act on behalf of another person under the circumstances specified. This power is given in writing by the principal to someone else and lasts through the incapacity of the principal, until death or until revocation by the principal.

A DPA is considered by many to be an estate planning tool for the elderly—particularly if there is concern about incapacity from illness or senility. But I suggest that a DPA is a wise planning tool for all adults. Why? Even young and healthy people are sometimes incapacitated.

Let's say you have disability insurance to cover the loss of your earnings while temporarily incapacitated and you already have joint banking accounts with your spouse. Without a properly drawn and executed DPA, the spouse will still find it difficult, expensive, and time consuming to obtain a court-ordered power of attorney for tasks that may arise during an incapacity, such as

(a) negotiating a mortgage loan, (b) selling a jointly held mutual fund or, (c) performing other transactions requiring the participation of both of you.

The principal must execute a DPA while he or she has the legally defined mental capacity to do so. Before you spend the money and time to have a power of attorney drafted, review your situation with your financial adviser so you know what duties you want each proxy to take on.

PLANNING FOR DEATH TAXES—FEDERAL AND STATE

Although I am speaking primarily to Americans in *Wisdom and Money*, the suggestions in this subsection apply to anyone living anywhere in the world who may be subject to estate taxes.

When it comes to avoiding the dreaded bite of death taxes, most people focus their attention on Uncle Sam. Many people adopt sophisticated plans to eliminate or minimize their federal estate-tax liabilities. While the federal government's estate-tax bite is very steep at the time of this writing—up to 55 percent of the taxable estate—Congress may yet phase this out over time. But do not get too comfortable at that news. Bear in mind that you are more likely to be estate-taxed by your own state than by the federal government. This can come as a big, bad surprise for anyone inheriting or planning an estate who is not fully informed.

You can find out about current estate-tax systems in your state by talking with your financial adviser and/or contacting the agency in your state that administers this tax. If you don't know what agency that is, call the office of either your elected state representative or senator or the governor's office in your state's capital city.

• Trusts

From a legal or tax perspective, a trust is a separate entity from the person who arranges one. A trust structure can aid you with your desired giving while minimizing taxes in ways other estate planning tools cannot.

For example, in a properly structured, separate life insurance trust, the trust owns a life insurance policy on you. It receives, manages, and distributes death proceeds according to the provisions and instructions of the trust document. This can be a very valuable estate-tax minimization tool. It can also ensure a particular estate objective at the same time. You can find out about life insurance trusts by talking with your financial adviser, attorney, and/or agent who handles your life insurance.

A living trust works in a similar way. One of the advantages of a living trust over other trusts is that you can control the trust's assets during your lifetime. What a country! Those who establish a living trust do so for various reasons, but one reason is almost always so that the heirs can avoid the huge hassles and publicity that are sometimes involved in probate proceedings (a court proceeding in which the validity of a will is determined).

PLANNED CHARITABLE GIVING

Planned charitable giving is an aspect of your overall financial planning that covers two areas of your true prosperity at once. It cares for your assets and it gives to others. Because this tool is particularly useful in estate planning, I have waited until now to explain it.

When you employ the tool of planned charitable giving, you continue your commitment to giving—while you are alive and afterward. Beneficiaries may include existing charitable endeavors or some future vision of yours or someone you care about.

With this tool you designate some of your assets and/or income items to become the property of qualified charitable organizations. You may pass on these income items or the title to the assets before or after your death, depending on the needs, desires, and planning ramifications for both the giver and the charity.

Planned charitable giving can save you a significant amount of income taxes both for you during your living years and for your heirs (in estate taxes) after you die. I strongly recommend that you look at ways to institute a program of planned charitable giving. To find more information on how to do so, talk to your adviser or search the web or talk to the organizations you are interested in giving to. Be careful about using advice from mutual funds vendors, since they have the bias of selling their funds.

WHEN A SPOUSE DIES

The death of a spouse sets off an avalanche of emotion. Suddenly the surviving spouse is alone and has to cope with major financial decisions: funeral arrangements, insurance claims, investments, and company benefits. Let me illustrate. An older woman who was a friend of ours had a particularly hard time. Her husband did not leave a detailed list of every step she needed to take. It was distressing to see her anguish and frustration as she sloshed her way through territory totally unfamiliar to her, which could have been easier to cope with had she been left with some instruction. This was at a time when she should have been free to grieve without undue hardship. Instead, she not only struggled through tasks but was sometimes taken advantage of.

When my father died, the above scenario did not occur. My father and mother had planned and prepared long before his untimely death. This was a great relief to my siblings and me. We watched our mother grieving deeply over her beloved husband of almost fifty years having passed into forever.

She was left without the daily companionship of the love of her life. But she was also left with a situation where all the preparations had been made.

I encourage you to leave the latter scenario behind you, not the former. Even with prior planning and preparation, when the spouse who dies is the one who carried most of the responsibility for managing the couple's finances, the surviving spouse may be in for a rough time. Suddenly, he or she must learn his or her way around finances and other related matters. Leaving your loved one a good road map is a kind thing to do.

• Beware!

There is one other important dynamic that follows the death of a spouse. Beware of financial, investment, insurance, and funeral company representatives who come out of the woodwork with off-the-wall advice. They can make a bad situation worse. (Sometimes these individuals are relatives!)

Widows or widowers often find themselves in an initially untenable situation after the death of their spouse, and when they take bad advice, however well intended, they end up making rash financial decisions that make their situation worse. Bad decisions can include selling their home too quickly, moving prematurely, or paying off their mortgage with the insurance policy's death benefit. Or unscrupulous product and service purveyors can persuade and coerce vulnerable widows or widowers into making unwise investments. For example, prepaying for your own funeral is often an unwise investment.

When you are the widow or widower, get advice from many sources and compare it. If you already have trusted financial advisers, talk to them. (This is yet another reason for having them throughout your life!) If you don't, ask around until you get several good references for the same adviser. Then listen to that adviser and take the time to think things through for yourself. Then, when the smoke clears, you will likely avoid finding yourself broke as well as in grief!

Two Simple, Wise Rules

Here are two simple, wise rules I believe every newly widowed person should follow:

1. Avoid making major financial or life-changing decisions in the early stages of grief. This usually means you should take at least a year or two to put any major decision into effect.

2. Preserve the inheritance, preferably keeping it liquid in conservative investments such as CDs or money market accounts for a period of time, until you are sure you are back in control of your emotions and ready to think things through rationally.

• First Steps

Some of the first financial steps to take after your spouse dies are to file your insurance and Social Security claims. Contact the Social Security Administration in Washington, DC, and applicable insurance company(s), requesting a copy of their written requirements and the applicable forms that must be filed (with supporting documents) to validate your claim for Social Security and insurance benefits. If your deceased spouse was a war veteran, contact Veterans Affairs in Washington, DC, or in your state's capital, to determine your eligibility for veterans' survivor benefits (disability and pension benefits). If your spouse left a letter of instruction on how to file these claims, bless him or her!

Next, as soon as you are able, I encourage the newly widowed to go through the same budget process I have outlined in this book. Despite how you feel about the situation, you will not be exempt from dealing with basic living necessities, including money-related ones. You will need to examine all your available resources to meet financial necessities, such as your spouse's employee benefits, Social Security benefits, and your income from investments. If you have not yet reached retirement age and you're not currently working, it may make sense for you to reenter the workforce, if your new budget is in need.

In time, perhaps after as long as six months to a year or more, the surviving spouse should begin to seriously consider long-term needs and goals. This involves estate planning, looking at any need to change investments, tax planning, retirement, updating the will, and so forth. Seek advice!

If you are new to being single, change your investments slowly. Take on only one or two new investment vehicles at a time—and only after understanding each thoroughly.

INSIGHTS

- A legacy of love is more valuable than a large financial one without love.
- The surviving spouse will be much better prepared if couples make financial decisions jointly in marriage.
- To ensure that the legacy you desire is left behind you, learn and apply the Philosophy of Wisdom and its 7 Laws of Highest Prosperity, especially the sixth and seventh ones, the laws of Preparation and Preservation.

Before proceeding to the next chapter, please consider and record your thoughts and work through the exercises on the following worksheet, Planning My Estate.

WORKSHEET 14

Planning My Estate

NOTES FROM READING THIS CHAPTER

PLANNING MY ESTATE

A. Note your dreams about what you wish to leave behind.

B. Note who your financial advisers are.

C. Note your adviser's advice on how to realize these dreams.

D. Note any specifics on what you have yet to do.

Take into account your needs to write or update your wills, your living will, your letters of instruction, your DPAs, trusts you want to form, and any program of charitable giving you wish to institute or change.

E. Discuss your plans, as appropriate, in a loving way with your spouse.

Don't forget to pray together as you discuss topics that involve your own mortality!

F. Use your follow-up system to renew your estate planning as needed.

15

Making Your Trail

The best is yet to be.

—Robert Browning

If by now you have embraced wisdom *and* money, you will have begun applying that wisdom to your use of money. You will have defined visions that will benefit you and others, bringing all within your reach more peace, joy, and fulfillment. You will have based your daily thinking and your actions and reactions on the Spirit within. You will have freed yourself from money's potential grasp by focusing on dreams and goals and by changing what needed to be changed in your habits and actions. You will have enabled yourself to be the person the Spirit means you to be, the person of your dreams. Becoming that person—or not—is part of the legacy you will leave behind when you leave this earth.

Your legacy is all that you create and build, little by little, during your unique walk, with or without God, on this earth. Some think of legacy as limited to the material goods and services left behind in estate planning. But your true legacy is more than that: It includes relationships and ways of thinking, acting, and reacting to circumstances. It includes choices to plan or not to plan, to follow through on plans or not to follow through, to begin again when things get tough or not to begin again. It includes living a dream that is selfish or selfless, a dream that is limited to looking at what you don't have or seeing all you have already.

I hope your legacy encompasses a selfless living of each circumstance as best you can, asking for forgiveness (from God, others, self) when you fail, so that you can apologize as needed and go on with the dream instead of getting stuck at one failure, however large or small. I hope your legacy is one of success in finances and in giving and in relationships—one of true prosperity based on heart-based thinking and wise actions.

I hope your legacy will include your wise example as well as healthy assets for those who depend on you. I hope it will include a program of generous charitable giving that offers others the chance to do some of the work that the world needs. I hope your legacy will pass on *Wisdom and Money*'s lessons. If you choose to walk the trail of life it teaches—one filled with love and with wisdom, honor, and hope—you will leave a bright trail for others to follow.

MAKE A TRAIL THAT LEADS TO LOVE

The 7 Laws of Highest Prosperity and all the suggestions offered in *Wisdom and Money* can help you along the path to financial security. They will also bring you to full prosperity if you take the advice to keep your focus on God and on the needs of others whom you encounter as you implement *Wisdom and Money*'s finance suggestions. You will find happiness through the material prosperity and through the love you give and receive in your lifetime. You will also leave behind you a rich legacy.

In a materialistic society like ours, especially, where there are so many possessions or achievements to crave, it takes courage and perseverance to "just say no" to that one more task—to instead spend time with family, cultivate friendships, express unconditional love for others through wise words and actions, set up ways to help those in need, and develop one's own relationship with the Spirit within. But the rewards in terms of an ability to give and receive love, to leave that shining path for those who come after us, far outweigh those from money and possessions gained in a selfish way and for self-serving interest.

MAKE A TRAIL THAT LEADS TO WISDOM, HONOR, AND HOPE

Building a life with the precious inner stones of wisdom, honor, and hope and the building blocks of the 7 Laws of Highest Prosperity does so much more than bring you peace and prosperity. We are made in the image of a God who is creative. We create too whenever we build—sow—anything. When we create in accordance with God's ways and instruction—in partnership with Him—we create greater things than we could ever imagine. We exhibit a wisdom we could never own with our human brains and heart. We remain faithful to an honorable criteria with the ease that comes from being Spirit-led. We create hope for others by our example and by our help. In all, we create a truly awesome legacy, step by step. Some of these steps are taken, for example, when

- we save prudently, so that a child may attend college to bring his or her talents to fulfillment;
- we work diligently without working obsessively, serving as a role model to all those who watch our progress;

- we seek wisdom from the Spirit, who will provide us with inspiration and also ways to share that inspiration with others;
- we invest wisely, so that we can live according to the dreams God has given us the ability to envision; and
- we pursue those dreams and goals in a way that leaves our whole life a useful legacy that glorifies its Inspiration.

Through your love, your discipline, your benevolence, your work, and your spirit—your wisdom, honor, and hope—you become part of the eternal message: creative Love is and always will be.

A life empowered by a connection at the heart to God leads to the greatest fulfillment, purpose, and significance. Because it is a life that shows His Love in the nitty-gritty of the most material aspects of each day.

LEAVE A GOD-LIKE TRAIL

No matter what your circumstances, financial or otherwise, you can take control of your money and your life. You can forge the unique God-like trail you are destined to walk if you'll only let yourself.

You've got your own inner voice asking you to step out in faith. You've got a loving God with arms outstretched. You've got encouraging teachers and examples all around you, if you open your eyes and ears to their voices. . . .

You still have voices telling you it's impossible?

It's kind of fun to do the impossible.

—Walt Disney

You still have voices telling you it won't matter anyway?

Act as if what you do makes a difference. It does.

—William James

You are still stuck in thinking that the future will take care of itself?

The future depends on what we do in the present.

—Mahatma Gandhi

You still think your life and your mind are just too empty or used up to start on a new path?

The mind is not a vessel to be filled, it is a fire to be kindled.

—Plato

You think you are not meant to be prosperous?

I came that you might have life and that you might have it more abundantly.
—Jesus (paraphrase)

You think you can't do it alone?

Come to me if you are laboring, overburdened, and carrying a heavy load. Learn of me and discover that I give rest, answers, and help.
—Jesus (paraphrase)

Getting your life on course is not impossible. You do matter. What you do today matters. Your dreams matter. Your walk with God matters. This is what Jesus says about how much you and I matter to God:

For God so greatly cherishes each of us, He willingly gave His only son, Jesus, so that any one of us who believes in Him shall not perish but have everlasting life.
—Jesus (paraphrase)

These last three stanzas from *A Psalm of Life* by Henry Wadsworth Longfellow may help you see this truth.

> *Lives of great men all remind us*
> *We can make our lives sublime,*
> *And, departing, leave behind us*
> *Footprints on the sands of time.*
>
> *Footprints, that perhaps another,*
> *Sailing o'er life's solemn main,*
> *A forlorn and shipwrecked brother,*
> *Seeing, shall take heart again.*
>
> *Let us then be up and doing,*
> *With a heart for any fate;*
> *Still achieving, still pursuing,*
> *Learn to labor and to wait.*

Before closing Wisdom and Money, *please consider and record your thoughts and work through the exercises on the following worksheet,* Starting Today . . . .

WORKSHEET 15

Starting Today . . .

NOTES FROM READING THIS CHAPTER

STARTING TODAY . . .

A. Read the following.

If you have read through Wisdom and Money *but have not managed to work up a plan, this worksheet is designed for you. Or if you have worked up plans but they are not quite realistic enough to help your situation, this worksheet is for you too. Or if you have made a lot of progress and want to make more, this worksheet is for you as well.*

Please read the following.

Coming Down From the Mountaintop

Up in the dizzying atmosphere where we fly with passion under our wings, we can easily become lightheaded, caught up in the wonder of spiritual connectedness. In a sense, we must leave the earth in order to begin our journey, to begin our work. But we cannot possibly stay there if we hope to truly fulfill our heart's desires—we have to come back to earth and breathe. For many, this return is too dense—too depressing—too daunting—and their dreams stay in the clouds. If you want your financial dreams to have substance, fruition, and the power to touch others, there is simply no alternative but to come down from the mountaintop, put your feet on the ground of the real world, and start going.

B. Write at least one thing you want to accomplish.

Don't give up if you don't yet know how to do this one thing. Write it anyway.

If you cannot think of what your one thing will be, read on:
Start with *anything*—one insignificant thing you've been putting off:

• Give generously to someone who needs the money more than you.

• Pay off a debt.

• Save a hundred dollars.

• Open an account in a mutual fund.

• One dream.

• One word of encouragement you meant to say.

Anything! Just get the wheels in motion.

C. Remind yourself that a life is built one step at a time.

Achieving a small thing or reaching out that first time will provide momentum. Momentum will give you the courage you need to take another step, make more connections. Before you realize it, you will find that, step by step, you are moving down the path you always wished you could travel.

Remember this advice:

If you have built castles in the air, your work need not be lost; that is where they should be. Now put foundations under them.

—Henry David Thoreau

D. Write your plan to take this step.

So stop now, take a breath—and answer these questions truthfully in the spaces below. In each case, write at least one thing. Then add to the lists as you are led. Best wishes!

1. What is one thing I must do differently—starting today—to create lasting benefits for myself and others whose lives I influence and impact each day?

2. What will be my first small step in that direction?

3. When will I take it?

4. (If appropriate to the situation:) Whom will I ask to advise me on how best to take this step?

5. Whom will I ask to hold me accountable to this step? (Whom will I tell that I am doing it, so that they can ask—on a certain date—if I've done it)?

6. What is my follow-up date?

7. (When you are ready, answer this question:) What will be my next step?

May Wisdom and Money *give you courage to take one step, and the next, and the next. . . . And may you let the Spirit of God lead your heart every step of the way.*

AFTERWORD

I hope *Wisdom and Money* has helped you in your search for inner peace, happiness, and joy, and in the financial planning needed to realize your particular dreams and goals.

If you were once on the end of the money personality spectrum that unwisely believes that amassing material possessions, status, and other false symbols of success will fill inner emptiness, I hope you have dropped that misperception and embraced the Philosophy of Wisdom and its 7 Laws of Highest Prosperity that inspire generous giving, forced saving, disciplined spending, and wise investing.

If you were on the other end of the money personality spectrum and were neglecting to even plan to meet long-range needs for yourself and those who depend on you—either denying the need for that chore or intending to "get to it" sometime in the future or hoping someone else would do it for you—I hope you have begun to find the joy that comes with accepting responsibility and reaping such planning's benefits, both financially and in your spirit-person.

If you were in the middle and had areas of lack of knowledge or of misunderstanding, I hope you have begun to progress in the knowledge and understanding required to reach your dreams and goals.

I hope you now have few, if any, residual traces of the bitterness, greed, and selfishness associated with a materialistic handling of money tearing at your soul, life, relationships, family, career, and business if you own one. I hope you now see that it takes managing more than money alone to leave behind the dead ends and the trails of false promise. I hope you, like Sam the wood gatherer in the fable *7 Laws of Highest Prosperity*, will forge ahead on the path to true prosperity and true hope.

Never forget that this hope comes from returning God's incredible Love for you with love for Him and for each creation He loves so much. It comes from setting His priorities in your life and from the sense of purpose these priorities bring. It comes from loving others, giving generously, furthering your understanding of His ways, and understanding that He wants a life of abundance for you.

Remember that to receive that life of abundance you must prepare for it according to the steps set forth in *Wisdom and Money.* Then you must accept it with gratitude—and share it. You must nurture it wisely so that it can grow to feed and comfort you, your family, and others. Finally you must preserve that abundance so that it can continue to serve. This is true prosperity, and it is easy to find when we stay in touch with the Spirit through prayer and apply His sound principles of heart-based thinking each day, living by wise habits.

Wherever you are, however you are feeling about your successes and failures, remind yourself that faith and money *are* compatible. You need only choose to learn how to intertwine them correctly to accomplish great good.

When we meld our faith and money, the distance between the haves and the have-nots grows closer and we all move to common ground. This sort of faith in action becomes a healing force that spreads out to fill genuine need, solve real-world problems, and create emotional, spiritual, and economic abundance. Indeed, reaching out to others in this way is one of the most deeply rewarding experiences we humans have the privilege to enjoy.

In *Wisdom and Money* I often use my father's life choices as my example. When he died in 1995 I reflected deeply on the value of the life I was living compared to his. That was a landmark event for me, a major turning point. His life challenged me to a deeper partnership with God, to make the remainder of my own life count even more for what really counts! I pass that challenge on to you.

Let God become a transcendent, transforming influence in the core of your being, the most significant guiding force in your thinking, the standard for conduct in every dimension of your life. Then welcome His truth, justice, and loyalty into your life—in your dealings with money and material resources as well as in your personal, business, and financial interactions.

You will soon notice kindness, humility, compassion, forgiveness, mercy, and unconditional and sacrificial love taking over in ways you could not imagine. The vacuum we all sometimes feel inside will be filled to overflowing, and the Golden Rule that is at the center of all Jesus' teachings will be lived.

My prayer for you is that you open your heart and mind to expansion. Take a chance on something that, while exciting in concept, seems too uncontrollable in outcome. Let go of the predictable. Live the whole contents of *Wisdom and Money.* You will find yourself living worry-free and building treasure on earth and beyond. This heavenly treasure, after all, is the only investment that is eternally safe. Trust in the living God, rather than money. Delight in the Lord. Give Him first place in your life. Live by His Word. Then He will abundantly give you the desires of your heart.

When those gifts include money, use that money to do good. Be rich in good works. I encourage you to give generously, out of your abundance, to all those whose lives you touch.

Thanks again for purchasing *Wisdom and Money*. My prayer for you is, "Through the power of His indwelling Spirit, may the God of hope make you genuinely prosperous—filling you abundantly with life's greatest riches—His peace, unconditional love, and wisdom."

Now is the time for you to build a life of significance and true prosperity and make your own trail for others to follow.

APPENDIX

Sources for More Information

Note: These suggestions on sources for more information are meant to help you become more informed. I recommend you talk to your financial adviser as well. These listings are not meant as endorsements. For that reason, sources listed are in alphabetical order within their topic.

Please ask around for advice and keep notes on where you find the best information.

In case you're new to the internet, some basic search engines are:
> http://www.excite.com
> http://www.google.com
> http://www.msn.com
> http://www.yahoo.com

Please also note that the addresses of some websites have "www" in them and others don't.

Chapter 4—Relationships and Money
Advice on Communication

Look for books that give advice on communication, especially communication between the sexes.

Some good ones are:
> John Gray, Ph.D., *Men Are From Mars, Women Are From Venus*
> Deborah Tannen, Ph.D., *You Just Don't Understand*
> Bob Yandian, *One Flesh*

and books by:
> Larry Burkett
> Dr. Creflo A. Dollar and Taffi L. Dollar
> T. D. Jakes
> Dave Ramsey

Chapter 7—Forward Budgeting
The current federal tax tables can be found by calling the IRS at 1-800-829-3676 (1-800-TAX-FORM) and requesting form 1040 and instructions or by downloading from their forms and instructions website at:
http://www.irs.gov
or from their Forms and Publications site:
http://www.irs.gov/formspubs/index.html

Chapter 8—Forced Saving
What's important on balance sheets
Information on what's important on a balance sheet or a profit-and-loss statement of a business (bank, investment fund, etc.) where you're planning to put your money can be found at:
http://www.uschamber.com/sb/sbresources.asp?p=
P06/P06_7035.asp
Or you could go to:
http://www.uschamber.com
and click on the link "Manage Your Business," then "Financial Statements" (under "Financing"), and "Balance Sheet" of "Income Statement" (this is another name for a profit-and loss statement).

You might also look at:
http://www.personalwealth.com
This takes you to:
http://www.businessweek.com
where you can click on "Personal Finance."

Chapter 9—Spending Wisdom
For budgeting help/financial advice
Crown Financial Ministries has free resources on their website:
http://www.crown.org
Their counselors also will give financial advice limited to budget or debt conferences in some geographical areas. To find out more about this particular service, call 1-800-722-1976, or go to:
http://www.crown.org
and click on "Local Church" (at the top) and then go to the "Financial Counseling" section. (Note: These counselors are volunteers trained by Crown Financial Ministries in a course accepted by the Certified Financial Planning Board of Standards, Inc., for twenty hours of continuing education credit for CFP licensees.)

Another helpful website is:
http://www.daveramsey.com

Helpful books can be found in the personal finance section of almost any bookstore, privately owned or chain. Some websites are:

> http://www.amazon.com
> http://www.bn.com
> http://www.ipgbook.com (Independent Publishers Group)

In addition, your library may have free access to online book searches like *Books in Print.*

You can use your internet search engine, too, to search for personal finance information. Be careful!

Refinancing

To calculate cost to refinance your home, so that you can decide whether you'll save money by doing so, you can use computer home bookkeeping software.

Websites of many software creators also give simple fill-in screens that will guide you to a decision on whether refinancing is for you. For example, go to:

> http://www.quicken.com

and click on "Home Loans" at the top and then on "Mortgage Calculators" or "Refinance Center."

Other sites that will help with this are:

> http://www.hsh.com/usnrcalc.html
> http://www.bankrate.com/brm/calc_vml/refi/refi.asp

Or plug in "refinancing" in your internet search engine.

Auto Buying/Leasing

A common source for the so-called book value of new or used vehicles is the Kelley Blue Book. It is often available in public libraries. It can also be found online:

> http://www.kbb.com

Note: This "book value" can be either the Kelley Blue Book value—the suggested retail price, which is what the dealer will probably be asking and which is likely to be substantially higher than the price at which he will finally sell the vehicle—or the estimated *average* selling price, which can be found at websites like:

> http://edmunds.com

Factory invoice price (the price the dealer paid for a car) can be found from several sources, such as the CNN/Money Car Finder:

> http://configurator.carprices.com/cnn/makemodel.html

This site can also be found by going to:

> http://money.cnn.com

and clicking on "Personal Finance," then on "Money 101," then on "Lesson 17—Buying a Car," then on "Setting Your Target Price," then click on the link for CNN/Money's Car Finder.

Lease information

Lease information is available at:

> http://leaseguide.com

To figure the annual percentage rate the dealer is proposing you pay and any other aspect of the financial terms of a lease, you can buy software products that figure the rate for you, for example LeaseWizard, available, among other places, at:

> http://leasewizard.com

To evaluate your prospective vehicle for safety and frequency of repairs, etc., see the *Consumer Guide,* which comes out annually with slightly different names for both new and used cars. This book by the Consumer Guide editors can be bought or found at most public libraries.

Insurance

Comparing rates

To find sites that will give you free quotes on insurance coverage and rates, try searching for "property insurance" or "life insurance" or "health insurance" at your favorite internet search engine . . . and stand back!

Rating insurers

Some companies that rate insurers are:

> http://www.ambest.com   (A. M. Best)
> http://www.weissratings.com   (Weiss Ratings, Inc.)

Others can be found by plugging in "insurance raters" in your internet search engine.

See the section in this Appendix for chapter 11, "Funding Retirement," for how to find more information on Medicare, Medicaid, Social Security, and other government insurance programs.

Vacations

Talk to friends and travel agents.

Look for websites that help you save on transportation and hotels, and compare with what your local travel agencies can offer. Don't forget to look for package deals!

If you are attending a specific event, be sure to compare with the event host's special offers (when they exist).

Make use of frequent flyer miles and hotel frequent user benefits.

Some websites to look at are:
> http://www.all-hotels.com
> http://www.expedia.com
> http://www.hotels.com
> http://www.orbitz.com

And, of course, check the websites for the historical sites or cities or countries or convention and visitors bureaus in the areas you are interested in visiting.

Chapter 10—Funding a College Education

There are many free or low-cost tools available on the internet and from high schools and colleges, from state and federal government agencies, and from retail stores that offer computer aids and books on topics related to college education.

For financial aid

There are two basic information forms you may be required to fill out to apply for need-based financial aid. Your high school counselor should be able to help you sort these out for the colleges you are applying to. There *are* deadlines for these, so be alert!

1. The FAFSA (Free Application for Federal Student Aid)
> http://www.fafsa.ed.gov

2. The CSS/Financial aid PROFILE

There is a fee for filing the PROFILE, which is lower if you register online. Online address for the PROFILE is:
> http://profileonline.collegeboard.com/index.jsp

Or you can access it by going to:
> http://collegeboard.com

and clicking on CSS/Profile online.

Applicants must have valid credit card to apply online.

You can also call them for a paper form for an additional fee of about $2:
> 1-800-778-6888 (outside the U.S. call 1-305-816-2550)

Both the above sites have information as well as forms.

Other helpful sites are:
> http://collegeaidcounselor.com
> http://collegefinancingguide.com
> http://salliemae.com   (for college loans)

For books that will help you find financial aid and scholarships, try publications like the Barron's Educational Series, Peterson's guides, or guides by the Princeton Review publishers.

There are free scholarship databases such as:
> http://apps.absolutelyscholarships.com
> http://www.colleges.com/financialaid/-
>   scholarships/find_scholarship.taf/
> http://www.collegenet.com/mach25/
> http://www.fastweb.com

(On this website the student may complete a personal profile at no charge and receive updates about applicable scholarships via e-mail)
> http://finaid.org
> http://SRNExpress.com/index.cfm
> http://supercollege.com

Note: If you don't like receiving junk email, be careful how you fill out the profiles on these sites. Read their privacy policies carefully.

Books on scholarships can be found in bookstores or in the reference section of your public library.

For online information about colleges themselves, try typing the name of the college in your internet search engine or try plugging in the name of the college plus .edu in the address line in your browser (for example: http://www.harvard.edu). College websites usually tell you about the school itself, courses/majors offered, entrance requirements, admission process/dates, cost, and how to ask for printed information.

CLEP
To learn about the cost and process of taking the CLEP (College-Level Examination Program) test to get college credit without taking the college course, you can ask your child's college adviser or go online to:
> http://www.collegeboard.com/clep/

Chapter 11—Funding Retirement
Some online sites that will assist you in planning your retirement are:
> http://www.quicken.com

The American Association of Retired Persons (AARP) can be found on-line at:

http://www.aarp.org

It has helpful links, one of which is a retirement calculator found at:

http://partners.financenter.com/aarp/calculate/-
us-eng/retire02a.fcs

Or call AARP at 1-800-424-3410.

Social Security

For an estimate of what you will receive if you retire at 62, 66, or 70, based on your past employment history, request a Social Security Statement of Earnings and Benefits (Form SSA-7004), either by calling the Social Security Administration (SSA) at 1-800-772-1213 or writing to them at Social Security Administration, Wilkes Barre Data Operations Center, P.O. Box 7004, Wilkes Barre, PA, 18767-7004.

You can also go online to request this information. Go to the Social Security Administration website:

http://www.ssa.gov/

and click on "How to . . ." (left side of page); then click on "How to Request a Social Security Statement of Earnings and Benefits"; then either follow the directions to fill in the required form online (during the hours specified on the site) or, if you prefer, print out the form so that you can fill it out and mail it to the address listed above.

Other government programs

For certain needs (such as application for Medicare) you must visit your local Social Security office. More complete summaries of Medicare, help with locating your local office, and answers to questions that this book doesn't cover may be found at:

http://www.medicare.gov

or by calling the Social Security Administration in Washington, DC, toll free, at 1-800-772-1213 or by going to the SSA website given above.

Call your Medicare carrier about bills and services. The phone number for the Medicare carrier in your area can be found in the "Helpful Contacts" section of Medicare's internet website:

http://www.medicare.gov

Besides the contact information provided above, if you have unanswered questions about Part A (hospital insurance) of Medicare, you can call your Fiscal Intermediary, whose phone number for your area can be found in the "Helpful Contacts" section of the internet website:

http://www.medicare.gov

If you are eligible for benefits from the Railroad Retirement Board, you can call your local RRB office or 1-800-808-0772.

The Department of Veterans Affairs website is:
>   http://www.va.gov/

To learn about government programs/benefits you can also contact your congressman or go online to the U.S. government's searchable database:
>   http://www.firstgov.gov/

Your congressman can be found through:
>   http://www.house.gov/
and your senator through:
>   http://www.senate.gov/

For state-administered programs (like Medicaid), see the government pages in your local phone book or look for your state's central website, which will help you find the sites for each branch of its government. Often, you can plug in the word or words that describe what you're looking for and specify a search within the state government web pages. If not, try sending an email to a similar site you do find.

Or you can learn about Medicaid eligibility, coverages, and find answers to questions you may have by visiting the internet website of the Centers for Medicare and Medicaid Services at:
>   http://cms.hhs.gov/medicaid/consumer.asp

Your local representatives to state legislature should also be able to help.

The government site:
>   http://www.firstgov.gov/
also has links to local sites. Under "Agencies" on the left, click on "State, Local & Tribal." Then click on the link for your state or other local link.

Chapter 12—Saving Taxes
To study tax law on your own, look at:

Tax-topic-intensive books at bookstores

Tax planning and preparation books by J. K. Lasser

Tax-topic-intensive books on the web or through your tax preparer or financial adviser

U.S. Master Tax Guide published annually by CCH, Inc., available through their website:
>   http://www.cch.com
For tax laws in your state, see the government pages in your local phone

book, or go online to the official state website for your state, or to the U.S. government's searchable database at:

> http://www.firstgov.gov/

Chapter 13—Investment Wisdom

For continuing written guidance, read magazines and newsletters like:
Money
Kiplinger Finance Newsletter

You can also go to:

> http://www.investopedia.com/

and click on "Tutorials," and then on whatever topics interest you.

To locate a financial advisor:

Call the Association of Certified Financial Planners: 1-888-CFP-MARK or visit the ACFP website:

> http://cfp-board.org

They also have tips on hiring a financial adviser.

Go to the following website:

> http://www.daveramsey.com

Free advising for debt and budget only is available through Crown Ministries (listed in chapter 9 section of this Appendix.) They also have advisers on financial planning for a fee.

Investment model information

Investment model software can be purchased on websites like:

> http://cpateam.com
> http://gravityinvestments.com
> http://laportesoft.com
> http://toolsformoney.com

Software and/or printed material on investment modeling can also be purchased inexpensively from computer retailers.

Mutual fund companies and other financial service and financial professional organizations offer free printed material on investment modeling. Be sure to remember that this may be biased information.

Austin Pryor's *Sound Mind Investing* offers information on investing, mutual funds, etc.

Chapter 14—Preserving Your Estate

Laws on documents you can leave behind

For state statutes describing in some detail the circumstances for implementing a living will, see your state's official website, or try going to:

> http://www.firstgov.gov/

and following the link to the state. (The process for finding that link is given in the state-administered-programs section under chapter 11 of this Appendix.)

Information on estate planning

Call the American Association of Retired Persons (AARP) at 1-800-424-3410, Monday-Friday 8 A.M.–8 P.M. Eastern Time or write to them at AARP; 601 E St., NW; Washington, DC 20049. They can be found online at:

> http://www.aarp.org

Your state government may have agencies with websites that give information on aging, estate planning, etc.

For example, in North Carolina you can go to the North Carolina Cooperative Extension website,

> http://www.ces.ncsu.edu/resources/

and click on Family and Consumer and then click on "Legal Issues." You can then browse through a "slide show" about aging that covers advice on a wide variety of applicable topics, including living wills and estate planning. On this website you can ask about legal issues surrounding aging and receive an answer online from an expert (credentials listed with the answer), for example, "Is a will that was written in New York valid in North Carolina?" or, "Should I purchase my mother's home so that she can be on Medicaid while in the nursing home?"

State estate taxes

If you do not have an adviser or if you want more information on the estate taxes levied in your state, contact the agency in your state that administers this tax.

If you don't know what agency that is, call the office of either your elected state representative or senator or the governor's office in your state's capital city.

About the Author

Cecil O. Kemp Jr. grew up on a small farm. He and Patty, his childhood sweetheart, have been married over thirty years. Their two children are married and have given the Kemps four grandchildren.

In 1971, Cecil graduated from college and began his professional career as a CPA working with one of the world's largest accounting firms. At twenty-three, he became chief financial officer of a public company and, before thirty, became its chief operating officer. From 1982 to 1998 the Kemps owned and operated many successful businesses, including a financial and investment services group of companies that managed over $100 million for several thousand individuals and businesses.

As a result of lessons learned from Cecil's near fatal accident in 1993 and introspection following his father's unexpected death in 1995, the Kemps sold all their businesses and have focused their energy full-time on life and financial coaching, business consulting, writing, publishing, speaking, and retreat ministry.

Cecil's books offer wisdom and inspiration for the heart and hope for every season of life. In addition to *Wisdom and Money*, he is the author of these:

INSPIRATIONAL PAPERBACKS

Rock the Boat: Defying Sacred Cows to Become a Truly Great Leader
Roots & Wings: The Keys of Parenting Excellence
7 Laws of Highest Prosperity: Making Your Life Count for What Really Counts!
Success That Lasts
The Inner Path to True Greatness
The Key to Relationship Excellence: Unlocking the Door to Success in Any Relationship
The Secret Meeting Place
Wisdom Honor & Hope

Cecil is also the creator and principal writer of:

The Hope Collection Gift Book Series

A Book of Hope for the Storms of Life: Healing Words for Troubled Times

A Book of Hope for Mothers: Celebrate the Joy of Children

A Book of Hope after Retirement: The Best Years Are Ahead

A Book of Hope for Students: Dream Big, Dream Wisely!

A Book of Hope we're Forgiven: The Healing Power of Forgiveness

A Book of Hope on Prayer: Key to Successful Days, Lock of Secure Nights

A Book of Hope on Abiding Faith: Rediscovering the Rock of a Meaningful Life

A Book of Hope for Lasting Peace: Inspiring Thoughts for Possessing Real Hope & Security

A Book of Hope for Parents: Inspiration & Wisdom for Successful Parenting

A Book of Hope for Leaders: 86 Day Guidebook to Leadership Greatness

A Book of Hope for Shaping a Life of Honor: How to Live a Life of True Excellence

A Book of Hope for Higher Connection: Truth, Inspiration & Wisdom for the Searching Soul

A Book of Hope for Achieving True Greatness: 26 Keys to Lasting Success

A Book of Hope for Relationship Heartaches: Wisdom & Inspiration for Mending Broken Hearts

A Book of Hope for a Better Life: Inspiration Today From Reflecting Back & Looking Within

A Book of Hope for Loving Unconditionally: The Power & Passion for Living Life Fully

Approach to Writing

The books of Cecil O. Kemp Jr. challenge humanist philosophies and the wisdom of modern culture.

The core value of loving, caring for, and focusing on God and others is featured in all the books. Relationship with God through faith in Jesus and allowing His Spirit to live within are portrayed as the keys to achieving true greatness: life, relationship, and leadership excellence and success that lasts.

The books offer sound counsel and real hope based on the Bible's unchanging principles of eternal truth. These are embedded in a positive and powerful message that comforts, encourages, heals, instructs, and inspires.

Kemp values what is important in the here and now, and in eternity, for individuals and for the relationship, family, and organizational units upon which a caring society and culture rest. Thus he points readers first to spiritual reconciliation, renewal, and restoration, then to selflessness in daily living and working.

He is humbled to have the God-given call, privilege, honor, skills, and resources to produce works of literary distinction that focus on traditional values and contribute an extremely valuable perspective on the genuinely great issues of modern life.

He is proud that his books not only offer a view through the eternal scope and practical, sound solutions that stand the test of time, but openly fly in the face of materialism, intellectualism, man-made religion, and other empty humanist philosophies.

In promoting the values and priorities of eternal truth that run counter to popular culture, he produces books that are suited for a broad audience—readers of all ages in all places in the world who are open-minded and sincerely searching for what he calls the truly better way of living and working.

NOTES

NOTES